DATE DUE

A LIFE IN TWO WORLDS

A LIFE IN TWO WORLDS

The Autobiography
of Beatrice Bishop Berle

Walker and Company, New York

Note: *A Life in Two Worlds* is a personal account, based on the author's diaries kept over the years. Every effort has been made not to repeat the economic/political emphasis of her earlier work, *Navigating the Rapids*, and of the forthcoming book on Adolf A. Berle being written by Professor Jordan Schwarz.

Copyright © 1983 by Beatrice Bishop Berle

*All rights reserved. No part of this book may be
reproduced or transmitted in any form or by any
means, electric or mechanical, including photocopying,
recording, or by any information storage and retrieval
system, without permission in writing from the Publisher.*
*First published in the United States of America
in 1983 by the Walker Publishing Company, Inc.*
*Published simultaneously in Canada by John Wiley & Sons
Canada, Limited, Rexdale, Ontario.*

ISBN: 0-8027-0743-2

Printed in the United States of America

10   9   8   7   6   5   4   3   2   1

Book design by Laura Ferguson

Library of Congress Cataloging in Publication Data
Berle, Beatrice Bishop, 1902–
    A life in two worlds.

    Includes index.
    1. Berle, Beatrice Bishop, 1902–   . 2. Physi-
cians — United States — Biography. 3. Politicians'
wives — United States — Biography. 4. Berle, Adolf
Augustus, 1895–1971. I. Title.
R154.B49A34   1983   610'.92'4   [B]   83-7033
ISBN 0-8027-0743-2

Foreword ≈

Adolf Berle died twelve years ago. We had been married for forty-three years. Ever since his death, I have been wanting to write about our marriage. It was a very special relationship, which brought happiness and fulfillment to us both.

In the course of the many rewritings of this book, I have found that I was writing not only about us, but also about my early life and about the changing world in which we are living; hence the title *A Life in Two Worlds*. However, marriage is still the central theme of this book.

The privileged old New York family into which I was born at the turn of the century was deeply Francophile — and intent upon maintaining a pre–World War I standard of manners and conduct. There was an established code of behavior, which everyone knew and understood. Those who broke the rules knew that they were doing so. There were few gray areas.

Today the world is full of gray areas. The means through which one's ideals may be realized are not clear; still, that is not sufficient reason to give up these ideals.

Soon after our first meeting, Adolf called me Playmate. Playmates and lovers we became and continued to be until the end. We shared our dreams, our many activities, and many friends, and we raised three wonderful children, whose children, our ten grandchildren, are promising young people. Within the framework of our love and respect for each other's individuality, Adolf realized a measure of his great creative powers, and I became a physician.

To the children, grandchildren and great grandchildren of
Adolf and Beatrice Berle—
> *"This above all: to thine own self be true,*
> *And it must follow, as the night the day,*
> *Thou canst not then be false to any man."*
> *Shakespeare*
> Hamlet, *Act 1, Scene 3*

Contents

Early Days ≈

≈*1*

I was born in Lenox, Massachusetts, on August 6, 1902, an only child. My parents had wanted a boy; sometimes they called me by Father's name—Cortlandt. I often wondered why I was born. It is hard to imagine that my Mother, the beautiful Amy Bend, ever wished to become pregnant. She used to tell me pregnancy had spoiled her figure. In her eyes all matters female—menstruation, pregnancy, childbirth—were disgusting. Femaleness was so abhorrent to her that she insisted on having a hysterectomy before the age of forty, declaring that the pain associated with menstruation was intolerable. I can still see myself at age six or seven, a tiny figure dressed in white, trotting along in the street trying to keep up with Father on the way to see Mother at the hospital. Of course, I knew nothing about the operation—the "facts of life" were not revealed to children in those days—but I felt that something was wrong, he held my hand so tightly.

A flashback to this scene came many years later, when I overheard Father's voice, anxious and angry, saying, "Amy, you shouldn't have done that." Mother's chest was covered with bandages; she had just undergone plastic surgery to lift her breasts.

It is true that Mother was a great beauty. According to Edith Wharton, to be recognized as a beauty in the 1880s and 1890s was a "gift" that in the eyes of New York justified success and excused a certain number of failings. It was a career, and Mother was still pursuing it the last time I saw her, when she was fifty-six. Body culture and body worship are not new, but in the early 1900s, with less body visible, much was left to the imagination, and young men could indulge their fantasies. A few years ago, I showed a miniature painting of Mother to an octogenarian of my acquaintance. With tears in his eyes, he exclaimed, "I only saw her once, when I was a small boy. I never forgot her. She was so beautiful — the most perfect complexion and those blue eyes, like forget-me-nots."

The miniature is in my hands. I see the blue eyes, the porcelain-like complexion. The evening gown is held at the shoulder line by a tiny strand of rosebuds and forget-me-nots; a tulle scarf floats over the shoulders — this is a doll, not a woman; perhaps a goddess to be worshiped from afar. She liked me to call her Venere — Venus in Italian, a language we spoke together sometimes.

I also have a photograph in which she is holding me at arm's length like a puppet. Perhaps I should have been one, but that is not my temperament.

Father was quite different, a brilliant, dynamic man, born with a silver spoon in his mouth. He obtained a law degree and a doctorate in political science from Columbia University but never practiced either profession. When he applied for a position in a law firm, Mr. Parsons, my paternal grandmother's second husband, had discouraged him. Young men of independent means, he told Father, should not seek paid employment; they would be taking bread out of the mouths of less fortunate youths — a rationalization current in the 1890s and early 1900s. So Father became a sponsor of the Wright Brothers and a discriminating bibliophile and print collector — at a time when the species was dying out, he remained a charming dilettante.

Father was among the first Berkshire residents, if not the first, to import and drive a French motorcar. Motoring was a real adventure then. Each time a drive was planned, it was necessary to inform the authorities of the direction in which the vehicle would be proceeding, so that farm vehicles and horseback riders could take their precautions. A Lenox town ordinance dated August 19, 1901, read,

> ... No person shall ride or propel, or cause to be propelled any vehicle other than those propelled or drawn by horse or persons upon any of the streets or ways of the town inside of the Fire District at a rate of speed greater than 8 miles per hour nor outside of the Fire District at a rate of speed greater than 15 miles per hour and any person violating this by-law shall be punished by fines not exceeding $100 or by imprisonment not exceeding 10 days.

Before World War I, family life among those who considered themselves upper class was very different from what it is today. Children were not included in their parents' day-to-day lives; they lived in a separate world of their own, run by nurses and governesses, and were presented to their parents only at stated times. Probably my situation was somewhat exaggerated in this regard. I have been told that the English nanny who took care of me was once reprimanded because Mother considered that the ribbons to my bonnet were not properly pressed.

I have no recollection of this woman. She must have been replaced by a Frenchwoman when I was very small, since French was my first language. Indeed, most upper-class children were brought up by French mademoiselles. At the turn of the century a group of Americans living on the eastern seaboard identified with the European aristocracy, from which some of them were descended. Accordingly, to be a part of my parents' circle one must be well bred and of good family. A "good family" had money—old money, not new money. How long did it take to age new money? I never found out, but I know that it was not as long as it took to age Madeira; according to Father, this wine must have sailed around Cape Horn and be more than fifty years old before it was fit to drink.

In the eyes of my grandmothers, Vanderbilt, Whitney, Harriman, and Rockefeller money was new money, only one generation old. Those people were nouveau riche, ostentatious, and vulgar. But as the old rich became less rich and the "nouveau" became richer, the former soon became absorbed by the latter, to the mutual satisfaction of all concerned.

Most of the "good families" were either Francophile or Anglophile. My parents were Francophile. They spent six months on the Continent and six months divided between New York and the Berkshires, never becoming complete expatriates.

They wished me to be educated like a French aristocrat but also to attend American schools.

In my early years, the French influence prevailed even while we resided in America. I had a French governess, Mother had a French lady's maid, Father had a French valet, and the search for a French chef was neverending.

My parents spoke only French to me. I remember experiencing difficulty understanding English when I first attended the Brearley School and in learning the American method of doing long division, which was different from the French.

My French accent in English must have been fearful and wonderful; my classmates roared with laughter imitating my rendering of William Blake's poem "The Tiger."

> Tigerrr, tigerrr burrning bright
> In dée forrests of dée night

Not only did we speak French at home, but we lived in a French house.

[3]

Fifteen East Sixty-seventh Street had been built for my parents by Ernest Flagg, an architect trained at the Beaux Arts in Paris. This house is now the seat of a fashionable bridge club. A few steps up from the street, the heavy wrought-iron door backed with glass leads into the front hall, which opens upon a vista of the white marble stairs, leading to the drawing room and the library floor.

The reception room on the ground floor has been converted into a bar. (How horrified my parents would have been. Gin was anathema to them. Civilized people drank only good French wine and champagne.) This room was an exquisite reproduction of a small French eighteenth-century salon, with rounded corners and oyster-white-painted walls hung with Aubusson tapestries. It was not a room for children; I was not allowed in it except on special occasions, as when my godmother, Coco, was visiting.

Coco was a large woman with a deep voice, lifting up and smothering in her embrace the little girl who had been sitting up straight, legs outstretched, in the Aubusson *fauteuil* awaiting her godmother's entrance. "Sit up straight; stand straight" were the constant admonitions; "no lounging, no slouching." Grown-ups did not lounge, and children were to be seen and not heard, but I did not mind it in this room, for there was a lot to be seen and quite a lot to be heard. Mother, for example, saying to Coco, "I will not receive a divorced woman in my house," and Coco acquiescing. The name of the lady, I do not recall. Perhaps it was Mrs. O. H. Belmont, the notorious divorcée of the period. While the two ladies were deep in talk, I was enjoying the scene portrayed in the tapestries. I slid off the *fauteuil* with La Fontaine's fable *Le Corbeau et le Renard* on it, whispering to myself *"Maître Corbeau sur un arbre perché/tenait en son bec un fromage."*

My attention shifted to the Aubusson tapestry on the wall — a woman was carrying a child on her back and having her fortune told, and a little girl (I, Beatrice) was sitting on the ground near the sheep and oxen. Soon we would all be skipping down the *allée* toward the château far away. There was the fire screen also, an Aubusson tapestry with a boy and girl sitting together. This was the picture of *"le petit* Bayard" who came to play with me sometimes.

Just then the French clock on the mantlepiece, whitefaced between two gilt columns, struck three. Coco was getting up to say goodbye; they were still talking: Mother: "Poor Ellen Speyer — she has lost her money."

Coco: "Well, she married a Jew."

Mother: "I know. Poor Ellen, what could she do after she lost all her money? Jimmy is really very nice. He is our pet Jew and gets invited everywhere. He's not pushy like a lot of Jews. He doesn't seem to have a lot of family whom he wants to introduce into New York society. Or maybe he's just bright enough to understand that one Jew in New York society is enough. Otto Kahn is building a huge house up on Ninety-first Street next to the Burdens and Hammonds, but of course, they won't receive him."

Turning to me abruptly, she says, "Beatrice, it is time to get dressed for dancing class."

I went upstairs to be dressed; the white dress trimmed with Irish lace, the wide Roman silk sash, pink, blue, and white, tied around my middle with a large bow in the back. All this was the fashion for little girls at that time. I liked the crescent-shaped gold pin studded with tiny pearls that held the bow; it was a gift from Grand-mère, "too extravagant for a little girl," Mother had said.

Dodsworth, a dessicated white-haired gentleman in tails, was the director of the dancing class. He had taught Mother, and other young girls preparing for the cotillion, twenty-five years ago. The ballroom floor where the class was held was marked off in squares of light and darker wood. Under the baton of a plump woman, to a rhythm more like that of a military march than the cadence of "The Blue Danube," we stood at attention, heels together, feet at right angles, pacing the waltz in three dissected steps: one, two, three.

My governess and I always walked down to Forty-ninth Street, but we were brought back in Mother's town car. It was painted dark blue with red penciled lines around the doors. The body resembled a brougham, compact, closed, and intimate. Mother was very proud of this French car, which could turn right around on Sixty-seventh Street without backing.

That day, wet snow was falling. Two men sat on the box (the driver's seat), the chauffeur and the footman in smart navy-blue coats with brass buttons and detachable brown fur collars (made in France). A little awning could be rolled down if the weather was considered sufficiently inclement (that day it was not considered so); otherwise, the men sat upright in the open air as they had in carriage days not so many years before.

It was suppertime when we got home. There was a dinner party on for that evening. Mademoiselle and I ate at a little table in the dining room at five-thirty. Father was just opening the wall safe and the butler was taking out the gilded silver candelabra. I loved the plates with the gold-festooned border and centered initial and the Baccarat gold-rimmed wine glasses for sherry and claret, monogrammed DWB, my grandfather, and CLW, Catherine Lorillard Wolfe, my great-great aunt. The champagne glasses were my favorites—no gold rim but clear crystal with scattered rosebuds printed in the glass.

I enjoyed dinner-party evenings because then Mother called me to fasten

[5]

her bracelets as she was dressing. There were many, of gold with small pearls or diamonds, but the "broken hearts" was the interesting one. There were twenty-five charms on this one, attached to a small gold chain. "Twenty-five proposals," Mother would say proudly, "before I met your father and really fell in love." The charms were mostly little gold hearts, but there were a tiny golden pug and a small gold fish.

"Who were your beaux?" I asked.

"One was an English lord, but I wouldn't live in England. Another was an Italian count with no money, another a French marquis. There were a couple of American stockbrokers in New York society, but I wouldn't marry a man who goes to Wall Street every day. Businessmen don't know anything about Europe."

I used to wonder why Mother and Father had not married before the age of thirty. The family legend, which no one contradicted, held that Father, a shy, studious young man in contrast to his more sociable brother David, had never looked at a girl until he met the beautiful Amy Bend. It was love at first sight, *le coup de foudre*, so the story went. But as I grew older I wondered—by the time Mother married, most of her contemporaries had already paired off. Was it that she enjoyed the game of being pursued and not giving in? The gossip sheet of the period, *Town Topics*, noted that "Miss Bend had been engaged so many times." Or had the Europeans discovered that, after all, she was not an heiress, her father, George Bend, a former president of the New York Stock Exchange, having lost his money in the panic of 1893?

That evening, as I was snapping on the last bracelet, I heard Father call, "Donkey, come and help me dust the books, but mind you don't drop any." He called me Donkey—a pet name, it's true, but it meant he did not have a high opinion of my intelligence.

Only since I had passed my eighth birthday had I been allowed to dust the books. The library occupied the entire front of the house, thirty feet wide, with three French windows, bookshelves from floor to ceiling, and glass doors with double locks to which only Father had the key. A portrait of Mother dressed in pink satin was over the fireplace. Of course, at that age, I was not allowed to touch the medieval manuscripts and could only marvel at the blues, reds, and gold in the nativity scene as Father held a book open to let me look. I was given a clean white cheesecloth duster, which Father took out of a drawer. He opened one of the cases filled with sets bound in red morocco or brown calf—Molière, Racine, La Fontaine. I was expected to take out one book at a time, pass the duster gently but firmly over the binding and the edges, place the book on a nearby table, dust the back of the empty shelf, then replace all the books in order. Here were La Fontaine's fables, the ones portrayed on the tapestry chair downstairs. I sat down and looked for *Le Corbeau et le Renard.* There he was, silly old crow, dropping the cheese into the fox's mouth. I giggled to myself. The book slid to the floor. "Donkey," my father said severely, "how stupid you are! I told you not to drop the books." I burst into tears and ran up the two flights of stairs to my room.

On the third floor there was a smaller room with one window where Mademoiselle and I slept. The larger room with two windows was the playroom, with a large dollhouse and an armchair full of costume dolls. There was also a bookshelf filled chiefly with books of *La Bibliothèque Rose* — sappy stories about little girls, *Les Petites Filles Modèles,* and more entertaining stories about naughty children, like *Les Malheurs de Sophie,* about a little girl who endured frequent whippings with bundles of birch sticks.

After my bath, I was supposed to go right to bed — lights out at seven-thirty. Sometimes Mother and Father came up to kiss me good night, but they did not come up on dinner-party nights. As the grandfather clock on the stairs — a hoarse, friendly old thing — was striking eight, Mademoiselle and I peeked over the banister to watch the guests parade in to dinner. Mother went first, in pink satin like the dress in the library portrait, a tiara over her lovely hair, and elbow-length kid gloves, which would be drawn back from the hand or removed after she sat down to dinner. The gentlemen were all in tails and white ties, of course. Father and a lady in white satin with silver spangles and silk fringes brought up the rear. The dining-room doors were closed by the two footmen in livery — red waistcoats and blue coats with gold buttons, also made in Paris. All very grand, like the pictures in some of Father's books, I thought. *"Allez vous coucher bien vite,"* Mademoiselle admonished.

The bedroom door was ajar, so I could hear the voice of the housemaid, Agnes, a recent Irish immigrant with a brogue and a mass of auburn hair piled on top of her head. "Did you notice the master's shirt — was it all right?" she asked Mademoiselle.

"I couldn't see very well," was the reply.

"I hope it was," Agnes went on, "or poor Charlotte [the laundress] will get the sack."

"Perhaps she will anyway. That horrid Claudine [Mother's personal maid, a Frenchwoman] carries tales about her to Mrs. Bishop. She tells tales about everyone — about this poor child, too."

Father's stiff collars and stiff shirts were always an issue. Somehow they were never quite right—too much or too little starch. The next morning, as I went into Mother's room in the front of the house to say good morning and goodbye before going to school, Claudine, a redhead with a big bosom, was talking a mile a minute about the way Charlotte was neglecting her work. She had been out all the previous afternoon when she should have been taking care of the shirts. Mother listened to it all, declaring that if this went on Charlotte would be dismissed without a reference.

The atmosphere was like that of an Italian court. Tittle-tattle, one servant intriguing against another—claiming for instance that a piece of silver had been stolen, thus hoping to rise in Mother's favor by taking advantage of her suspicious nature. In this instance, it was not Charlotte but Claudine who got fired. True, she was French and dressed Mother's hair quite well, but she had body odor, a fault Mother could not overlook, especially after Agnes, the housemaid, complained about it. Finally Father got tired of the constant bickering and hired a housekeeper. "That way, Amy, you will not be troubled with these details. The housekeeper will be responsible for managing the servants." That did not help matters as far as I was concerned—the housekeeper was just one more person to report to Mother that I had spilled cocoa on my clean white frock.

Father's dressing room and bath were in the back of the house, at the end of the hall from Mother's room. I stopped there also to say good morning. This morning after the dinner party, he was out of sorts: the champagne had not been sufficiently iced; Mrs. C. with the fat bottom had sat in one of the best Louis XVI *fauteuils* in the salon and they almost had to break the arms of the chair to get her out of it; the guests had stayed too long. The established rule was an hour at table, thirty minutes for the gentlemen with cigars in the library while the ladies were in the drawing room, another thirty minutes when the gentlemen returned to the salon and were assigned to sit and converse with the ladies next to whom they had not sat at dinner, and home shortly after ten. Last night they had stayed until ten-forty-five.

The floor of Father's bedroom was strewn with collars—not enough starch, he complained as his valet held his trouser leg and put on his shoes. "Study hard" were his parting words to me. "I was always first in my class. See you this afternoon, but don't drop any more books and don't be late for school." At that time the Brearley School, where I was enrolled, was at Sixty-first Street and Park Avenue, a short walk, on which Mademoiselle accompanied me.

After school I went to lunch with Angel and Aunt Beatrice in their apartment on Sixty-second Street. "Angel" was my maternal grandmother, a sweet old lady. Aunt Beatrice, Anti Bi (pronounced Auntie Bee) as I called her, my other godmother, after whom I was named, was four years younger than Mother and very different. She did not marry until 1917, when she was more than forty. Her husband, Henry Prather Fletcher, a career diplomat, became ambassador to Belgium and to Italy. The diplomatic life, striped-pants variety, was Mother's dream, not Father's. He had a poor opinion of Fletcher's brains and considerable hostility toward Anti Bi, who was known in the family as "the suffragette." Anti Bi was interested in the suffrage movement but never to the extent of getting herself chained to a post for the cause, as some more militant women did. She was not her parents' favorite. She was everything Mother was not—a competent and active committee woman—and she was not beautiful. Even so, Mother was very fond of her.

While lunch on weekdays was brief, since Anti Bi soon left to join the building committee of the Colony Club across Park Avenue, a Sunday meal with Angel was a real treat—roast beef, Yorkshire pudding, and chocolate ice cream.

On Sunday mornings, we attended Grace Church, at Tenth Street and Broadway. Grace Church was our family church. We owned four pews. My grandmothers each had one, Father had one, and Uncle Isaac Townsend, Angel's brother, owned the fourth. Sometimes, I sat with Mother and Father in his pew. The fur from my white bunny coat shed on Father's oxford gray coat, and I fiddled with the buttons on my long white leggings while he scribbled on the card that asked for donations for colored missions.

Most often, I sat with Angel, my maternal grandmother, in the Austen pew, the second from the front. David Austen, Angel's grandfather, had been co-chairman of the building committee of Grace Church when it was established in its present site at Tenth Street and Broadway in 1848.

As soon as I got into the pew, I unlocked the little drawer under the shelf and took out Aunt Amy's prayer book and hymnal. They were bound in red leather with a thin gold line around the edge, and inside was written her name, Amy Townsend, in a large running hand. Aunt Amy, Angel's older sister, shared this pew. She never married, and she was a great traveler at a time when single ladies were not globetrotters.

Globetrotter she was, as I learned later when Baedeker guide books for Greece, Egypt, Syria, and Holland (1897 edition) came to me through her will. She was also a "lady" of her time, an active member of the Colonial Dames and of the group of lady "visitors" of Mount Vernon.

I felt very important finding the places in the prayer book for my two elderly relatives. The clear, pure voices of the boy sopranos in the choir seemed to reach to the summit of the Gothic arches, and I never tired of looking at the mosaic of Christ in the center of the stone reredos over the main altar. He was hold-ing out his hands: "Let the little children come unto me." I knew that I was included.

The reredos was one of the many gifts Catherine Lorillard Wolfe had made to Grace Church. Great Aunt Catherine died in 1887 when Father was seventeen. She had exerted a great influence on him and was responsible for his interest in collecting books and works of art. She was, Father added proudly, the only woman on the founders' committee of the Metropolitan Museum of Art. Here in Grace Church the evidence of her benefactions was all around me. She had built the chantry and Grace House, and contributed to raising the spire and building the organ and the stone doorway leading to the sacristy. The copy of her portrait by Cabanel, a French portrait painter, hung in Grace House. The original is in the Metropolitan Museum, and we also have a copy in our home on Nineteenth Street. For me, Catherine Lorillard Wolfe is the only ancestor who counted; she was and still is a "presence." She believed what her father had taught her: "Wealth is a sacred trust to be administered in the fear of God and for the benefit of hu-manity." Grand-mère, Father's mother, had continued the tradition, giving the open air pulpit in memory of her husband, and a stained-glass window in the north transept, which I was looking at as the service was ending and the choir boys were filing out.

I longed to be with Grand-mère, who was already hurrying out. Every Sun-day afternoon she was driven down to her mission in Catherine Street, where she read the Bible to seamen, a bunch of violets pinned on her chinchilla muff. She was always alone in my great grandfather Japhet Bishop's pew. I was never allowed to sit with her. Although we had been singing "Love Divine, All Love Excelling," it made no difference. My grandmothers were not on speaking terms. Mother hated Grand-mère. Ours was not the only family feud; the Winthrop and Trevor grandmothers, friends of my parents, did not speak to each other. Although young Mrs. Winthrop had recovered completely from a postpartum psychosis, and her daughters were normal, the Trevors were accused of not hav-ing disclosed that there was "insanity in the family" before marriage with the Winthrops. But there were two granddaughters in that family, one for each grandmother on Sundays. There was only one of me.

Even after I was grown up, I never was able to find out what Mother's hate was all about. "Why, why?" I would ask.

Mother would turn to Father and say, "Your mother insulted my mother. It was all on account of Beatrice. I don't want Beatrice to have anything to do with her."

Father would not answer. In practice this meant that as a child, I was taken to visit Grand-mère only two or three times a winter.

Grand-mère was married at eighteen to my grandfather, David Bishop, a man twenty years older. David died in 1900, and Grand-mère almost immediately married John E. Parsons, a widower who became my godfather. He died in 1915. Grand-mère lived with him in his house at 30 East Thirty-sixth Street, opposite the Morgan Library.

On the occasions when Father took me to see Grand-mère, he usually stopped to visit Miss Belle Greene, the adviser of J. Pierpont Morgan. She was a great expert on books, and although the conversation was above my head, I retained the impression of lively and spirited talk while I shuffled my feet impatiently, wanting to get over to be with Grand-mère.

Grand-mère's house, in contrast to ours, always seemed very dark. The heavy velvet portieres and shades were drawn even during the day. We entered the parlor on the first floor, and Grand-mère took me into her arms. As soon as she released me I went over to the table with the miniature silver objects — a piano, a tea set, little chairs. I was allowed to play with them while mother and son talked.

"Have you heard from David recently?" Grand-mère asked.

"No," was the reply. "I expect he is having a good time in his château in France."

David was Father's younger brother, a bon vivant who lived in France all the year round. Grand-mère adored him.

Though Uncle David rarely came to the United States, I remember his visits to Lenox, when our otherwise silent house would be enlivened by a gay laugh that infected both my parents. I remember his showing off by breaking a pack of cards between his powerful hands — hands that were deft in handling the reins of spirited horses as well as the steering wheel of a French automobile swerving in and out among the Berkshire ruts.

I was setting the miniature tea kettle on the silver tray, when I heard Father call abruptly, "Time to go."

Grand-mère gave me a big hug and a box of Maillard chocolates filled with orange cream. She said to Father, "You're not going to leave that poor child alone in a hotel with her governess while you travel over Europe with Amy in the spring? She is so lonely. I feel sorry for her."

Father frowned but did not reply. I suppose Father and Mother construed this type of remark as interference. It served to fan Mother's continuing hatred.

≈≈ *2* _____

We were going up to Lenox for Christmas. I loved the snow, and coasting, skating, running by myself to the cow stable, where Francis the milkman taught me to milk cows and I drank the foaming warm milk, sometimes milking directly from the cow into my mouth. I loved the barn, too, where one could jump from the loft into a mass of loose, fragrant hay below. I rode a stubborn little black pony named Coucou, and later a donkey who brayed so vigorously that I wondered if his sides would split. Coucou could also be harnessed to a two-wheeled dog cart, in which Mother and I went out together. Her cocker spaniel, Red, with an unfashionably long tail, sat between us, and Mother said we must teach him to understand French. Later, when I was about fourteen, we had two Alaskan malamutes; I harnessed them to a toboggan, and we went racing through the snow.

Christmas was a big occasion, with a large Christmas tree at least twenty feet high in the horse stable, lighted with candles and decorated with fragile German-made ornaments, glowing balls, and a painted Santa Claus ascending in a gauze-covered balloon. The milkman played a live Santa Claus and helped Mother distribute the presents, one for each man, woman, and child in the families who worked on the estate — about fifty individuals altogether — presents which Mother had bought and which we had wrapped and labeled together.

But the Christmas when I was nine turned out to be very sad. On December 11, 1911, while we were in the midst of the present-wrapping ritual and Angel was sitting with us by the fire, the telephone rang — a comparatively rare occasion in those days. The operator relayed a cable from France. "It's David — he has shot himself," Father said.

Dead silence, broken only by Angel's quiet remark: "I'm so sorry, Cortlandt." That night I took the little pearl necklace and the little case that Uncle David had given me and put them under my pillow. I liked the case better than the necklace. It was plum-colored, the size and shape of a small English muffin split in two, lined with turquoise velours; on it were embossed gold letters I could trace in the dark with my fingers: D.W.B. to B.B. The carriage clock Mr. Parsons had given me struck ten before I fell asleep.

Following his father's death in 1900, my Uncle David had used his inheritance to buy a house in Paris and a château near Reims. There he lived the life of a French aristocrat, entertained the ten best guns in France with a shoot of two hundred partridges and fifty pheasants, and drove around in the newest models of French automobiles.

His mistress was an actress, to whom he left a considerable sum of money in his will—a legacy that Father did not contest. But why did David commit suicide? Another family mystery that was not discussed with a little girl.

I was taken to the funeral in Grace Church and we drove out to Greenwood Cemetery in Brooklyn for the interment. It was a gray December day. Mr. Parsons and Father supported Grand-mère as she put one foot in front of another going up the incline to the family plot. She leaned, appeared to sink against the granite stone, a heavy black veil over her face. I walked over timidly, and she took my hand into hers. Was Mother there? I don't remember. Though she hated Grand-mère, she had been friends with David.

The words of the committal service, so often repeated since that day, remain in my mind. "In the midst of life we are in death. Of whom may we seek for succor but of Thee, O Lord? Who, for our sins, art justly displeased." Grand-mère pulled herself up and dropped a bouquet of violets into the grave as a shovelful of wet earth hit the coffin with a dull thud.

The rest of that winter we spent in New York as usual, and I attended the Brearley School. We left for Paris in April: Father, Mother, Mother's personal maid, Father's valet, my governess, and I, plus a dozen Vuitton trunks. We always traveled on the French Line. Before World War I, the *Provence* was the flagship. Captain Poncelet took a fatherly interest in me, and I remember my glee, and his picking me up in his arms, when he discovered the paper *poisson d'avril* I had pinned on his back one April Fools' Day. For reasons that I did not understand, although Mother was not seasick, she remained wrapped in her deck chair most of the time. Father and I were excellent sailors and proud of the fact, making horrid remarks about the seasick Mademoiselle, and later, an equally seasick Fraulein, who came when I was ten.

In Paris we stayed at the Ritz, not exactly the place for a child to run, skip, and jump—running was the prerogative of the Aga Kahn, who, clad in white shirt and shorts, was the precursor of today's joggers as he trotted up and down in the hotel garden. I was taken to the Champs-Élysées, where I watched little boys guiding their toy sailboats in the pond while those on the shore intoned, *"Mon petit bateau a-t il des jambes? Mais oui, mon gros bêta; sans cela, il ne marcherait pas."* (Does my little boat have legs? Of course, dumb bunny; otherwise, he could not walk.)

In the Champs-Élysées there was "Guignol," the Punch and Judy show, a lively performance where the children shouted to warn Guignol and his red-nosed companion Gnafron that the gendarmes were coming around the corner. At the merry-go-round, the children were given a pointed spike to pull down a brass ring as the horse went by. The prize for the child who caught the greatest number of rings was a *sucre d'orge*, a long candy stick to suck into a point — the equivalent of our lollypops. I was never a winner.

In May and June my parents were off on their travels to Italy or North Africa. They had many friends among the Italian aristocracy. In fact, a cousin of Father's had married an Italian papal prince. My governess and I spent this time in Saint-Germain-en-Laye, forty-five minutes by train from Paris (now twenty minutes away via the new Métro).

Louis XIV was born in Saint-Germain; a gold-and-blue cradle medallion over the old hunting lodge, now an expensive restaurant, commemorates the fact. Saint-Germain is famous for its mile-long terrace with a view of Paris; today many high-rise buildings overpower the winding Seine below, and Montmartre is seen only dimly through mist and smog. The terrace, graveled and planted with rows of stately horse chestnuts, is a fine example of the formal style in which little is left to the imagination but an impression of clarity and order prevails. There are a few unimpressive limestone statues eroded by dampness and dirty green moss. Vercingetorix, the Gaul, with spear, boots, and a shock of long hair, is still there, although his name at the base of the statue is not longer visible. This was the man who defied the Romans — my hero and also the hero of the little French girls who skipped rope around him many years ago.

A *grande allée* at right angles to the terrace was the site of a spring fair when I was a child. That was my great delight. Grand-mère, not my parents, always provided me with pocket money — two ten-franc gold pieces stamped with a chanticleer. I kept them in the innermost compartment of my *porte monnaie*, a small accordion-fold purse of dark leather, with many compartments. The small gold pieces made me a rich little girl. I could go to the fair about four times during the season, play the tombola, perhaps win a goldfish, ride the merry-go-round, and buy *guimauve*, that gooey pastel pink, mauve, yellow, and white French version of marshmallow. There were also *sucres d'orge*, bigger than those I never won at the merry-go-round in the Champs-Élysées, wrapped in silvered blue paper with fringes at each end.

From one of these jaunts Fräulein and I walked proudly home, she leading her little fox terrier, I carrying a small glass container with a goldfish. Home at this point was 42, rue Voltaire, a boarding school where my governess and I were *pensionnaires libres* — paying guests. We left the terrace grounds where the fair was held and went past the château where Louis XIV held court until he moved to the more magnificent Versailles; then we went down a side street past the barracks where the sentry in red trousers and blue vest did not refuse to smile at the little girl marching along with her goldfish bowl.

Rue des Ursulines, originally, renamed rue Voltaire after the revolution, was one of these side streets. Number 42 had been the dwelling of the duc de Rohan. In later years, I often heard his proud motto quoted by my husband, Adolf: *"Roi je ne puis; ministre je ne veux pas — Rohan je suis."* ("I cannot be king; I don't wish to be minister — I am Rohan!")

When I was a child the massive entrance door was always closed and surmounted by a heavy stone cross. After the French Revolution it became a girls' boarding school; Hortense, the daughter of the Empress Josephine, who became the wife of Louis Napoleon and the mother of Napoleon III, was educated there. She was said to have left her mark — an *H* scratched into a window pane in the *cour d'honneur*. Of course, we girls believed that this scratch was authentic.

Later in the nineteenth century, the building was taken over by a small religious order of teaching nuns. By the time I came, in 1911, the nuns had been exiled by the anticlerical government and the boarding school was run by a lay director and took in paying guests in addition to the regular students.

I loved the place. Since the massive door was never opened, to enter, it was necessary to pull a rusty crooked wire almost buried in the corner of the street wall. The sound of a tinkling bell followed, and then a wrinkled face would peer through the grate and a small door would be opened into a courtyard in which the nasturtiums bloom eternally in my mind's eye. Under the *porte cochère* a half-open door revealed the chapel, with a statue of the Virgin against a blue sky. It would be surrounded with white lilacs in the month of May, the month of Mary.

On the left was the *parloir*, which was always locked, except when parents called here for their children to take them out on Thursday afternoons and Sundays. It was a hideous place with small straight-backed chairs and polished floors, shiny and slippery as the first black ice on a Berkshire pond. The *parloir* — literally translated, the talking room. How could anyone talk in that room?

Beyond, the tree-lined *cour d'honneur*, through which the religious processions filed, led to the main building and to *l'escalier d'honneur*, a stairway with a wrought-iron banister. *L'escalier d'honneur* stopped in front of a double-paneled door, and this was the door to our rooms. My governess occupied what had probably been the antechamber of the duke's apartments. My room was larger and had been converted by the nuns into a chapter room, or meeting room, before the convent was abolished in 1905. A strip of narrow benches lined the side walls, very convenient for spreading toys and keeping the nougat from Montelimar that my parents sent me. I slept on a narrow iron bedstead in the middle of the room.

A washbasin with a cold-water pitcher and slop bucket stood against the rear wall. As a good American, I was supposed to have a bath every night. A little maid brought up a pitcher of hot water and poured it into a rubber tub with flexible sides. It took just one little push with the foot to flood the room. Once, the maid poured the hot water into my goldfish bowl accidentally—or was it intentionally?

Two big French windows overlooked the *parc*. My governess and I had our meals alone in a small dining room. The regular *pensionnaires* ate most of their meals in silence while one of the teachers read from the lives of the saints. From time to time, on days when conversation was permitted, I was invited to join the students in the refectory.

I joined them every day at recess. We played in two hedged gravelly plots, skipping rope and shouting jingles: Alexander the Great (double turn of the rope) had a horse (another double turn) named Bucephalus (double turn). Alexander the Fat had a cat named Attila, and so on. But the real game was croquet. Not lawn croquet, as played silently and aggressively by Secretary Hull in Washington during World War II, but croquet played by sixteen girls constantly quarreling and arguing, balls running in, out, and over deep holes from which a ball must be lifted out by hand and replaced on the uneven ground. When the bell sounded for return to class, mallets were put down by the balls, the game to be continued at the next recreation. The renewed game always started with an argument and an accusation that someone's ball had been shoved into a hole.

On rainy days we played in a big, noisy hall with a stone floor. This hall had been built by the nuns to join the two palaces and overlooked a yard where a patient blindfolded horse walked around and around turning a wheel to supply the energy that brought water from the well. In this yard was the bathhouse, where the regular *pensionnaires* took their weekly baths under supervision.

At four o'clock we stood in line to get our *goûter*, or snack, a piece of hard bread and a chocolate bar—ten centimes.

At four-thirty one of the young maids jumped on the chain attached to the bell outside the recreation hall and pulled with all her might. The noisy clang marked the end of recreation. When the *pensionnaires* returned to class, the *parc*, as it was called, and which was sheltered from the street by an eight-foot wall, became mine, mine alone. It was my dream world, in which people, places and centuries merged.

First I sat on the green bench under the Judas tree and watched the pink flowers fluttering to the ground. This was the tree from which Judas hanged himself. Through the large open windows, I could see the girls in their black aprons sitting behind desks stained with purple ink, and I could hear the pens scratching, with the supervisor at a high desk calling *"Silence, mes enfants."*

The *perron des roses* was only fifty feet away. I only half-heard the sound of the tinny pianos and the metronome ticking as the girls practiced; that was unimportant. For me this was the moment every afternoon when I imagined Hortense de Beauharnois coming down the steps, not leaning on the railing lest she prick her fingers. She curtsied to her mother, the Empress Josephine, and the two with measured steps walked down the *allée des iris.* They were escorted by two pages, who held up their trains lest they become dusty on the white chalk walk. I was waiting for them at the bottom of the alley, where they stopped a moment to enjoy the lilacs — no lilacs, even New England blossoms, were ever as hauntingly perfumed.

Beyond the *allée des iris* there was a patch with two unpruned apple trees — this was Jeanne d'Arc's field where the blessed Saint Margaret and Saint Michael spoke to her through the branches.

A shaded walk of beech trees, *la grande allée,* brought me back to the main building. On the way I hesitated to climb a little rocky elevation covered with ivy on top of which stood three wooden crucifixes. That was Golgotha. I rushed back into reality, to the vegetable garden bathed in sunshine. The wall was lower here. The top could be reached by walking up a little ladder. This I did, and, dressed in little boys' shorts long before this was considered an appropriate costume for a girl child, I ran up and down the top of the wall. The *directrice* was scandalized, but in the background, unbeknownst to me, was a nun known to us as Mademoiselle Mulot, who had returned clandestinely to the convent and who was saying, *"La pauvre petite Américaine* is lonely; let her have a little fun."

Eventually it was time for lessons for me also; calligraphy, writing sentences and letters over and over again carefully between double lines, pages at a time; French grammar; dictation; French history and geography. These lessons were in preparation for the semiweekly sessions of the Cours Dieterlen in Paris. The Cours Dieterlen and other similar institutions were places where French children studying at home with governesses went to test their progress twice a week. These institutions were considered the equivalent of day schools. I was taken there on the train from Saint-Germain by my governess. About twenty of us sat around a large table covered with green carpeting, like a casino gaming table. The governesses sat around the walls behind the girls. Each girl had a little brown box in front of her. The teacher, at the head of the table, asked questions. The correct answer was rewarded with a little red chip, which the student promptly inserted into her brown box. At the end of the day Madame Dieterlen, in a violet dress with a wasp waist, her black hair pulled tight away from ivory temples, came in with her record book. We opened our boxes and counted our chips, and the numbers were entered in purple ink in Madame's book. My chips were very few.

At the end of the year the chips were added up, and those who had the most were rewarded at the "*distribution des prix*," receiving a crown of laurel and one or more red-bound books with gold designs. I never achieved a prize at the *cours*, but the kind ladies in Saint-Germain, as a reward for work done during the summer, did give me two books; one was a translation of *Evangeline* by Longfellow. The other was a novel, titled *All Alone*. The heroine of *All Alone* was a lonely girl who led a life of many difficulties, but the story ultimately had a happy ending. She married and lived happily ever after. This was to be my story, but of course, I did not know it then.

May was the month of Mary. Each of the big girls, those about fourteen or so, wore a wide blue ribbon over her black apron. They were the children of Mary. On the appointed day, the children who were to make their first communion were dressed like brides, all long white dresses with white veils over their faces. The rest of the students walked down under the linden trees in the *cour d'honneur* to the chapel. Each girl wore a little white cotton-rose crown on her head.

It was my greatest desire to take part in this procession. My German governess at the time was a Lutheran. The *directrice* recognized that I was a Protestant. There was no desire to convert me. I pleaded to be allowed to walk along in the procession. I wanted desperately to belong, not always to be on the outside looking in. Finally I was given a little crown of cotton roses and proudly marched along with the other children.

Late June each year brought us through Paris on the way to the seashore in Normandy, to Cabourg or Deauville, while my parents were off again. For several summers I had some real playmates—Jean, Paul, and Suzanne. I wore shorts just like a boy, and a sailor blouse with a big blue collar. We built sand fortresses and a big sand boat, and we waded into the water fishing for shrimp, pushing nets along the sea floor. Fishermen with big nets went in up to their waists, but we were not to go into water higher than our knees; we'd get our shorts wet and our German governesses would scold us.

These women must have had a hard time, for we were French chauvinists.

Foolish kids—we refused to learn German. Jean, Paul, and I read the Hansi books, which demanded the return of Alsace-Lorraine to France, so the idea of war was not outside our consciousness. We flew a toy French flag over our sand ship, and when the order for mobilization came in August 1914, we went to the station to see the soldiers off. As the crowd was waving goodbye to the boys piling into the trains, I saw a pale face, convulsed, a sobbing woman holding a babe in her arms, grabbing a man's hand stretched out the window as a trainful of recruits got underway. This picture remained with me for years, recalled over and over again in my mind's eye but now faded—pictures of wholesale slaughter have replaced it.

Fifteen days later Father appeared. I don't know where my parents had been traveling when war broke out, but they managed to get to England and Father crossed the channel from Southampton to Le Havre, taking me back to England with him. The German governess was left to fend for herself. We never heard from her again.

In London, I felt very sad, worrying about France and the war. France had become and remained something like a goddess whom I worshiped and to whom I wrote some very bad poetry. My parents were concerned with a more immediate question: how to find another governess for me.

This time it was an Englishwoman, Miss Ruby. Little Miss Ruby was barely five feet tall. She was not pretty—an English governess is not supposed to be. She was not severe nor distant. She loved me and, unlike some English people, was not afraid to be demonstrative. She was proper, certainly. "Your drawers," she insisted, "must always be intact or carefully mended so as not to shock the policemen in case you are picked up in an accident."

Miss Ruby was a loyal British subject, and the doings of His Majesty, King George V, and the glories of the British Empire under Queen Victoria were part of daily conversation. The royal family was her family. Father teased her, and I joined in. She stuck to her guns. Miss Ruby came by her love for the empire naturally, and in the long run she won, as through my adult life, because of Miss Ruby's loyalty, I have felt I could understand something of the British feeling for the crown. She was born about 1880 in Georgetown, British Guiana, where her father was a British civil servant and her mother ran a school for the daughters of British colonials. She was sent "home" to England to school but did not return to Guiana, since "I could not stand the heat." For a woman of that background, to become a governess was natural.

≈≈ *3* _____

When we returned to the United States, after the Battle of the Marne in the fall of 1914, I went back to the Brearley School but remained emotionally involved with France and followed the war news, marking the advances and retreats on the Somme front with little pins on a map in Father's room. Father put in the pins with me, and when the United States entered the war, he talked about joining up, but he never did. Maréchal Joffre's visit to New York was a great event. Grand-mère took me to the Metropolitan Opera to hear him speak. Joffre was my hero, the savior of France. I held Grand-mère's hand and shouted "La Marseillaise" while trying to restrain my tears.

On the streets of New York, I always looked at the French soldiers, flying aces, blind and crippled veterans. I wanted to do my bit to help the war effort. The Red Cross assigned individual soldiers as godsons to American ladies who knitted socks for them and wrote them letters. Mother was a great knitter and taught me how to turn heels in a sock.

The war summers were spent in the Berkshires with Miss Ruby while my parents traveled in California a good part of the time. The distance between us did not diminish.

Since the death of Grand-mère's husband, Mr. Parsons, in 1915, Mother had relented somewhat so that I was able to visit Grand-mère more frequently. She lived in the house in Lenox in which I was born. The piazza, where no one sat, was lined with pots of climbing Canterbury bells, white and blue. On hot days, the windows of the house were closed, the shades drawn. The house was cool, filled with the rich scent of double white peonies, dropping their petals on the stairs. Grand-mère, still in black, mourning for my Uncle David, spent a good deal of her time in the large drawing room upstairs with many photographs of David: one of him dressed as Romeo on the occasion of a fancy dress ball; another in front of his château; yet another showing him leaning forward from his chair as if he were speaking to us. One day when Father and I went to see her, we found her sitting at a table idly fitting pieces into a jigsaw puzzle. Her head was leaning to the side. David's snuff boxes and a variety of silver trinkets were on the table in the center of the room.

"I have such a headache, Cortlandt. I can't stand it."

"Have you seen a doctor?" Father asked.

"No doctor here can help me," she said plaintively. "Only Dr. G., that Russian in Paris. I want you to send for him."

"It will not be easy, Mother—you know it's wartime."

"Please, Cortlandt, do that for me."

Eventually Dr. G. came over and Grand-mère improved. Hypnosis, massage, medication—I don't know—but Father was not very sympathetic and pointed out that she was wasting a lot of money on that "quack."

When Grand-mère felt well, she went out driving in an open victoria. She came down the steps holding a small black parasol and was helped to her seat by George, the butler, who carried several small open brown baskets filled with cotton wool in which nestled three or four greenhouse peaches or nectarines. These Grand-mère was taking to sick or less fortunate friends. Occasionally, I would drive with her, but I found these drives slow and boring except at the start, when Tom Riley, the coachman, snapped his whip and touched the horses slightly on the rump so that they gave an imperceptible jump forward, and off we would go.

There was no need to take peaches to the neighbor across the road, since Mrs. Sloan had a greenhouse of her own, larger than Grand-mère's, and so did the owners of a ridiculous reproduction of Versailles at the end of an alley of poplars between Stockbridge and Lenox.

The greenhouse, like most greenhouses and gardens at the time, was run by Italian immigrants. Johnnie, born in Calabria, was secretly bent upon spoiling me. "Now see here, Miss Bishop, this is the key to the peach house, hanging on the nail behind the door so no one will come in and steal the fruit." With a big wink he hung the key on the nail. I did avail myself of this half license, but not too often!

Angel, my other Grand-mère, spent a month at Elm Court, the sprawling "summer cottage," presided over by Mrs. Emily Vanderbilt Sloan, who married Henry White, the diplomat, after the death of Mr. Sloan. Mrs. White was an erect little lady who lived a disciplined existence within her luxurious surroundings. When I bicycled down to visit Angel, who was having breakfast in bed at eight-forty-five, Mrs. White was starting off on her morning walk, accompanied by her white-and-black Great Dane, Pilor.

During the summer Mrs. White's daughters, Mrs. Hammond and Mrs. Burden, came to visit. Mrs. Hammond, the mother of John Henry Hammond, the now-famous jazz critic, held reunions of the women for whom she had conducted sewing classes when they were girls, and their parents were employed as gardeners. Diligently, sincerely, she inquired about their lives and served ice cream and cake.

Mrs. White had many grandchildren who were also visitors at Elm Court.

Adele Hammond and Sheila Burden were my contemporaries. At fourteen and fifteen we were still children, and treated as such. This meant that we did not have the evening meal with the grownups but ate at a small table with the housekeeper in the dining room while Stride, the English butler, six feet tall, and the equally tall footmen were setting the table for eight-o'clock dinner.

Dinner at Elm Court and in other similar houses of the period was always black tie for the gentlemen and dinner dress — long skirt, short sleeves — for the ladies.

Adele, Sheila, and I played tennis, and on rainy days Sheila taught Adele and me how to play poker on the porch under the gigantic elm, which has since succumbed to the Dutch elm disease. Sheila had learned to play poker from her older brothers. Hers was a special kind of poker in which one small white chip was specially prized and deuces were always wild.

The most exciting adventure, however, was climbing into a glass-enclosed lookout on the roof. It was reached by an inside ladder from the top floor. We poked our heads through the trapdoor and climbed onto a platform. The door closed after us, and we sat up there squeezed together munching stolen cookies, watching great thunderclouds gather all around us, lightning playing over the hills and lake. A clap of thunder, then a downpour. We were a bit scared, but dry.

School and College ≈

≈*4* _____

In 1917, Miss Ruby returned to England to "do her bit" for king and country. I never found out exactly what her bit was but believe it had something to do with food processing. I was desolated. For the two years following, we exchanged weekly letters. When the war ended, my parents and others tried unsuccessfully to arrange for her return to the United States.

Apparently I did not keep her letters, but those I wrote her were returned to me after her death. They gave the picture of a lonely child whose emotional life was wrapped up in a romantic feeling for France and a longing for this woman across the seas whom she felt was the only person who loved her and understood her. Sheila Burden, Adele Hammond, and the Schieffelins, who lived on Sixty-sixth Street, were friends, but at this juncture in my life I was not as emotionally involved with them as I was with Miss Ruby. My Brearley classmates remained on the fringes, because my parents did not allow me to visit in the homes of girls whose parents they did not know. Apparently the parents of Brearley girls were unknown to them! So I waited impatiently for my sixteenth birthday.

Sixteen was an important birthday when I was growing up. Girls who reached the age of "sweet sixteen" put their hair up, wore silk stockings, and attended small parties with boys in groups of six or eight—picnics, automobile rides, visiting in parents' homes. My hair was short. I did not care about stockings and knew nothing about boys, but sixteen was the legal age for obtaining a driving license in Massachusetts.

Father had taught me to drive a car when I was twelve years old, he and Mother having decided it would be safer for me to drive myself than to trust Félicien, a former blacksmith who, although a licensed chauffeur, frequently drove into the ditch. At that time, it was legal for a young person to drive a car if accompanied by a licensed operator, so Félicien sat by my side until the day of freedom arrived on August 6, 1918. Now with my own license I could go out by myself in the open French car Father let me use. It was painted bright red, with two bucket seats in front and a single seat in the back. I liked to drive through the woods with the four dogs — Mother's police dog, Lupo, the two Malamutes, and my cocker spaniel. I would stop the car by the brook and let the dogs run while I read, prayed and meditated, or just walked barefoot in the stream. I was gradually learning to use these hours alone and not to feel sorry for myself. After my confirmation in Grace Church, I experienced a conversion and felt that God was very close to me. I attended the early communion service and derived great strength from this practice. Entries in my diary for this period reflect my sense of peace and greater self-control. Henley's poem "Invictus" — "I am the master of my fate; I am the captain of my soul" — expressed these feelings.

Equally important was the experience of visiting in the homes of other girls. Up to this time I had not stayed overnight in anyone's home, so that I had no basis for comparing other people's family life with mine. Later I learned that they, too, had problems, but as I knew them then, their homes appeared to be all that I suddenly realized mine was not.

Adele Hammond lived in Mount Kisco. Her mother had the social prejudices of her class: Jews were not received. But she had a sense of social responsibility. Hers was the generation of women to which Eleanor Roosevelt belonged — women who had been educated by governesses, had not gone to college, but married well, brought up their families, and engaged in charitable works. Frequently they lacked critical judgment in selecting the causes that they supported, but they were sincere. This criticism is hindsight; when I was a girl all that mattered was that Mrs. Hammond cared for me as if I were her own daughter. In her home, there was laughter. We romped up and down the house and in the garden playing horse with John Henry, the young brother who became a leader in the jazz world, encouraging young musicians regardless of race, creed, or color. Robin, the butler, was our friend, not a bearer of tales to curry favor with the mistress. Mr. Hammond was a man of great good sense and understanding whose support became invaluable when I was planning to go to college.

That summer I also visited the Schieffelins in Bar Harbor. That visit was what used to be called a house party, and an equal number of boys and girls were invited. There was singing, horseback riding, tennis, and sailing. Adele and Sheila each had a beau, but I never knew who was supposed to be my beau. Perhaps it was Jay Schieffelin, a beautiful youth of twenty with a tenor voice that moved me deep down inside when he sang "It's a long way to Tipperary." I followed him like a little puppy dog, but he paid no attention to me. Still, it was all wonderful, and on the night train back I cried because it was all over. Pouring out my heart in letters to Miss Ruby, I wrote of my longing to develop a family life of our own. I must learn to love Mother and Father more. It was with the greatest anticipation that I waited for their return from California. This did not take place until September. Mother arrived alone. I was on the train platform to greet her and hugged her very hard.

Mother's arrival brought the household situation to a head. Miss Ruby's successor, a Mademoiselle, had come to blows with the housekeeper because the latter refused to serve us raspberries, though there were plenty in the garden. In spite of Mademoiselle's desire to leave immediately, I had succeeded in maintaining an uneasy equilibrium between these two women until Mother's return. Mademoiselle departed the day after Mother arrived home.

She was a sad creature whose sorrows were never revealed to me. I did not love her but felt sorry for her. I respected her learning — it was she who introduced me to Voltaire and Jean-Jacques Rousseau. The week after she left us I learned that she had died — suicide over an unfortunate love affair with a French *poilu* was the rumor. Who knows?

After Mademoiselle's departure, Mother tried to fire the housekeeper on the grounds of disrespect and conspiring with the Japanese servants to steal the family silver. Since Mother did not seem to be able to do this by herself, Mr. Buckingham, Father's secretary, was called in for the final act. But all the fuss did not matter to me. For the first time, Mother and I were alone together. We rode horseback, we laughed, we made chocolate custard in the little playhouse Grand-mère had built for me. But what Mother seemed to enjoy most was caressing Lupo, the police dog. He had a huge basket against the window in the living room in which he could lie stretched out on a flowered mattress. Mother would sit on the floor, petting him and brushing him by the hour in the evening while I read aloud to her. At times I wished some of this attention could have been directed to me, but this was only a passing thought; I felt during those few days that the wall between us was breaking down.

Although I told Mother I had never been so happy with her before, she did not seem to understand and this happy interval was of brief duration. The school year would be starting in October and I could not live alone with the servants in the Sixty-seventh Street house. A new mademoiselle must be found. Mother took the unusual step of going to New York herself to find one. This was my view of the new one at the time: "A bigoted old woman whose chief interest lies in over-

[25]

seas missions. She talks all the time, but I must admit she is well versed in French history and literature."

Father came home early in October and I took it upon myself to stay in the Berkshires to meet him at the train, in other words to miss school in New York. The war was not yet over. My interest had not diminished, and now that the United States was also a combatant, I kept insisting that Father must do something. He said he was considering a situation in the judge advocate's office; then in a dramatic tone he went on, "I cannot leave you and your mother."

I protested, "You can trust me—I will take care of Mother. I will do my part. It will be for you, for Mother, and for France." Nothing came of it.

Two weeks later, the influenza epidemic reached such proportions that my parents decided to keep me in the country. It was mid-October. I went walking in the woods with Father, the leaves, gold and red, dropping casually in the still air. We shuffled along the paths pushing the leaves before us and laughing. Suddenly our eyes met, and he took my hand and embraced me. It was as if we had never met before. We looked and looked into each other's eyes lovingly all the way home. The following day he took me for a drive up to Bennington, Vermont. I was ecstatic, worshiping him all the way. The circle of fire that I had always imagined as enclosing Mother and Father and separating them from the rest of the world was opening up, and they were lifting me up to join them. All this had happened in a month's time.

Miss Ruby continued to be my confidante:

> I think Mother has a most beautiful nature. She is so absolutely unselfish and so loving. She loves with all her heart, and she must have somebody to love her and do things for her. I don't think Mother has ever grown up, and there is a freshness and simplicity there that I have never found in anyone else. She is like a beautiful vine who needs to lean against a sturdy oak, and in return for the little protection, she gives all her love, her whole self. There is something too beautiful about her for this world. You see, I am only beginning to know Father and Mother intimately.
>
> I have quite a different feeling for Father than for any other person in this world. He and I must be very much alike, for we have reached a perfect understanding. He is a most intelligent and clever person. I cannot place his brain capacity too high. He is well aware that in many instances (and that gives him a most childish delight) he has done something or found out something important, but he does not follow through. That is, he never developed a sense of purpose. I don't know why, at least that is the only way I can explain the fact that he has not

made a mark in the world. Few people really understand him. Mother does not—in fact I really do not know who does, there are so many things in him which, had he had somebody like you in his youth, might have been brought out and put to good use.

But it turned out I was not the only star on Father's horizon. The beautiful Irene with auburn hair and a silken voice came to visit. Father and Mother had met her in California. She bewitched us all. With me she talked about France; with Mother it was knitting and Lupo; with Father it was motoring and rare books. Father and Irene went on long drives together. She seemed to understand him, and teased him when she thought he was eating too much. This delighted Mother, who was concerned about his weight, and Irene's remarks appeared to amuse him also.

Platonic friendships between men and women were not unusual in our world, and Mother and Father considered that these were part of upper-class civilized living, but Irene, I learned very soon, was different. Father was forty-eight, the age that a man, according to the French expression, becomes possessed with the *démon du midi* (literally "demon of noon"; the midlife crisis). When we returned to New York in November, after the worst of the influenza epidemic was over, I overheard Father talking to Irene on the telephone. His tone of voice and the expression on his face were somehow different—more like the way he had looked at me that day in the woods.

In the evening, I found Mother in her room in tears. "Your Father is in love with Irene," she sobbed. I was deeply shocked. It could not be that a love of twenty years could come to an end and that the circle of fire should break in another place. How could Father love Irene more than Mother? Mother in my eyes was so much more beautiful. I really do not know what happened finally; Irene returned to England soon after the armistice, and I never heard of her again.

≈ 5

How I was to get to college became my chief preoccupation. We were twenty-one girls in the class of 1919 at Brearley. Seventeen expected to go to college. Mother disapproved of college. She expected me to be a French *jeune fille* and to marry well. A good match was not defined exactly—probably a diplomat. "Do not marry a stockbroker," Mother said. "They are very dull and uncultured. Do not fall for a man with a title, for they are fortune hunters."

To keep up the French side of my education, the Brearley curriculum was supplemented by a number of private tutors. I studied French literature, composition, and history with a Mademoiselle at home. French diction and deportment were taught by a retired member of the Comédie-Française, a superb teacher. Deportment meant learning to enter a drawing room gracefully, to make a deep curtsy without falling over! In those days a *jeune fille* was expected to curtsy when introduced to an older lady, but she had to wait to become a young married lady before a gentleman bowed over her extended hand and kissed it ceremoniously.

Good diction came through learning by heart and reciting the majestic pentameters of Molière, Racine, and Corneille and phrasing the verse as if it were music. One of my Brearley classmates was also fluent in French, and we gave a small poetry recital in Angel's apartment. We played the scene from Molière's *Le Misanthrope* in which the prude (Arsinoé) and the coquette (Celimène) joust in subtle irony.

At home, I also had private lessons in Italian and Spanish and received religious instruction, learning the catechism—"My duty toward God and toward my neighbor." This included doing my duty in whatever station to which it pleased God to call me—not a revolutionary creed. Unfortunately, music lessons were not included—Grand-mère wanted to give me a piano, but Mother said I was tone-deaf and I had better stick to languages.

These studies were designed to prepare me for the French Baccalauréat. I wanted to be French, but I wanted to be American, too.

My parents' extreme snobbishness was not going unchallenged. In Lenox on summer afternoons, in Father's library, I had read Rousseau. "All men are born equal and good. Society generates evil." Following the recommendation of Miss Anne Dunn, a teacher of English at Brearley, I got up at six o'clock in the morning (lights were out at 9:00 P.M.) to read Bertrand Russell's *Proposed Roads to Freedom*. By what right were my parents wealthy? was the question I started to ask. To answer that query and others like it, I must study more. I must go to college over Mother's objections. Father did not oppose the idea, but he gave me no active support. Both he and Mother were again out of reach, within that circle of fire which I could not penetrate.

There were endless discussions, which went something like this:

Mother's question: "Why do you want to go to college?"

My reply: "I want to learn. I want to do something worthwhile in the world."

Mother: "Nonsense. You will become a bluestocking and no man will look at you. Men can't bear women who think they know everything."

(It seems that the term *bluestocking* is no longer used. My grandson, a Vassar graduate, had never heard it. "Did you mean liberated?" he asked. "Perhaps," I replied.)

"Anti Bi," Mother went on, "never went to college. She has accomplished a great deal—she married a diplomat."

I protested, "Anti Bi keeps telling me she wishes she had gone to college and that I should go. Things are different now than they were with you, when going to balls was the only occupation. Elsie Clews Parsons went to college. She is a doctor of philosophy, and she writes books."

Mother: "She is the kind of bluestocking I am talking about. Her hair is always falling down her face, she is sloppy, and she doesn't take care of her children. Lissa, who came to skate with you last winter, has no manners. I don't want you to have anything to do with her."

Elsie Clews Parsons had married the son of my godfather, John E. Parsons, Grand-mère's second husband. She was a distinguished social anthropologist at a time when the field did not yet exist. In 1906, she published a book called *The Family*, an ethnological-historical outline, a textbook for use in college courses. Certain passages in the chapter entitled "Ethical Considerations" make interesting reading even today:

> We have given late marriage and the passing of prostitution two alternatives, the requirement of absolute chastity of both sexes until marriage or the tolerance of freedom of sexual intercourse on the part of the unmarried of both sexes before marriage, i.e., before the birth of offspring. . . . It would seem well from this point of view to encourage early trial marriage, the relation entered into with a view to permanency but with the privilege of breaking it if it proved unsuccessful and in the absence of offspring without suffering any great degree of public condemnation.

Much space is devoted to child rearing and to the importance of parental care and nurture.

Unfortunately I met Dr. Parsons only casually and did not read her book until I was in college, so that I was never able to discuss her theories with her in person. She was a brave woman, for although criticism of her views never ceased, she continued going on field trips and contributing to scientific journals. She bore four children. One of these was Lissa of the spotted skirt and poor manners, now deceased, who paradoxically never went to college and who married a man of good family, whom she divorced.

A tale, no doubt apocryphal, circulated among Mother's friends about ten-year-old John, Elsie's son — was that he once cut his finger on purpose so that his mother would come out of her study to care for him.

In spite of Mother's objections I persisted in my efforts. I carried out a lengthy correspondence with C. Mildred Thompson, the secretary of admissions and also professor of history at Vassar College, who was to become a dear personal friend of mine, my husband's, and my daughter Beatrice's. Most of my Brearley classmates were choosing Bryn Mawr, but I was interested in Vassar because I wanted to make a fresh start. Also, it was only seventy miles from the Berkshires. Eventually I was admitted to both colleges.

Mother continued her opposition. My pleas were to no avail. I cried myself to sleep on more than one occasion and was almost reaching the point of giving up, when I told my troubles to Mrs. Hammond, who promised to intercede in my behalf. But the best advice came from Mr. Hammond: "Be calm, sit tight, and smile." It worked.

The great day came in September 1919. Mother wept as I left the house, but she did not scold. Father drove me over from Lenox and deposited me in an off-campus house where some of the late registrants were to live. "You have your own way to make. You have a great opportunity," he said in dramatic tones as he got into his car and drove off. I do not recall being homesick; I was just thrilled, especially by the library and the introductory course in European history given by Miss Thompson.

The library was even better than Father's — open shelves upon open shelves, with tables at which one could sit and read! The English department also had great teachers — Miss Wylie and Miss Winifred Smith.

In those days, freshmen were allowed one weekend a month away from campus, and ten o'clock was the hour for returning to the dormitory. All this, of course, did not bother me; it was a great deal more freedom than I had at home. There were simple pleasures such as walking to the cider mill (about a mile and a half) in the fall and sleeping out on the hill in the springtime. The seniors were very kind to me, treating me and caring for me like the child I was. Caroline Ware (class of 1920), who later married Gardiner Means, co-author with Adolf of *The Modern Corporation and Private Property*, became a good friend.

My own classmates played a minor role in my life, and there were only three or four with whom I remained in contact after college. Once again, the professors, notably Miss Thompson, were my closest friends.

At the end of freshman year, the spring outdoor play was the great event for me. I worked the lights, sliding colored isinglass squares over floodlights in the dewy, sweet-smelling May nights.

Then came the agonizing drawing for rooms, selecting roommates, and forming the groups that would go into each of the dormitories. I was alone, and so was another forlorn girl, who had straw-colored hair, a prominent nose, and thick lips. We hardly knew each other, but we decided to risk rooming together. She came from a small town in the Middle West. Her father was the owner of a shoe store, her mother was fat, and all three spoke with a nasal twang. Mother would have called them "common, not in your class," but for me this was immaterial. "All men are equal and good." This was Rousseau's doctrine, which I espoused wholeheartedly.

We drew a three-room suite in the corner of Lathrop Hall. I was very naïve and obtuse. In spite of my faith in Rousseau, the cultural and social differences between my roommate and me made her very unhappy. I am afraid that I was quite unaware that she was miserable and demanding of an affection that I did not feel. A visit to our home in Lenox, for which I had obtained grudging permission from my parents, reduced her to tears. We both withered under Mother's disapproving glance. Fortunately at Vassar, Mildred Thompson rescued us, and in due course I moved to a single room.

≈≈ 6

I had been waiting impatiently for the end of the term and a return to France, to Saint-Germain, where I had stayed before the war, to hear French spoken around me. I knew that I spoke as well as any French girl. The Normandy farms' thatched roofs, the children in their black aprons, the *bec-de-gaz* (gas-lamp posts) — all these had featured in my dreams for the past five years. The fact that I did not know any people there did not appear to bother me. I had lost track of Jean, Paul, and Suzanne and at this time Mademoiselle Mulot, who was to become so important in my life, was still only a shadowy figure. The garden in Saint-Germain was my secret world, where for years I had walked in my imagination before falling asleep. I had smelled the lilacs, picked the *bigarreaus* (the big cherries), felt the heat on the chalk walk with the Empress Josephine, and sat quietly in the ivy grove at the foot of Our Lady's statue.

After the war, the French government relaxed the anticlerical regulations. The nuns were able to return to the convent, although they did not wear their habits in the classroom. The rooms that I had formerly occupied were put back to their original use. The *salle des chapitres*, with the narrow bench lining the wall where my dolls had been assembled, was taken over by the religious congregation for their meetings.

Becoming a regular boarder was not desirable. Both my parents, who were heartily in favor of the baccalauréat, and the nuns agreed that *"la petite Américaine"* needed a little more freedom, so it was arranged that I should live with a governess in a pension in the town of Saint-Germain and spend the day at school. I cannot recall who this governess was; dear Miss Ruby was unavailable.

This "semester abroad" ltook place in the spring of 1921, after I had persuaded Vassar to grant me college credits for my work in France.

French education, then and until the upheaval of 1968, was much more structured than education in the United States.

The baccalauréat, which marks the end of secondary eduction in France and is the passport for entrance to a university, was considered equivalent to the first two years of college. The situation is somewhat different today, since the standards of the better American colleges have risen and those of the baccalauréat since the 1968 revolution have relaxed somewhat. Still, even today, the baccalauréat, the *bac* as it is called, is important.

The essay is the center of the examination. Abstract conceptual thinking is stressed, in contrast to American pragmatism. Parents and grandparents compare notes on the theme subjects with the same fervor with which enthusiastic Harvard men discuss football scores. There are those who claim that the travail associated with childbirth is not as hard on parents as the baccalauréat — painless, natural baccalauréat has yet to be invented.

The division of the baccalauréat for which I was preparing was Latin and modern languages. This involved French literature and composition, history and geography, and English and Italian as second languages.

There were four of us studying with our tutor, Mademoiselle Mulot, for the *bac* — Geneviève, Germaine, Simonne, and myself. Simonne was my special friend. She had a protruding, discolored eyeball and was blind in that eye. This was a congenital defect that her parents had neglected, since she was a girl and the family did not have the means to give her a substantial dowry. Her brother would inherit the title and the property. The nuns had a well-established solution for this type of problem. Simonne was to enter a religious order and become a teacher. This she did.

I saw Simonne several times after she had taken her vows and found in her a simple gaiety and sense of peace that had been entirely absent in our earlier association. Unfortunately, she died of tuberculosis a few years later.

The other two girls also found their own way. Geneviève, brilliant and a ball of fire, went on to graduate work and became the principal of a French *lycée* in Algeria.

Germaine, the daughter of the painter Maurice Denis, a precursor of Cézanne, remained in Saint-Germain and raised a fine family.

We had one strong bond in common that was maintained through the years. Mademoiselle Mulot loved us, and we loved her and continued to visit her until she died fifty years later. At the age of twenty, Geneviève Mulot, the only daughter of a physician, felt she had a vocation and decided to enter religious orders, a career her parents could not contradict. Shortly after she took the veil, the nuns were obliged to leave the country, and they took refuge in England. Just before the war, Mademoiselle and others had returned to Saint-Germain, operating as lay teachers and gradually taking over the direction of the establishment until they could do so officially after the war. She was the one, unbeknownst to me, who had befriended *"la petite Américaine"* years before, had encouraged my running up and down the garden wall and permitted me to take part in the religious procession. But as mentioned, she and the other nuns held firmly to the point of view that *"la petite Américaine"* came from a Protestant background and was not to be converted to Catholicism.

She was a superb teacher with an incisive, logical mind. More than that, for me she became a guide, counselor, and friend. A woman with a deep faith in God, she believed that the teacher must develop both the mind and the character of her pupil. This she called *"la formation,"* the molding of character.

In the late afternoons, Corneille and Racine were put aside. Mademoiselle and I walked up and down the *grand allée, "bras dessus, bras dessous"* (arm in arm), her supple body clad in a black dress. Her long, expressive fingers, her burning dark eyes in deep sockets, and her eloquent speech held me spellbound. The nuns wore their habits only when they were in the cloistered part of the building, and they continued to be called Mademoiselle by the students. As shafts of sunlight filtered through the beeches, we paused and sat on a mossy little bench and discussed authority. She had taken the vows of obedience, chastity and poverty—her life was bound by *"la règle,"* by authority, but within that framework she never ceased to think her own thoughts, successfully challenging the narrow minds who put the Old Testament and Pascal on the index. How could she be a teacher if she had not read these books? she argued.

I told her of the many infuriating rules set down by my parents. Although after World War I, even "nice" French girls walked alone in the streets of Paris, Mother forbade me to do so and clinched her veto with the phrase *"Cela ne se fait pas"*—it is not done. "You cannot go against your mother's commands," Mademoiselle would say. "You should try to persuade her." (Note that I never succeeded.) "But you can always keep on thinking for yourself, and you can never afford to be bitter. Bitterness and hate destroy the soul. You may have to fight when it comes to the most important decision in life, that is, in regard to marriage. Do not let your family marry you off." This celibate woman, whose experience of the world came through literature and through talking to young people like me, had very definite ideas about the role of women and the quality of marriage. Woman is to be the companion of man, the mother of his children. Companionship means the sharing of a common life and of intellectual interest, not subservience to the man. Above all, each must respect the other's personality. Marrying well does not mean money or position, but mutual love and understanding.

Kissing me gently on the forehead, "the most noble part of the face," she would say, "I believe you are learning to cultivate *la vie intérieure*—the inner self where you commune with God and pray every day. Prayer is not asking little favors, but practicing the presence of God. You are like a rosebud that will probably not come into full bloom for another ten years." I married Adolf seven years later.

Italian was taught by a very myopic *signorina*: her glasses, inadequately held in place by a black ribbon, were always falling off her nose. She would read passionately from Dante and Leopardi so that the cadence of the great poets has remained with me through all these years.

The day of the baccalauréat, we went up to Paris. A mass had been said for us in the chapel. Mademoiselle did not go with us, for she was not allowed to leave the convent. She was confident that we would pass. We had all worked hard, she said, and we were well prepared; we had not been *"chauffée"*—"warmed up"—or crammed at the last minute.

The written test took place in what appeared to me to be some kind of garret at the Sorbonne. The day was very hot. A *pion*, or proctor, walked up and down between the aisles to prevent us from cheating. I was shocked. In those days, at Brearley and Vassar, the honor system worked; cheating was unheard of. (Apparently this is no longer true.) Teachers would make a point of leaving the room from time to time to prove that we were trusted. In the attic at the Sorbonne, in spite of the *pion*, notes were passed back and forth between students.

For me the Latin version was the most difficult part of the examination. When reading Virgil at Brearley, we were expected to understand the meaning of the text and to make a rough translation. In France under the guidance of Monsieur Colonnier, the Latin teacher, we wrote a *version latine*. To perform this exercise, a piece of lined copy-book paper is folded down the middle, lengthwise. On the left-hand side about thirty lines of an assigned Latin text are copied; on the other side of the fold is written the student's French translation. The translation must be in correct idiomatic French and must not cover more space than does the Latin. Naturally, the Latin words will be spaced a little farther apart, but this device is not very elastic, and a strict construction of the text is imperative. A fat Latin-French dictionary was part of the necessary equipment and was brought in to the final examination. I had two copies, one in France, the other in New York.

After the examination, as Monsieur Colonnier was standing in the courtyard of the Sorbonne, I proudly and gratefully presented him with my copy of the dictionary. He almost dropped it. "How can you afford to part with so precious a volume?" he exclaimed.

"I have another copy in New York," I explained.

"How is it possible? It costs fifty francs."

Monsieur Colonnier was the only male member of the faculty at Saint-Germain. A dedicated, overworked, and conscientious teacher, he taught boys in a Jesuit school and came to the rue Voltaire two days a week for the advanced students. We knew that he had five children, and we learned later that two of them became Jesuit missionaries in Madagascar. He was frugal, like the ant in La Fontaine's fable *La Cigale et la Fourmi*. His children were not allowed to go to a *patisserie* lest the taste for chocolate éclairs and other delicacies grow out of bounds and he not be able to keep up with their demands.

After his astonishment and embarrassment over my gift had subsided, he embraced the dictionary, and the five feet of him strutted across the courtyard. I fear the gift did not provide chocolate éclairs for André, Élisabeth, Jean-Pierre, Geneviève, and Françoise.

Several days after the written examination, the candidates returned to the Sorbonne to learn the results. Those who had not passed the written were not admitted to the oral examination. Out of probably fifty candidates in my group, only a small handful passed the written. Those whose names were not called shouted, and were about to mob the examiners sitting behind a balustrade in the lecture hall. *"Evacuez la salle!"* (Clear the hall!) thundered the professors. In marched the Garde Républicaine. Order was restored, and the examination proceeded.

The candidate's whole family may turn up at the oral, but since the several examiners sit behind a long, high table and the student stands below like a supplicant, those in the audience cannot hear; they can only study the expressions on both sides of the table. Monsieur Colonnier was there, and so was Father. Dear Capitaine Poncelet of the French Line, in full regalia and decorations, was pounding the floor with his cane as the *"recalés,"* those who had not passed, were evacuated by the gendarme. To the satisfaction of all concerned, I passed with *mention bien*, that is, with honors.

≈ 7

_____

The day after the baccalauréat, Father, Mother, and I were lunching together. Lunch at the Ritz was always an event. I was very happy — the flames had parted, and once again I was within the circle. Father always commanded the best table and the undivided attention of Olivier, the maitre d'hôtel. The Aga Kahn and other dignitaries could wait. Father came first. Olivier was bending over Father's shoulder, pencil in hand. "I recommend the sole grillée today. I know Monsieur and Madame like it, and I expect Mademoiselle does too. By the way, congratulations, mademoiselle. You should be very proud of passing your *bachot* with *mention bien*; only a few young French people achieve that." We all beamed.

While Olivier was dissecting the sole, lifting out the backbone, and passing a reconstituted fish to each of us in turn, I announced in firm tones, "Mother, I am going to the Louvre this afternoon."

"Haven't I told you a *jeune fille* does not go out alone in Paris? I will send my maid Josephine with you."

"But Mother, that was before the war. Now everyone goes out alone. L., the daughter of the Marquise de B., goes all over Paris by herself. Besides, I am grown up now. I have my *bachot*."

"As far as I am concerned, *cela ne se fait pas*. It is not done." How I hated that phrase. But there seemed to be no escape. Mother sent her personal maid to trail after me — Josephine was fat. I didn't care if her feet hurt. I walked as fast as I could and kept a good hundred feet ahead of her.

Most of the time I went out with Father. We went to the Comédie-Française frequently. The repertory then and now included classical plays; Molière, Racine, Corneille. I was thrilled listening to the declamation of some of the great pieces I had learned by heart, and I repeated the lines under my breath. *Le Bourgeois*

Gentilhomme, discovering that indeed he was speaking "prose," always raised a chuckle.

Father enjoyed the classics also but did not know the texts as well as I did. "I guess, Donkey, you learned something preparing for the baccalauréat," he grinned as we came out of the theater and went for a stroll in the Palais Royal. We both enjoyed looking at the window displays of decorations from all countries — red ribbons, blue ribbons, gold medals, magnificent crosses. Father seemed a bit wistful. I suppose he longed for a Légion d'Honneur so that he might wear a slip of a red ribbon in his buttonhole.

But the most privileged and the most looked-forward-to outing was a visit to the bookshop, 44, passage des Panoramas, over which Monsieur Edouard Rahir presided. Father was a small collector, but he was a discriminating one. Incunabula (books printed before 1501), French books printed in the eighteenth century, and *livres des provenances* (books that belonged to special people and bore their coat of arms stamped on the binding) formed the base of his collection. Monsieur Rahir, a legendary figure in the book world, was very selective in his choice of clients. He and Father were friends. The relationship between agent and client can be very special — there is, of course, the jockeying between both parties to agree on a fair price but more important is the growing mutual respect and the interchange of ideas that takes place between agent and client over the years.

On the outside, 44, passage des Panoramas was very unpretentious, with a couple of ordinary leatherbound books in the window. Opening the door into the shop was followed by a sharp metallic ring; an oldish man in a black suit appeared and looked suspiciously on the intruder. A few words were exchanged, and the stranger left; but if the visitor was a friend, Monsieur Francisque shook hands, beamed, and announced, *"Monsieur Rahir arrive à l'instant."* Monsieur Rahir, also dressed in black with a little black goatee and dark eyes set in deep sockets, emerged and the conversation about the last auction sale began in earnest.

The shop was lined with glass-enclosed bookcases from ceiling to floor. There was a large bare table in the middle, and small straight chairs were brought in from the rear if a book was to be examined. On this particular day the conversation between Monsieur Rahir and Father was rudely interrupted when I, who had been leaning against a bookcase, suddenly slid to the floor under the table. I was mortified.

It was Monsieur Rahir who rescued me and helped me to my feet, while I could hear Father muttering under his breath, *"Mon Dieu, que tu es bête."* Monsieur Rahir addressed me as if nothing happened. "I understand, Mademoiselle, that you were preparing for your baccalauréat in the establishment in Saint-Germain which had formerly been a boarding school attended by Queen Hortense, the daughter of Empress Josephine and mother of Napoleon III."

"*Oui, oui, monsieur,*" I replied eagerly. "And I have seen the pane of glass on which she is supposed to have scratched her *H*."

"I can show you much better than that," Monsieur Rahir smiled. Three chairs were brought out and then a large volume with an *H* and a crown stamped in gold in the middle of the Moroccan red leather binding. There were gold lyres in the corners. "This is a volume of romantic songs that the queen had ordered especially and dedicated to her brother Prince Eugene. She loved music and flowers."

So my dreams of Hortense walking down the *"allée des iris"* in Saint-Germain were not altogether fanciful, I thought as I caressed the binding and outlined the indented *H* with my fingers.

By this time Father was mollified, and the conversation between the two gentlemen followed its usual course.

Mother had her own interests. With a car and a chauffeur of her own, she drove to little shops in remote parts of Paris where she picked up presents for Angel and Anti Bi—presents like marabou feathers, fans that would be placed on the edge of the Metropolitan Opera box in New York the following season. She also bought beautiful sheets for her bed, uniforms for the footmen, and other "essentials" for her artificial life. These were then stashed in the twenty numbered trunks that lined the hall in front of her suite at the Ritz.

Occasionally I went with Mother to the dressmaker, and in my eyes she emerged more beautiful than ever. She was my Venus, as she liked to be called. I hated dressmakers, but I really enjoyed being fitted for a riding habit at Busvine's, the best tailor in Paris. There were also perfectly fitted riding boots from a bootmaker on rue Saint-Honoré. While shopping, Mother did not forget Red, her cocker spaniel. He was to be outfitted with little red rubber booties with black snap buttons. Naturally, when Mother tried to put them on back in Lenox, Red refused to allow it.

In Paris, Mother and Father had a special activity of their own, the purchase of new pearls for Mother's necklace. This was before the days of artificial pearls. Mother wore her necklace all the time—even at night, when she would slip it into a chamois case which she hung around her neck. The constant contact with body warmth was said to increase the luster of the pearls. Apparently this necklace was started when Mother and Father were first married, and now every year they added a pearl or two, discarding one of lesser quality.

[38]

The pearl merchant would arrive at the Ritz and unwrap his treasures. Each pearl was in a carefully folded package of fine tissue paper to which was attached a small tag with the price and weight noted on it. They were laid out on a black cloth while we three looked on and fingered them delicately. Each was about the size of a robin's egg, slightly irregular, with the feel of silk on stone and an almost imperceptible golden sheen that would become more golden with wearing. Father and Mother would then compare them with those on the necklace and decide upon their comparative worth.

I looked on, but I had no desire to own such a necklace. How could one run or play tennis, with such a big string around the neck? Besides, I had a necklace of my own with less-than-pea-sized matching pearls, which Uncle David had given me. A necklace of the kind Mother wore must be restrung from time to time. Mother did this herself. She was an expert, and I enjoyed watching her. Each pearl had to be separated exactly from the next by a special knot without a great interval of silk being visible, so that each pearl could be seen individually and yet be a part of the whole.

While in Paris we sometimes drove out on Sunday to the château of the Marquis de B., about ten kilometers beyond Versailles. The marquise was an American, a childhood friend of Mother's. Everyone knew that the marquis had married her for her money and had made good use of her fortune in restoring the château.

She was a lonely woman and had never succeeded in getting beyond a formal relationship with her French relatives. Courtesy can be cold comfort after twenty years. The marquis was a good shot, enjoyed the races, and took great pride in his property. Their daughter, Leta, was two or three years older than I and was engaged to a marquis.

One Sunday we played a foursome at tennis—Leta, the young marquis, her fiancé, the Comte de S., and I. The Comte de S. asked me if he might call. A few days later he appeared at the Ritz with a box of chocolates. I was delighted. What is more lovely than a box of French chocolates? The box is wrapped in white paper, pleated on the top like a skirt, and tied with a colored ribbon. It may be gold cardboard or, as in this case, the lid may carry a tapestried reproduction of a gallant scene—shepherdess with crook, shepherd kneeling at her feet. At last we come to the chocolates, round ones, square ones, all in straight rows divided by gilt-cardboard partitions.

The Comte de S. was a quiet, soft-spoken man with a slight limp, the result of a war wound. He had nice tastes and was a client of Rahir's. Father came in as I was telling him about Queen Hortense's collection of "romances." The young man rose to leave at the end of five minutes, since Father's manner was less than cordial. After he had left, Father said, "I don't like that man. I don't want you to see him again." I decided not to make an issue of this, since we were leaving for Brittany at the end of the week.

The following day another young Frenchman, whom I had met in New York through the Burdens, called with his sister and invited me to dine with them. I was given permission; the sister, being thirty years old, would act as chaperone. After dinner we went to a nightclub on the Left Bank. It was noisy, and I was not greatly amused. When we returned Father was furious and told the young man he had no business to take his sister and me to such a vulgar place. I, too, was furious since I had already made up my mind I did not care for that kind of place and did not need Father to tell me so.

At last we were off. Touring western Europe by car was Mother and Father's favorite pastime. Since the days before my birth, when Gabriel's horn sounded through the Berkshires to warn pedestrians and horses off the roads, Father had had many custom-made cars. This one was a Hispano Suiza, with solid top and open sides. The luggage was carried on the roof. Mother and Father's trunks were custom-made to fit in the rounded corners. Alphonse, the chauffeur, Mother's personal maid, and I each had a suitcase. The whole was covered by a tarpaulin.

Father always drove. He was a superb driver. Mother sat in front with him. I sat behind him, map in hand, hoping to steer him faultlessly through towns with which he was usually more familiar than was the Michelin guide. The maid sat in the other corner, and Alphonse sat in the middle.

I felt very close to Alphonse. His only son had been killed in the war, and as he spoke of him, his eyes would fill with tears and the picture of the troop train I had seen going off in 1914 would rise before me. "We had such hopes for him, my wife and I. We thought he could pass his baccalauréat and become a lawyer, not just a workman like me. You are lucky, mademoiselle. You have two fine parents, and you have your *bac*." I tried to dispel the shadows by letting the wind take my thoughts as we raced through the French countryside, and an unexpected shower washed my face clean.

Saint-Malo was our first overnight stop. This is a gray-walled town from which Jacques Cartier started for America in 1525. In the evening, the Bretons sat open-mouthed watching a new phenomenon, a film projected against the old fortress wall. The following day we stopped at Cancale, famous for its oysters. Father and I sat at a wooden table on the wharf, sucking them up noisily and drinking white wine, while Mother looked on disapprovingly.

Tréguier was the next relay, the home of Joseph Ernest Renan, whose life of Jesus I had read aloud to Mother. Renan was a nineteenth-century rationalist. He was the first to present Jesus as a man, and his poem *"La Prière sur l'Acropole"* extolled the virtues of the Greek worship of reason. Here in the square of the small Breton town, I looked at his statue. The inscription at the base of his statue in the square read, *"La foi qu'on a eu ne doit jamais être une chaine."* Freely translated, this meant "Let not the faith that you no longer hold be a chain." The square was crowded with peasants in their native costume filing into the little church to attend mass. I followed them in saying to myself, faith, remember, is not superstition or credulity. "Faith is the substance of things hoped for, the evidence of things not seen" (Hebrews 11:1).

Morgat, at the far western end of Brittany, south of Brest, was our destination. It was a small village on a half-moon beach with one hotel where French families spent a vacation month not doing anything in particular.

Father took me for short drives into various little inlets. Some are so well protected that palm trees grow down to the sea. One delighted me especially — the hamlet was called Sainte-Anne. Legend has it that Saint Anne, the mother of Our Lady, with Mary Magdalen and John the apostle, landed there after the crucifixion. Did she come here from Saintes-Maries-des-Mers south of Marseille, where the fortress church in the marsh is the holy site for a Gypsy's annual pilgrimage? Who knows! It does not matter. I enjoy the mental picture of a charmed and sacred open ship being wafted improbably across the seas regardless of the laws of navigation.

In Morgat, we went bathing together, the three of us, Mother rather gingerly, wearing a large hat to protect her from the sun, and I joyously, swimming vigorously with Father as we ducked each other. There were days when I felt very close to both of them. I read aloud to Mother (that summer it was Victor Hugo's *Les Misérables*) as she knitted or strung her pearls, and we were very affectionate. Sometimes Father hugged me, saying, "There is no one with whom I feel more at home than I do with you." At other times he seemed very distant. I was realizing I must try to understand him if he was to understand me. This must be because he had always been his own master, I said to myself, and no one had ever contradicted him.

After two weeks at Morgat, we crossed France en route for Aix-les-Bains in Savoie.

Aix-les-Bains was one of the fashionable watering places in the nineteenth century. To go for a cure, to take the waters, was a folkway scorned by most Americans — in fact, Saratoga Springs, although probably medicinally as efficacious as other springs, never had the vogue of places like Baden-Baden, Karlsbad, Vichy, or Évian. Of course, in Europe, the attraction was not just the waters, but the accompanying régime designed to encourage a righteous, sober life and to rest the liver! Every day the guests gathered at the fountain, drinking large glasses of water at appointed hours, walking around and around, flirting, and playing baccarat in the evening.

Some also took the baths. Mother was one of these. Every morning, two men carrying a litter enclosed by heavy striped red-and-white curtains called at the Grand Hotel. Wrapped from head to toe in a white terrycloth bathrobe, Mother stepped into the litter and was carried to the bathhouse about a mile away. After the bath and the massage, the litter bearers might pause for a moment at the flower market while Mother purchased several bunches of mountain cyclamen. These little flowers are much smaller than those of the same name that grow in our greenhouses. They are picked early in the morning in the mountains, tied together tightly with twine, wrapped in wet moss and packed in a small wicker basket. Their delicate perfume has never ceased to haunt me, and their color came alive for me again years later when Adolf gave me an evening dress *couleur de cyclamen.*

Father did not take the cure but drove his sports car up and down the mountain passes, which he had climbed on a three-wheeled bicycle when he was eighteen. In the afternoons, if he were not off on a day's excursion, he would take Mother and other friends out for a drive and tea, and sometimes I was invited to go along.

One afternoon Father drove us all down to Le Grand Port, on the shores of the Lac de Bourget. It is a beautiful lake surrounded by mountains rendered famous by Lamartine's verses, which every French child knows by heart. As the sun was setting behind La Dent du Chat, a dark outline against the twilight, I rowed myself, reciting aloud.

> *Ainsi toujours poussés vers de nouveaux rivages*
> *Dans la nuit éternelle emportés sans retour,*
> *Ne pourrons-nous jamais sur l'ocean des âges*
> *Jeter l'ancre un seul jour?*
>
> . . .
>
> *O temps, suspends ton vol et vous heures propices*
> *Suspendez votre cours;*
> *Laissez nous savourers les rapides délices*
> *Des plus beaux de nos jours.*

Always driven toward new shores
carried into eternal night with no return,
Will we never be able to drop anchor for a single day
into the everlasting ocean?

. . .

O time, suspend thy flight, and you auspicious hours,
suspend your course.
Let us savor the swift delights
of the most beautiful of days.

On my return I saw the grownups sitting in the shade, and I came in on a fascinating conversation between Mother and the Marquesa dei Chiusi, one of Mother's bathing companions, and the Marquese Sommi Picenardi.

"Amy," the marchesa said, fixing her golden lorgnon on me, "I don't see why you let that child go to college. Doesn't she realize that the more helpless a woman is, the more a man will do for her? What she needs to learn is to become attractive to men." The gold-handled lorgnon scanned my sunburned nose, uncurled hair, ill-fitting white dress, flat shoes. I blushed crimson. What could I say?

Mother replied, "I can't do anything with her. All she learns at college is to think she knows better than anyone else."

Sommi was a little more kindly. Speaking rapidly in Italian and adjusting his monocle, he said, "Marriage is important, of course, but you have to meet the right people. Take me, for instance. My first wife died five years ago. I am broke. I have a beautiful *castello* and I am going to marry your rich friend Dorothy. She has a lot of money. She wants to be a marchesa and to live in a castle. I love my old place. It's been in the family for five hundred years and is full of antiques. I am sure we will be very happy together."

Father said nothing and tried to switch the conversation to the trip he was planning for the following day. He was going to take an English lady, Anne K., whom we had met recently, to the Galibier, a day's excursion with great views of the mountains. Would I like to go too? he asked. Of course I would.

Lady Anne was very cordial and asked me for tea several days later, wanting to know about college life. It seems she had a daughter who was thinking of going to college in the United States. "You know, don't you, that your father adores you and is very proud of you. He talks about you all the time when we are together."

I beamed. Still unsure of myself and of Father's feelings toward me, I was so happy to be told again of Father's love for me that the possible significance of

Anne's relationship to him escaped me entirely. I had forgotten that Irene had made the same remark two years before.

≈ 8

The end of August was approaching, time to return to Vassar for my junior year. Father and Mother both expressed regret, saying how much they would miss me. They usually returned to the States in late October or November, but this time Mother came home alone. She was concerned about Angel, who was growing old, forgetful and suspicious, wandering around her apartment, a bunch of keys in her hand, trying the closet doors, often not able to find the right key, then accusing the maid over some object that was missing. Mother was sure the maid was dishonest, so she was fired, and in spite of Anti Bi's attempts to show Mother that she was unfair, the whole rigmarole would start all over again with the next maid.

Mother was haunted by the fear of growing old. Although Mother was only fifty-one and looked much younger, Angel's wrinkles, gray hair, failing memory, and stumbling gait at age seventy meant only one thing to Mother: Someday she, too, would become old, and her beauty would fade. There was little I could do to reassure her. Why didn't Father come home and help Mother? I wondered. The reason soon became apparent.

Getting the mail at Vassar was always a scramble. In midmorning between classes, we rushed to Main and practically climbed over each other, trying to reach our mail boxes. One brilliant November morning—I remember it so well —there was a letter from France in an unfamiliar but characteristically slanting large English hand. Inside was a snapshot of Father and Anne seated against a background of trees, Father all smiles, Anne hanging on his words. "Beatrice dear. Here we are, having a wonderful time. We have seen Loches, Chinon, Blois. It has been one of the great treats of my life. The past two months have been heaven for me. He talks every day about you. I long to have you both here. You must know what I think and feel about him. I suppose I ought not to but I just can't help it. I love and adore him. I am wretched away from him. I have never been happy before."

I was stunned. It was no use pretending that this was just another friend of the family's. This was serious, a more possessive woman than Irene. Where did this leave Mother and me? What had happened to the circle of fire that encircled my parents and within which I had so recently been admitted? Somehow I must try to help Mother, but I could not be angry with Father—I loved him more than anyone in the world. These thoughts flashed through my mind like lightning as I rushed down the walk to my history class—there were no cuts in those days.

Father came home soon after I received Anne's letter. He said nothing. I said nothing. He seemed preoccupied, not his usual buoyant self. Coming into the library in Sixty-seventh Street one day, I found him standing before an open drawer gazing at a large photograph of Anne. Our eyes met. We both blushed. He jammed the picture into the drawer, shut it, and locked it, and we glided into talk about the Book of Hours he had recently purchased. "How odd," I remarked, looking at the prints of the Dance of Death, "that Death takes each one in turn, beginning with the pope and the king and down to the beggar, but the queen comes last. Are women less sinful?"

There was no comment.

Over Christmas in Lenox, things seemed normal again, on the surface. Mother was happy with her police dog, Lupo, and Father was climbing snowdrifts, showing off his new Caterpillar-tread vehicle. During the Christmas vacation I went to parties at Adele's and Sheila's houses. The parties were called "coming out" dances—no longer "balls," as they had been in Mother's time. The custom has not altogether disappeared. Coming out is an odd survival, a watered-down version of placing a girl on the marriage market. When a girl reached the age of eighteen she made her debut in society. This meant that she was presented at a tea or at a dance to her mother's friends, who presumably had sons and daughters of their own. It amounted to saying, "My daughter is ready to get married, and I want to make sure that she meets eligible young men from her own social class."

I was never a debutante, for which I was not sorry. My lack of social grace had been made very plain by both my parents. To use the French expression, I was gauche, that is, awkward. Adele and Sheila invited me to their debuts, whither I went clad in the appropriate white satin dress overlaid with tulle. Mother had taken me to Worth in Paris, where she, her mother, and the leaders of American society had had their dresses made for their coming-out parties. I stood for three fittings while the *midinette*, her mouth full of pins, expatiated on the beauties of this hateful dress. The price, ninety dollars, was paid out of my allowance.

[45]

The dancing classes that we had all attended in the Burden and Hammond ballrooms on Ninety-first Street, where the coming-out dances were being held, did not prevent me from being a wallflower. The dances were usually preceded by a dinner at a girl's home to which she invited two or three young men to ensure herself of a couple of dancing partners, but I knew no one to invite, and my parents were not going to give a dinner for me. The custom of "cutting in" meant a constant changing of partners in the middle of the dance floor. A really popular girl could hardly get around the ballroom floor without a young man's cutting in. A young man hesitated to cut in on an unpopular girl lest he be stuck with her for the evening. Sometimes he winked to a friend in the stag line to come to his rescue or the girl, realizing the situation, pleaded weariness and asked to be deposited next to one of the chaperones sitting on gilt chairs around the ballroom. This last was my tactic.

At midnight, couples went down to the dining room for scrambled eggs, sausage, and ice cream. Here, once again, Mr. Hammond came to the rescue and took me to supper. Mother and the marchesa were right—I was a bluestocking. But none of us could foresee what a chance encounter might bring.

Throughout my college years, when I was in Paris I was chaperoned every inch of the way, but since Father and Mother continued to follow their usual routine, sailing for Europe in the early spring and returning in the late fall, I crossed the ocean there and back on a French Line ship alone. Apparently Father decided the French Line was sufficient chaperone! He recommended me to the captain, at whose table I sat, and to the stewards. The chef, a large man, appearing even larger than life under the traditional cap topping a rubicund face, had also been enlisted. From him I learned to make an excellent onion soup, which remains a part of my repertoire to this day, but we both gave up on the omelette. "The trouble is," he said, exasperated and twisting his perfectly waxed moustache, "your mother never sent you out to the sandbox with a skillet when you were five years old; that is the time to develop the proper wrist motion; at nineteen, it is too late."

On a voyage home I had the good fortune to meet Alexis Carrel at the captain's table. Alexis Carrel was a short, stocky man with a round head, rimless glasses, and incisive speech. Through the culture of chicken hearts, he had been the first to perpetuate life in the test tube. In 1912, he had been awarded the Nobel Prize for his work on vascular sutures and the transplantation of tissues and organs. At the Rockefeller Institute (now Rockefeller University) he was not popular with his fellow scientists, in part because of his rather snobbish attitude, but also because he believed that phenomena, imponderable and as yet immeasurable, existed. This was the era when, for scientists, that which could not be seen through the microscope did not exist. Carrel claimed that the miracles at Lourdes were real and was greatly interested in the medieval mystics and the experience that we now call extrasensory perception, quite convinced that a universe beyond our senses exists.

Usually I joined him on the the top deck at sunset. The day before we were to land in New York, we watched a superb sunset together. The sky looked as though it were in flames, with layers upon layers of reds and oranges on the horizon. As the sun was sinking into the ocean, Carrel told me the following legend: "At the foot of a lighthouse lay a small village. When the peasants ran out of oil, the lighthouse keeper gave them some of his oil so that they might have light. They had light—but the lighthouse ran out, and the great ships foundered. That man was a poor sentimentalist. Do not be like him. Few people have brains. *You* have a brain," he concluded. "That is not your fault; you have a good heredity, a good French education. You know how to use your brain."

I was about to reply, when we were joined by a young friend of his, G. D., who became my first serious beau and who introduced me to Adolf two years later.

Beginning of Independence ≈

Senior year at Vassar was full of interest. I was majoring in history and English, spending many hours in the library reading a great deal. *The Medieval Mind* and *Thought and Expression in the Sixteenth Century* by Henry Osborn Taylor were among the books that influenced me most. Later the author became a close friend.

The history department at Vassar was a strong department and continued to be so when my daughter attended the college twenty years later. This strength came from the leadership of three women scholars, Lucy M. Salmon, C. Mildred Thompson, and Eloise Ellery. Lucy Salmon, a quiet, soft-spoken, white-haired, dumpy lady usually dressed in blue, which brought out the color of her blue eyes, conducted a seminar for seniors entitled The Materials of History. It was known as "Miss Salmon's laundry lists," because we were encouraged to consider *all* artifacts, not just public documents, as materials of history to be scrutinized and considered in a context with other sources. Most of all we must know the origin of these artifacts. Take the much-vaunted Chinese laundry lists — what could we learn about the habits and living conditions of the customer and the laundryman from the study of these scraps of paper?

The students wrote what were called "topics," taking notes on little blocks of paper, noting the author's name and the title and page of the book cited in the left of the red margin. For instance, when we studied the French Revolution, Miss Salmon or in this case her student Eloise Ellery, now a full professor, would probe, "You are writing about the French Revolution. The author you are citing was a member of the Convention. How would you expect his account of the beheading of Louis the Sixteenth to differ from that written by a French emigré of the time?"

Miss Salmon was modern in other ways — she did not believe in marks: Either you worked as a scholar or you didn't. Since giving out marks was a requirement at the time, she always claimed that she did so on the basis of random selection. I never quite wanted to believe that, since I always got an A.

From time to time students were invited for Sunday breakfast with Miss Salmon and the college librarian, Miss Underhill. Miss Underhill was not as stout as Miss Salmon, and her principal feature was a hawklike nose. At home she spoke rarely and definitely played second fiddle to Miss Salmon, but in the library she was the chief. Everyone knew that the open-shelf system of the Vassar library was among the best in the country. Miss Salmon and Miss Underhill lived in downtown Poughkeepsie in an old, rather dark frame house with bookcases in every corner.

Sunday breakfasts were called for 9:00 A.M. A classmate and I took the trolley and attended the eight-o'clock communion service in a downtown church, arriving on Academy Street at the appointed hour.

To accept the honor of these breakfast invitations required considerable fortitude. Then for me came the ordeal—too much to eat in the early morning. Grapefruit, sausage, eggs, doughnuts, and I forget what else. Miss Salmon would talk to us about her forthcoming book: an analysis of newspapers as materials of history. All this sounds dull when described fifty years later, but it was not so, and these conversations and other history classes taught me the importance of the evaluation of evidence.

Miss C. Mildred Thompson, with whom I had corresponded before entering college, taught the history of the American Civil War, using the same principles of the evaluation of evidence as did Miss Salmon. Since she had been born and raised in the South, this meant her having to shed many early prejudices. So it came about that gradually I stopped being a militant French girl and became an American with a deep love for France. The Hansi books that I had read as a child before the war—showing Alsatian children guarded by German soldiers—fell into perspective: They were propaganda intended to promote the reconquest of Alsace-Lorraine by the French and to breed hatred for the Germans, the "Boches." I had been swayed by the propaganda and had lost the opportunity to learn German.

Napoleon also fell out of favor with me. I became an ardent pacifist—the League of Nations was to be the instrument for world peace. But there I lost something of the ability to evaluate evidence, and could not appreciate or foresee the seeds of war contained in the Versailles treaty, as did Adolf, the man I married.

Much as I love France, I became aware that the opportunity to continue the independent life I was learning to live at college would not be available in

France. Mademoiselle Mulot had shown me by her example that it was possible to maintain a free mind within a cloistered environment. But even so, I could not see myself able to do this in my parents' French milieu, and I longed to lead an active, socially useful life on my own.

The development of an independent spirit on my part was something Mother feared and deplored and the principal reason for her objection to college. From her point of view, she was quite right, as my subsequent actions showed.

The fall of my senior year I spent almost every weekend with Grand-mère in Lenox. She was so happy to see me that it hurt, but on every visit I could see that she leaned more heavily on her nurse's arm and that her breathing was more labored. Her family physician, a devoted and competent clinician practicing in Pittsfield, told me that he considered her condition serious. I do not know whether he advised my father in Europe. Though Mother's hatred for Grand-mère had relented somewhat, Father was not exactly attentive to his own mother.

The room that was mine over the weekends was situated at the other end of the hall from Grand-mère's. On Columbus Day weekend I had fallen asleep reading "O Wild West wind, thou breath of autumn's being," and I was awakened by the nurse. "Come quickly; the end is near." I hurried through the big drawing room, noticing the gleam of David's silver snuff boxes in the penumbra. Grand-mère lay on her side, eyes closed, her breath coming in short, irregular fits and starts. The black heart-shaped locket hung loosely around her neck. I opened it to show her David's picture and lock of hair and kissed her lightly on the forehead. She opened her eyes. I thought I saw a faint gleam of recognition.

In a few moments she was gone. I sank sobbing to the floor. This was the room where I was born. Father and Mother were somewhere in Europe. When no immediate answer came to a cable sent to their forwarding address in Paris, Dr. Slattery, the rector of Grace Church, who had been like a son to Grand-mère after his own mother died, made all the funeral arrangements with me. It would have been possible to defer the final interment until my parents returned, but this was my Grand-mère, who loved me and whom I loved. I would honor her. Father did not seem to care, and only last summer Mother had sat on my bed with a look of hate in those blue eyes, repeating the same old refrain with no explanation, "My mother was insulted by your father's mother. It's all your fault."

Wearing black with a black sailor hat, its crown encircled by a crepe band, I walked behind Grand-mère's coffin up the main aisle of Grace Church—alone. I do not remember who the other mourners were. This was not the first family funeral I had attended in Grace Church. As a small child there had been Uncle

David's, then five years ago that of Uncle Cort, Grand-mère's elder brother, and only last year that of the grande dame, Aunt Amy Townsend, Mother's aunt after whom she was named and who had been so insistent that I join the Colonial Dames and was so proud of escorting visiting royalty around Mount Vernon. Snobs all of them, Grand-mère also — such were the mores of the times! My thoughts turned to the many Sundays I had sat with Angel and looked over to Grand-mère alone in the pew that had been my great grandfather Japhet Bishop's, close to the stained-glass window given in his memory.

Dr. Slattery and I drove out to the Greenwood cemetery, and after the service I wandered around the family plot. There were Uncle David's gravestone and those of two first cousins of Father's who had died in France — three expatriates in one generation. Then a small stone — Catherine, a child, Grand-mère's daughter, named after Catherine Lorillard Wolfe.

I do not remember Father's reaction on his return two weeks later. Mother was furious. "If you had not been to college you would never have dared to do this; you would have waited for us." The relationship so carefully built up between us was shattered with one blow. I was crushed. My diary entry closed with this quotation from King Lear. "Better to leave undone than by our deed, acquire too high a fame when him we serve's away."

Things did not go well at home during the Christmas vacation of 1922. G. D., Alexis Carrel's friend whom I had met on the ship, came to call at Sixty-seventh Street. Father and Mother came in just as he was leaving. I tried to introduce him but was ignored. After he had left, Mother said, "Who was that awful mick? I wouldn't have a chauffeur who looked like that. I do not understand how you associate with such people. You were brought up to be a lady — you will never know the difference between a gentleman and one who is not."

Father: "Where did you meet him? He has no breeding!"

"Dr. Carrel introduced us."

Father was not impressed.

Mother: "This man is never to enter my house again. The title is in my name." Father said nothing. I was crushed.

G. D. did not enter Mother's house again, but he came to see me at Vassar. He was a well-educated Frenchman with an engineering degree, a sensitive, gentle person. Subsequently he became a full professor in an Ivy League college and rose to the rank of brigadier general in World War II. When I was elected to Phi Beta Kappa, he presented me with the key, a little jewel made to order especially for me, not a store key. The jinx was broken; I was no longer a wallflower.

Spring—commencement time arrived at last. On class day we marched across campus four abreast, holding the class banner, 1923, and singing. For one of the few times in my life, I forgot myself and felt at one with a group—we were strong, we were young, the world was ours.

President MacCracken's address stressed change as the fundamental condition of life, one of its most interesting and desirable manifestations. We, as educated women, should never abandon "the insistent inquiry into the meaning of life."

Other people's families were present for the whole weekend, but since my parents were abroad as usual I had not expected them and was glad that Anti Bi attended the commencement ceremony. In fact, in my diary I spoke of myself as a privileged young woman with a loving family, good education, good health, and economic independence, resolved to lead a socially productive life. This I hoped to achieve through "an intense cultivation of the soul, the strengthening and development of human relations, a study of different conditions of life." Rather priggish!

Immediately after graduation, I sailed for France as usual. As we were approaching the shore of France, I could hardly contain my excitement. Father, my beloved father, was coming out on the tender to meet me. There he was, running up the gangplank, trying to get ahead of the pilot, giving me a bear hug as he came on board, shaking hands vigorously with the stewards. At fifty-three he continued buoyant, energetic as ever, full of information on many subjects: history, art, architecture, wines, food, old books, aviation, automobiles—always the brilliant and charming dilettante. Alphonse picked up my luggage and stowed it in the Hispano, and off we flew—so it seemed! On the way to Paris, we stopped for lunch at Rouen and Father, talking fast and vigorously all the while, told me about his latest acquisitions, which included several incunabula.

To celebrate my graduation from college and my twenty-first birthday, Father planned a stop at the Hôtel de la Poste in Beaune. This is now a two-star, very elaborate, expensive restaurant run by a cool maitre d' in proper black attire. In the twenties it was different. Old Chevillot, the proprietor, and Father were friends. "How much your daughter looks like you!" Chevillot exclaimed as he and Father embraced French fashion. Father smiled, a lovely smile with his eyes as well as his mouth and illuminating his whole face. He seemed so simple, so childish, and so great. I just adored him.

As we sat under the grape arbor, Chevillot and Father planned my birthday dinner and selected a bottle of Hospices de Beaune, a case of which was to be shipped to New York.

Mother did not participate but retired upstairs to her room and ordered some bouillon. She did not care for rich food and considered that Father ate too much and was getting too fat.

The dinner was wonderful. I felt that Father and I were united once more, the episode of G. D. was forgotten, and a perfect understanding existed between us. The menu consisted of *pâté de fois gras, quenelles au brochet*, and roast partridge, concluding with a *bombe glacée pralinée*. There were a half bottle of Demoiselles Montrachet (a white burgundy) and one half bottle of Hospices de Beaune (red). I was allowed one glass of each and a swallow of Marc de Bourgogne, a brandy, at the end. Father drank the rest, saying, "Wine selection, wine tasting, and wine drinking are among the great attributes of civilization. Getting drunk is disgusting: *'Cela ne se fait pas'*"—it is not done, the final condemnation.

"You have all the advantages that come as a result of good breeding and good education," Father went on. "You must do something important, and you must marry a gentleman."

I agreed. I told him about Prexy's remarks on change as the fundamental condition of life. "I am going to change the world. To establish universal peace through the League of Nations," I boasted, and started telling him about a Czech-born Vassar classmate living in Geneva with her husband where both had a position with the League. They had suggested that I live with them and find a similar job.

Father was not enthusiastic. "You are too young. Why don't you go on studying at Columbia and live with us in New York?"

That is the way it turned out.

≈≈ *10*

In September I registered at Columbia. The level of teaching and the competence of the students were not up to Miss Salmon's seminar in historical materials. The subject of my M.A. thesis was a study of the arms race between France and Prussia in the 1860s that was followed by the Franco-Prussian war, both parties claiming that each was building up a defense that would act as a deterrent to war. An arms race inevitably leads to war, I concluded.

Meanwhile there were other problems. To develop a life of my own with college classmates and other young people was not so easy. Mother consulted Anti Bi, who played the role of the Lady from Philadelphia, the visitor in *The Peterkin Papers* who knows all the answers. Of course, I should meet people of my own age and of my own class, but since Anti Bi's husband had been United

States Ambassador to Belgium and Rome, she had lost touch with her New York friends. She would be glad to invite me as her guest at the embassy. This she did, and I had a fascinating time sightseeing in Rome but "did not meet anybody." Chance, not conventional social channels, provided new opportunities.

The next acquaintance came about through Berkshire friends. He was more than ten years older than I, well established in the field of chemical research, brilliant, impetuous, dominating—and Jewish. I was much attracted and almost swept off my feet. He proposed marriage. Although I deplored my family's anti-Semitic prejudices and disapproved of them, I could not deny their existence and their virulence. This man was a man in his own right—he would not be anyone's "pet Jew," which were the only kind Mother and her friends would tolerate. And Father, well, he had opposed every man I had met so far, and a Jew would have been worse. Marriage to a Jew, no matter how fine a human being he was, would have meant a complete break with my parents. I could not afford to destroy a relationship so carefully built up.

There was no one in whom I felt I could confide, so I had to work it out alone. Although my friend had many non-Jewish friends and later married a fine Gentile woman, he became both aggressive and bitter when confronted with anti-Semitic prejudices. "You are but an immature child. You have used me. You have no courage. If you really loved me, you would leave your family. You would not care what they said." I guess he was right; I was not prepared to forsake all others and cleave only unto him.

Father was always telling me that I must associate only with gentlemen. "What is a gentleman?" I asked.

"A man who is well bred," came the answer.

"That means you must know all about who his ancestors were?"

"Of course." Thereupon Father launched upon a long monologue on our family history. "We are directly descended from the DePeysters."

The DePeyster family were "Landheers"—that is counts and owners of fifteen villages in Brabant, not far from Liège, Belgium. At the time of the massacre of Protestants in 1572, they took refuge in Holland. Johannes DePeyster, the progenitor of the family in the United States, came to New Amsterdam around 1645. When the British took over and New Amsterdam became New York, Johannes held a number of offices, and his son Abraham was mayor of New York from 1691 to 1694, and later a judge of the supreme court of New York.

Abraham, known as de Heer, a title of magnates in Holland, took himself seriously, making no pretense of being a man of the people. He was civic minded, donating a tract of his own land to the City of New York to encourage the building of wharves. (It is now Maiden Lane, in downtown Manhattan.) The De Peysters married Van Cortlandts, Schuylers, Beekmans, Livingstons, people of British and Dutch descent who were substantial citizens in the Old World. My great grandmother's name was Catherine M. Van Cortlandt De Peyster. She married Japhet Bishop, who was descended from early settlers in New Jersey. The Bishops married into the Wolfe family, longtime vestrymen of Grace Church. Catherine Wolfe I have mentioned. On my mother's side, her great grandfather David Austen, whose pew at Grace Church I sat in with Angel, was one of the founders of the church. Angel was a Townsend (also spelled Townshend), descended from a family of mixed Saxon and Norman origin who were granted titles of nobility at the time of William the Conqueror. Charles Townshend was chancellor of the exchequer at the time of George III.

"The one responsible for the Townshend acts, losing the colonies," I interrupted.

Father: "Exactly."

Me: "What a bunch of conservatives. They were all well off, I suppose."

Father: "Of course, but as I have told you more than once, well-bred people never talk about money."

This discussion gave me a lot to think about. I could not figure out how to reconcile Father's views about "family" with Rousseau's and Bertrand Russell's views on equality; still I kept on trying to please Father.

Several months after this I met another visitor to the Berkshires, a penniless French war veteran with a *beau nom*. On consulting the *Almanach de Gotha*, the book in which the pedigrees of European nobility are registered, I found that he was descended from a crusader and was related to many European noble families, including the English royal family. "This proves that A. de S. is well bred," I said to Father triumphantly, showing him the pedigree, which I had copied out carefully. Father only grunted but permitted me to invite the young man to tea in Lenox and to dinner in Sixty-seventh Street.

The dinner party was not a success. Writing about it today, the whole thing sounds utterly ridiculous, but at the time we were all dead serious. The morning following the dinner party my father presented me with a list of the unpardonable sins committed by A. de S.

1. Rudeness — and tardiness. Three ladies were kept waiting fifteen minutes for dinner.
2. Mediocre intelligence, as evidenced by dull conversation.
3. Cold clammy hands clutching his starched bosom trying to hide a hairy chest. (A shirt stud was missing.)

The third offense was the most serious. For this there was no absolution, the bishop—my Father—declared. The bishop's lady concurred. A. de S. became another casualty. He was never to enter the house again.

After this absurd scene, I was still trying to think for myself, and I came to the conclusion that unfortunately this particular French aristocrat and war hero was proving himself unable to adapt to American life, where the immigrant starts at the bottom. If only I had understood this earlier, our relationship would have become less involved; if only I had my own home, we could have continued as friends. If only...if only... Once again I had hurt myself and another human being. Would I never learn?

Disturbed and depressed, I did not know where to turn. Walking up the trail behind the house in Lenox, I watched the white birch turn pink in the light of the setting sun. The air was cold, crystal clear. I prayed to God to give me courage. After a few moments of silence there came a great sense of peace. If only it were possible to carry that with me always.

This interlude gave me courage to try again and to introduce another college friend to my parents. We had both graduated from Vassar the previous year.

I wrote Miss Thompson:

> W. came for the weekend in Lenox. She arrived Friday about an hour before me. Mother whispered to me in the hall that W. was her idea of a schoolteacher (obviously not intended as a compliment). After dinner Mother stayed in the kitchen and did not sit with us at all. W. retired into the depths of silence. All weekend she did not look as if she could sit down anywhere; she perched on one foot, talked to the dogs and fled to my room when she got a chance. I did not help matters, though I made a few remarks trying in a forced way to bring W. into the conversation. Father, I don't think, addressed more than two words to her.
>
> When it came time to leave Father was standing at the gate bidding goodbye to Mrs. Beatrice Farrand [a woman of good family!], a fine landscape architect who had planned Edith Wharton's garden in Lenox and was working on a project for my parents. W. was also leaving. Looking from Father to W. I did not know what to say.
>
> "W., have you said goodbye to Father? Father, have you said goodbye to W.?"
>
> All the sweetness seemed to have gone out of my relationship with Father. Will the understanding we had together ever come back? All the time I was more keenly aware than anyone else of the things Mother and Father were criticizing silently: her clothes, and all the one hundred little things that go to make what is called taste. Then I realized also what misery it would be if I should fall in love with

someone who would not be able to manipulate his knife and fork in the proper way! I was trying to analyze my family's social code. They both love Alphonse (the chauffeur) but in his place. Dining, tea, visiting at home are for them social rites which may not be shared except with those who belong to the same class. The ability to perform these rites does not depend on birth, wealth, or education, but on a combination of all three. It can be acquired—i.e., Mrs. Vogel (née Siegel), now Marchesa Sommi Picenardi, is received everywhere in Roman society. According to my parents one knows the W. kind of people, but one does not ask them to one's house unless one lets them know one is doing them a favor.

To me, this point of view was then, and is now, revolting. I believe in privacy but once a person has crossed the threshold of my home, he is welcomed, and to be treated with respect. To the right of the front door at Konkapot, the house in Great Barrington that Adolf and I bought together, there is a Portuguese tile we also purchased together, which reads,

> My house has the most noble coat of arms.
> To receive without distinction both rich and poor.

Following this unhappy weekend, I concluded that I must make my friends independently and not invite to the house those people whom Mother and Father did not care to meet socially. It was too uncomfortable for everyone. But this was not to prevent me from choosing my friends and seeing them on my own. In due course, when I had my own home, W. and I renewed our friendship and she visited me frequently.

On a different level, life with Father was full of interest! In Lenox we visited Father Fisher at Shadowbrook, the largest of the "summer cottages" built by the Stokes family in the 1880s, which had recently become a Jesuit novitiate. Father was almost as fluent in Latin as the Jesuits and enjoyed speaking with them, as well as attending mass. The ballroom, the scene of costume balls in Father's youth, where he had come as the Earl of Leicester and David as Romeo, was now transformed into a chapel.

An indefatigable motorist, Father knew all the back roads of Berkshire County, and I enjoyed exploring them with him. He was frequently accompanied by Kelton Miller, the owner of the *Berkshire Eagle*, and together they persuaded the state of Massachusetts to purchase the old Whitney property, eleven thousand acres of lakes and forest, which is now October Mountain State Forest.

With Mother I went horseback riding; she rode side saddle and looked very handsome. Her old horse Kismet had been a polo pony, and I had recently purchased a lively American saddle horse. Followed by Mother's German shepherd, the two malamutes, Husky and Lasky, and Zut, my cocker, we formed quite a cavalcade as we cantered through the woods. Riding was best in the fall and in early winter, when we rode under the pine trees, shaking the newly fallen snow.

Back in New York, Father was planning to build an apartment house on land in Manhattan that he had inherited from his father. Thomas Hastings, a graduate of the Beaux Arts in Paris and builder of the New York Public Library, was his architect. I accompanied Father to the meetings at which he, his lawyer, and Hastings worked together trying to comply with the New York City building code while preserving some elegance of style. I also accompanied Father to meetings of the American Art Association, which he owned and where he was conducting negotiations for the sale of an important Italian art collection. He was insisting that he wanted me to be his partner in these various enterprises and that we could work together in the art business both in New York and in Europe. To please him I took some business courses during the school year 1924–25.

But for me the most precious hours were spent in Father's library. The key to the bookcases was mine. I was no longer confined to dusting but could spend a whole day browsing. At leisure I caressed the fine morocco bindings and reveled in the intricate designs of Clovis Eve, that master sixteenth-century binder. I was fascinated by the elaborate armorials of cardinals and princes but particularly by the books of Mesdames de France, the sisters of Louis XV. These I felt were directly connected with me, as Madame Campan was *lectrice* to Madame Adelaide before starting the school I had attended in Saint-Germain.

While reading in the library, I came across several editions of *Daphnis and Chloe*, a Greek tale by Longus translated into French. My favorite edition was bound in green, the flyleaf a salmon pink, and the text a fine printing from the press of Monsieur le Duc d'Orléans dated 1786, with colored illustrations of pastoral scenes taken from paintings especially designed for him. This book became for me an important part of what is now called sex education. The text and the pictures depicted in romantic but accurate terms the details of physical passion. This was not my only text, for I soon became acquainted with the works of Havelock Ellis, one of the earliest twentieth-century writers on sex—a good writer and a good scientist.

From the library, it was only a few steps to Sixty-sixth Street, for tea with Henry Osborn Taylor.

Taylor was both a gentleman and a scholar. I thought surely Father would find him interesting, but this did not turn out to be the case. When I brought Father to tea at the Taylors' the conversation between the two gentlemen was brief and stilted. Walking home, Father made no comment but did not suggest a return visit, nor did he invite Mr. Taylor to visit the library at Sixty-seventh Street. It took me a long time to puzzle out this situation, but I came to the conclusion finally that Father was jealous of those friends—no matter their age or sex—which I made on my own. Dr. Carrel, Mr. Taylor, and Dean Mildred Thompson were included in this group. Father wanted to share his friends with me but could not tolerate a situation that he had not initiated. This interpretation of Father's behavior seemed to fit the facts, and I accepted it, determined to pursue friendships on my own; tea with Taylor continued to be a weekly affair. He became my Prospero and I his Portia.

He and his wife, the Lady Julia, as she was known to her young friends, lived in a duplex apartment with a two-storied living room on East Sixty-sixth Street. There he served tea in front of a big wood fire. Among the privileged characters encouraged to drop in at five o'clock were the physiologist Lawrence Henderson, Dr. Alfred Cohen, a cardiologist, and a few young people, including a Vassar classmate and me. When the Lady Julia stopped briefly for a cup of tea, he twitted: "My wife—she is full of good works. I am not."

Bending over the low tea table, he drank tea out of the saucer just to be contrary. We laughed with him, but when he moved to the deep wing chair, joined the fingertips of both hands together, and began to talk more seriously, we listened attentively. He did not minimize the brutal aspects of human history but assured us, "The secret of life is to live highly, nobly, and beautifully. You must know the most beautiful things of all times so that you may continue to grow after you are thirty, forty—always."

With Prospero I discussed another of my projects. Since I could not live in Geneva with my friends and work in the League of Nations after obtaining my M.A., I wanted to study the *Truce of God*, a mechanism through which medieval lords agreed to maintain peace over a certain period of time within their domain without raiding their neighbors. "That is very ambitious," Prospero remarked. "In order to do that you must be fluent in medieval Latin and expert in reading manuscripts. These skills you can obtain only through study at the École des Chartes in Paris."

When I proposed this to my parents I once again hit the stone wall. "A *jeune fille* cannot live alone in Paris—*cela ne se fait pas.*"

What, then, should I do with my life? The constantly recurring question. Though I loved being with Father, I really was not interested in business. If I was to be a socially useful independent woman, it would be through a job or a profession of my own choice in America.

I do not recall how I found it, but before leaving for France in June 1925, I obtained a job with Harold Rugg at the Lincoln School. I was to assist in the writing of history textbooks for high school students. I signed a contract. Work was to begin in September. This assured my return to the United States.

The Family Drama ≈

≈ *11*

The years 1925 and 1926 turned out to be crucial for several reasons: The family situation came to a tragic climax; I changed my orientation toward life from a purely bookish outlook to an interest in the serious study of human beings and human society that eventually led to the study of medicine; and most important of all, I met Adolf.

The first meeting with Adolf was quite romantic. It came about through the intermediary of G. D., who called for me at Sixty-seventh Street on a lovely May evening. I had informed him of my parents' prohibitions, so he did not enter the house. We took the bus down to Washington Square to meet a friend of his, Adolf Berle, a young lawyer who was interested in history, as I was. Berle was thirty years old, had been a technical adviser at the Versailles Peace Conference when he was only twenty-four, and had resigned believing that the treaty was a breeder for future wars. Now he was writing articles on corporation law and had his own law firm. "A versatile and brilliant young man," was G. D.'s comment. "I am sure you will find him interesting."

Adolf was waiting for us, pacing up and down under the arch. After a formal introduction, G. led the way across Washington Square as the street lights were coming on. Erect, an irrepressible little wave on top of his head, rimless glasses, a small moustache — he was, as always, precise, reserved, and courteous. Adolf, carrying a thin cane made of Dominican hardwood, made only a few desultory remarks as we walked across the square. I wore a white rayon dress, streaked with red like a candy stick, tied with a red sash at the hip-level waistline, the skirt mid-calf length. This was the fashion of the time and certainly not becoming. To this day the dress hangs in the attic closet, its flimsy material shredding like an old corn husk.

None of the three of us was a master of small talk, so we were glad to reach the tearoom at Grove and Bedford Streets. The building was one of the last of the old Brevoort Farm. It still stands, a clapboard gray one-story structure with its entrance on a small court off the street. G. D.'s precise diary note, of which he gave me a copy, records this historic (for me!) time and place:

> Wednesday, May 20, 1925
> 6:45 PM 15 East 67th Street
> Dinner BBB, AAB
> Bedford & Grove Streets
> Greenwich Village.

It was Prohibition time. There was no drinking, at least not for us. The interior of the tearoom was quite dark, with tables coming out from the wall between solid benches and decked with sputtering black candles. G. sat across the table from Adolf and me. Within half an hour, Adolf and I were showing off to each other, leaving G.'s engineer talk of nuts and bolts far behind. Adolf spoke rapidly, the ideas following each other one after another with the force and speed of a mountain brook in the spring, ill concealing what I felt was a shy and sensitive nature. "I worked with Ned Channing at Harvard; I was a member of his seminar in American history, and I wrote the bibliography for one volume of his *History of the United States*."

Was he showing off? I asked myself.

I thought I could show off also.

"The seminar at Vassar on Materials of History was given by Lucy Maynard Salmon, and we learned to use primary sources. Henry Osborn Taylor, who wrote *The Medieval Mind*, came to lecture. I know him. He was a student of Henry Adams."

"So you must have read *Mont-Saint-Michel and Chartres*?"

"Certainly, and I mean to study the *Truce of God* and find a model for world peace."

"Splendid," Adolf replied. "We did not do so well at Versailles. I believe this treaty carries in it the seeds of future wars."

Adolf's opinion came as a shock. My training in history notwithstanding, in my eyes Clemenceau could have done no wrong.

We veered to other subjects, still talking a mile a minute, Adolf and I seeking to build up a pluralistic interpretation of history, G. insisting that economic interests were determinative in all human affairs. I suggested that the Crusades had a religious origin but was soon defeated by G. D. Adolf, brilliant and articulate as he continued to be throughout our life together, came to my rescue. The cathedral at Chartres was dedicated to the glory of God and came into being through the efforts of faithful people, he affirmed. Napoleon, I went on, was not motivated primarily by economic considerations but by personal ambition and his desire for power. Adolf agreed. "Power is always personal" was an idea that intrigued him through the years and that he developed many years later in his book on power.[1]

The meal was ending, the candles sputtering and dissolving in seas of gray wax over the dark table.

"Where are you going this summer?" Adolf asked as we were rising to leave.

"To France," I replied.

"You are lucky. I am going to the Caribbean, to Santo Domingo."

What for? I asked myself.

As a European-educated child, I had learned geography, could visualize Santo Domingo on the map, but had never heard of anyone's going there. My family and their friends went to Europe.

"The island of Hispaniola—one-third of it French Haiti," I said aloud.

"The first black republic," Adolf commented. "Columbus landed in Santo Domingo. There is an old Spanish cathedral in the center of the square. The island is important today because of sugar cane. I am counsel to the South Puerto Rican Sugar Company. This means that I go first to Puerto Rico by steamer, then cross the Mona Passage between Santo Domingo and Puerto Rico in an old freighter. The Mona Passage is the roughest bit of water in the Caribbean. On my last voyage the captain was dead drunk. The first mate had to take over. There were only four other passengers besides myself. We played poker all night to keep from being scared to death."

This is a totally different world from the one in which I was reared, I thought.

We left the tearoom and rode uptown on top of the Fifth Avenue bus in the sweet May evening. The conversation continued in a serious vein. Economics was not everything, Adolf and I insisted. A single cause could not, did not explain everything. This left G. out on a limb by himself!

When we got off the bus, the gentlemen walked with me to the door of 15 East Sixty-seventh Street. I rang the bell. (No one except my father had a latch-key.) Anna Nixon, the red-haired Irish housekeeper, opened the door immediately.

[1] *Power*, New York: Harcourt, Brace & World, 1969

"It is almost eleven o'clock, miss. Madam would not approve," she said, scanning my escorts through her sharp gray eyes as they turned down the steps.

The heavy door clanged shut. Anna locked the double lock. In the vestibule the tapestried chairs draped in dust sheets appeared like ghosts — grotesque in shape and posture.

Walking down the hall, my steps echoing through the deserted house, I reflected that G. had been the first to be ostracized by my parents, and several others had followed. Would Adolf Berle, this new acquaintance, be the next casualty? I was now twenty-three, two years out of college. I hoped to get married someday, but to whom? How? Through what social mechanism was I to meet the "right man" — an intelligent, honorable, idealistic, well-balanced man?

At this point in my reflections, I was startled by Anna Nixon, who was turning out the lights:

"Aren't you going upstairs, miss?"

I felt uneasy about going up the staircase in the dim light. Three flights to my room, past Father's and Mother's room on the next floor; the doors, fine French doors with brass handles, all closed, dust sheets upon dust sheets covering the chairs and the mezzotint prints on the walls. I remembered having nosebleeds as a child; once, a red streak trickled all the way down the white marble steps. I remembered also when Lupo, Mother's police dog, broke from his leash and leaped upstairs, leaving black paw stains on the steps. A footman, another Irish redhead like Anna, had shed his brass-buttoned livery, hurrying lest the housekeeper reprimand him, and run for a pail. Above all he feared that the lady's maid would find him negligent and carry the tale to Mother, who would fire him.

It had never been a peaceful house. I could name a succession of lady's maids who were court favorites. Germaine, French, large bosomed, red-haired, evil tongued. Josephine, Austrian, fat, gossipy, fawning. She lasted seven years. Now there was Edith Nixon, Anna's sister. Edith was a gray-eyed Irish girl only a few years older than I who had been hired as a chambermaid three years before. She had rapidly risen to the rank of Mother's personal maid and was the current court favorite.

All through my childhood there had been constant intrigues among the servants, who tried to curry favor with Mother's personal maid. Butlers, chefs, housemaids, and footmen carried tales on each other, on me, on my governesses. Anna Nixon was in control now. Would she be like that awful housekeeper who had made my life so miserable ten years before?

I walked over to the little elevator, its walls lined with red brocade. That also was a bit disconcerting; once, I had been stuck between floors for what seemed to be hours. This evening, on reaching my floor, I was comforted by the three hall clocks striking eleven in unison. My favorite played a jig tune.

I remembered the afternoon Father brought that clock back from the auction room. When he called me I was on the way to dancing school. He stopped my governess and me on the stairs. "Come and see." As he turned the small hands on the dial and opened the back, the brass cylinders revolved slowly and a gay jig rang through the house. The same tune was playing now.

Coming into my room, I saw Napoleon's picture on the wall. A warmaker, I was saying to myself. He is no longer my hero. Next fall in my new job I will be rewriting history textbooks.

This was to be my last summer with Mother and Father, but of course, I did not anticipate that.

The day before leaving Paris, we were planning our usual tour to Brittany across France by way of the château country en route to Aix, when I received the following note:

> Café Eden
> Santiago de los Caballeros
> Santo Domingo
>
> May 29, 1925

My dear Miss Bishop,

As you will see by the stationery, the appropriate note which should have followed shortly after our modest party of last week waited until the steamer got in. It is merely to say that I hope the acquaintance which G. brought into existence will continue for a long time and to give you fair warning that I shall put in for a share of your playtime next season. Good playmates are so rare. Also it was exceedingly sporting of you to chance a long evening with an absolute stranger in the depths of Greenwich Village.

...Scenes shift rapidly, and you might find me now ensconced in the garden of Eden (Fonda y Café), uncorking a bottle of Sauternes with the satisfaction that comes of a morning's hard travelling, a little hard work, and a bath and a change of clothing. The Republic is changed since I saw it last; we bowled merrily along in a high-powered car over a beautiful road this morning across a stretch of country which three years ago would have been negotiated only with three days' hard riding through trails, if at all. Somehow straight, paved roads are the symbol of colonial power—Rome, Spain, England, now the United States (though we don't call this a colony). It will be interesting to see whether the peace (in Santo Domingo) lasts, and the roads are kept up. If that happens, my faith in anti-imperialism, or at least my aversion to military pacification will have a material shock. But—someone cursed me in the street this morning and it developed that his father had been shot without trial in the last Marine operation hereabouts. I suppose the answer is that warfare is most deadly against the maker of it.

Faithfully yours,
Adolf A. Berle, Jr.

Santo Domingo seemed even more remote than it had on my first meeting with Adolf in New York, but I kept the letter.

≈ 12

That summer I enjoyed Aix, especially since there were no "competing" ladies on the landscape and I was Father's constant companion. Mother seemed content under the care of Edith Nixon.

Father and I started on our annual excursion over the Galibier Pass, 2,300 meters high, on a cloudless August day. Father always planned to reach the top of the pass for lunch. The lunch was packed in a wicker basket, and the *petits pains fourrés au pâté et au jambon* were wrapped in large white napkins. Fresh black figs, and peaches whose rose skin peeled easily, disclosing white succulent flesh tinged with pink, were topped off with a glass of Seyssel, the local white wine. After lunch Father drove through the tunnel and I walked over the top of the pass to pick tiny blue gentians.

Coming down into the foothills, inebriated by the pungent smell of hay at sunset after the day spent overlooking the sparkling, glittering snows of the Lautaret, I felt transported, reborn. I thanked God for the beauty of the world and imagined a sublime communion between the solitary soul and the great mountains in which the soul would be transported beyond this earth.

On reaching the hotel, we found Mother in tears. The nurse in charge of Angel had cabled "Come at once. Mrs. Bend irrational and unmanageable." Evidently Angel, whom we knew had been declining slowly, was suffering an acute psychotic episode. Mother was beside herself and could only repeat over and over again, "I don't want to get old like my mother; I don't want to lose my mind."

Father had always declined to take any responsibility for his mother-in-law and was quite firm. "It is no use your going back to New York. You cannot do anything for your mother. Let your sister take over." Anti Bi and her husband, Henry Prather Fletcher, were United States ambassadors in Rome. Competent as always, Anti Bi went home and settled her mother in a nursing home, where she lived until her death four years later, unaware of her surroundings and a great deal of the time not recognizing her daughters or me.

Unfortunately, Anti Bi's takeover did not satisfy Mother, who remained in a state of continuing indecision and conflict, feeling that she should go home to care for Angel. Father contradicted himself. At first he was saying that Mother should stay with him, to which I agreed, believing that Mother was incapable of handling this crisis. The next day, he would say, "It is your Mother's duty to go home and take care of her mother, but she must make up her own mind."

Edith Nixon's position was that Madam should stay with Mr. Bishop. It never occurred to Father that he might have gone with his wife to help her in this crisis. I tried not to pass judgment on my parents. I realized that Mother had never grown up, and I thought of her as a beautiful vine entwined around a sturdy oak to whom she had given her love, her whole life. How could Mother make up her own mind, when Father had always made it up for her? All her life she had avoided pain and responsibility. Everyone had helped her to do so, he most of all.

Although my parents were not enthusiastic, I managed to escape to New York in September to take up my job with Rugg. Late in October Mother arrived, accompanied by Edith but without Father. Why didn't he come too? Mother was irritable and depressed, visiting Angel in the nursing home almost daily. Frequently Angel did not recognize her. "Is this what will happen to me?" She repeated over and over again, "I don't want to get old, to get wrinkles." For Mother, now fifty-five, beauty was still a career. It remained so to the end of her life — the bone structure was good, and the delicate rose complexion, maintained with innumerable unguents, the blue eyes, and the blonde hair did not fade. For me, she was Venus. I was not beautiful — both she and her friends told me so — but this no longer bothered me now that I had made a number of men friends on my own.

When Father came home in November the situation did not improve. Mother was irascible with everyone — the gardener in Lenox and the chauffeur in New York, both old retainers devoted to Father, were threatening to leave. Father was greatly distressed, since the loyalty and admiration of those around him were a cornerstone of his life. "Your Mother," he said to me, "is alienating all my employees." I did not know where to turn and sought a change of atmosphere by going up to Vassar for the weekend to visit Mildred Thompson.

Mildred belonged to the generation of women scholars who never married and whose lives centered around their alma maters and their work. Highly intelligent, she had developed a great deal of worldly wisdom through her contacts with many students and later with political figures, including Eleanor Roosevelt. With her straight, graying reddish hair, pince-nez over a largish nose, and prominent front teeth, she could never have been called a pretty woman—some people found her austere. For those whom she elected to be her friends—Adolf and I and later my daughter Beatrice were among these—she was good company, affectionate, wise, and loyal always.

On this occasion I invited Adolf, who was back in New York, to join me as my guest at Alumnae House, thus postponing the day of his probable ostracism from Sixty-seventh Street. My parents had not met him yet. The weekend started with a lively discussion of the Versailles treaty and the following letter indicates that the visit was a success from other points of view as well!

> Dear Playmate [This was the first time he addressed me directly by that name.]... I have also to return thanks for your kindly and gracious hospitality of the week-end. It was a golden interlude which I shall long remember, all compact of Indian Summer sunshine and forthright youth in search of service to truth; of painted firs and brown hills against a mauve, reddened sky; of great serenity and philosophy won by years of patience; of jolly fireside, and profitable spirits. The kind of holiday Athene grants her disciples when she is not making war; but I have someone nearer than Pallas Athene to thank. Tonight I was asked by one of your friends who met us there what took me to Vassar; and I answered, that like most who went there, it was to get educated.

To introduce Adolf to my parents I knew I must prepare the ground carefully. Father was always telling me that I must marry a gentleman. I kept pressing him for a definition. "A gentleman," he declared solemnly, "always wears a top hat when he comes to dine with a lady."

This was going to be tested! The rules had relaxed somewhat, and I was allowed to have a little dinner party of my own on an evening when my parents dined out. I arranged a foursome—Adolf, his sister Lina, whom he called Starlight, and another young man, B. R.

The young men were instructed to appear in top hats.

"It is a game," I said. "Be sure to lay the hats on the hall table at the foot of the marble stairs."

Adolf's prescience was amazing—he guessed the real reason. We laughed about it together and agreed to play the silly game. The next morning Father remarked, "It does not follow that a man who wears a silk hat is a gentleman, but if he is a gentleman, he wears one."

Undaunted, a month later I decided to try a dinner party with my parents present. We always dressed for dinner, whether we were alone or receiving guests. This meant a dinner jacket for Father, a "tea gown" for Mother (a hostess gown today), and a simple evening dress with short sleeves for me.

There were no cocktails in 1925. My parents and I received the guests in the reception room downstairs. We were six—Mother, Father, Adolf, another young couple, and I.

"*Madame est servie,*" the butler proclaimed as he opened the double doors of the reception room.

We strolled down the hall to the dining room. This was an informal party, in contrast to those I had witnessed looking down the stairwell when I was a child.

Adolf sat next to Mother and made valiant efforts at small talk—the weather, the latest show on Broadway. Father spoke to the lady on his right about French architecture. She was the daughter of Ernest Flagg, a Beaux Arts graduate who had built this house for my parents at the turn of the century. Looking up to the mantelpiece, Father pointed with pride to two empty Madeira bottles dated 1866.

"The wine was a part of my father's cellar. In those days, before I was born, kegs of Madeira were sent around Cape Horn before they were considered fit for drinking and bottled."

For some reason this remark did not lead to further conversation. The atmosphere was somewhat constrained as the butler passed the grilled shad, and the liveried footman followed with the drawn butter. Later I wrote in my diary,

> I like this dining room; the original eighteenth-century French cartouches on the wall, the dark green French brocade curtains, the table linen—pure linen soft as silk, already thirty years old—the highly polished silver, the Dutch ancestral silver tankard in the center and the four silver candlesticks with their funny little fringed shades over the white candles. Dinner here is a beautiful form—one enjoys it like French pastry. My diet when I grow up will be composed chiefly of red meat.

After dinner, Father and Mother took the elevator to the library on the first floor and locked the door. They did not come down again and made no comment on the following day. The four of us—my friend Betsy, her husband, Adolf, and I, spent the rest of the evening in front of the fire in the reception room reading poetry aloud to each other:

Love's not Time's fool, though rosy lips and cheeks
Within his bending sickle's compass come;
Love alters not with his brief hours and weeks,
But bears it out even to the edge of Doom.

> William Shakespeare, Sonnet CXVI

The next day a little note came from Adolf:

> Your dinner party of Wednesday was a golden evening after all (I was frightened, were you?) and I hope I was not too dull for your parents, though I am afraid your mother was anything but amused. Seriously, for one minute, what is this queer barrier between generations which both sides seek to pass and never can quite define? Do we attack something or have we no common language; or have the older ones simply built a world and forgotten us? Precisely, as we cease to care for inclusion the problem solves itself and the job becomes that of clearing space in our world in which the elders shall have a place; for undoubtedly the world belongs in the main to us. . . . The one certainty is that eventually matters do right themselves but apparently only by fighting and understanding.
>
> Yours,
> A.A.B.

≈ 13

Adolf was drawing me gently into his world and invited me to dinner at the Henry Street Settlement.

"The settlement tends to be formal," he wrote. "It really is a lay convent of sorts."

His parents, whom I had met briefly, were there. It was Friday night, the prelude to the Jewish Sabbath. (The neighborhood was the place where large numbers of Jewish immigrants had settled.) The long, dark oak table, highly polished, reflected the light of the candles. There were about sixteen of us. Lillian Wald, a stately woman with penetrating dark eyes ("Madonna," as Adolf called her), presided over the salad bowl. Dr. Berle, Adolf's father, short of stature, dynamic in voice and manner, sat at her right. They carried on a lively conversation about Ramsay MacDonald, who as a struggling young labor leader had been a resident of Henry Street. He was now prime minister of England and had returned recently for a visit to the settlement. Mrs. Berle, a quiet, white-haired lady clad in powder blue, inserted appropriate remarks from time to time and inquired gently about the work I was doing.

At the other end of the table, Adolf was busy discussing a report on social agencies with the residents of Henry Street—some of them nurses, others living in nearby apartments. "The Catholic Big Sisters do one thing, the parish visitors of the local Protestant and Catholic churches do something else, and the health officer and social-service departments of the day nurseries and dispensaries do something else again. Surely there is duplication and the client falls between agencies? How can we get them working together?"

Courteously, from time to time Adolf asked for my views, but I was out of my depth. What a long way from Sixty-seventh Street! He was at home in both places. Could I become so?

After dinner, we walked over to the Henry Street Playhouse for a performance of *H.M.S. Pinafore* put on by residents of the neighborhood. Adolf pointed to the third-floor windows of an apartment, a few doors from the settlement house. This was where, on his return from Versailles, he lived with Paul Kellogg, editor of *The Survey*, a socially oriented magazine. A young banker occupied the apartment now and carried on the same role that Adolf had had, that of Henry Street resident—working at his profession during the day, participating in settlement activities several evenings a week. For Adolf, this had frequently involved legal work.

"I remember a young nurse a few years ago," he said. "She fell in love with me, but that is not the point. I defended her in an abortion suit. The state prosecutor claimed that she had not reported a self-induced or criminal abortion on one of her patients. The nurse pleaded she had taken the bleeding patient to the hospital for treatment following a spontaneous abortion.

"'How do you know this was not a criminal abortion?'" the prosecutor asked me.

"'The patient lifted a piano the day before,' I replied with aplomb. 'That brought about the abortion.'"

"'Case dismissed.'"

But the major activity for Adolf and other residents was running a boys' club. The club members were the children of recent Jewish immigrants from central Europe living in the Lower East Side ghetto where conditions of life paralleled those encountered now, alas, among blacks and Puerto Ricans in the South Bronx.

Adolf's club was unique.

"I read Shakespeare to them," he told me with enthusiasm. "Last spring I took four of the boys to a camp on the Hackensack River in New Jersey. It was one of those breathlessly beautiful golden-and-green days with a silent glory beyond art—to find that the boys, instead of being fairly staggered by it, as I always am, hardly took it in at all. On the other hand, a fifth youngster, who had been educated to that sort of thing, was really appreciating the splendor of it. One has not only to have qualities oneself, but also to have the faculty of interpretation—and that seems to be nothing less than a divine spark."

The fifth boy was Joel Landres, now a successful businessman, who never forgot the experience. Many years later, after Adolf's death, he wrote me, "Savants will write biographies of my friend which will establish his place in history. How I wish I could write a small tract which treated only with my friend's great heart and his lifetime of giving to the ghetto kids, me, and hundreds like me."

Returning to Sixty-seventh Street after that evening I realized that on Henry Street a window had been opened for me and that I was entering a brave new world. I could not imagine Mother at Henry Street. Father possibly—probably not. I would have liked to tell them about my experience but could not find words. They would not have understood.

I could not see the way, either, to ease their situation as the tension over my grandmother's condition mounted day by day. Mother found it increasingly difficult to visit the nursing home. Father reproached her for not going more often. Then, leaning on Edith's shoulder, Mother would burst into tears. "Soon I will be like my mother. All you and Beatrice want is to put me away." Father would either snap back or walk away. I was in the middle.

I tried to analyze the situation, writing in my diary,

> Clearly Mother had never grown up, but neither had Father. He and her parents had always spread pillows before her so that she might not hurt herself if she chanced to fall. She did not succeed in running a house, so he hired a housekeeper and that responsibility was removed. She suffered pain during menstruation so she had a hysterectomy. The world called her "the beautiful Amy Bend." She has had to keep up that reputation. It still remains her greatest preoccupation—massage, facial and body, colonic irrigations, raw carrots, curl papers, that has become her life, and the fear of growing old dominates her every mood. This makes it impossible for her to think or speak of anything else and so she finds fault with everyone.
>
> Father is not exactly helpful. He has always had his own way, loving and caring for her as if she were a beautiful doll, until he reached middle age and sought a different kind of relationship. I feel they are victims of deep lack of understanding arising from his having spoiled her.

I felt great pity for Mother. When she was sweet and affectionate and begged me to tell her about what I was doing, I remained tongue-tied. I would have liked to tell her about Henry Street, for instance, but more than likely she would have countered with "I don't want you to associate with that kind of people. They are Jews." I knew she was capable of love and tenderness, but the things that mattered to me only disgusted her and made her unhappy. I could try, but I would never be what she would have me be. If an understanding grew sufficiently, I could give her some of the things she wanted without letting her know the things she could not understand. "It is a terrible thing in private as in public life—once the policy of censorship is started, it grows increasingly rigorous," was my conclusion.

With Father it was different. Where at first we had retreated each into his own corner, we were coming together again, taking refuge in each other as Mother was isolating herself more and more, saying that Father and I were conspiring to "put her away." *Put away* was the term she used over and over again. Father and I were both innocents—we had not read Freud! Not until my visit to Dr. Riggs did I obtain some understanding of the meaning of these words for Mother. Her mother had been "put away" in a nursing home. Mother was getting old; men would admire her no longer. Her daughter, whom she had never loved, was an immoral girl who was conspiring with her own husband to "put her away."

Usually after dinner the three of us went to the library and occupied ourselves with Father's books—a family activity that persisted even in the midst of the turmoil. One evening, I was cutting out descriptions from catalogues to file them in the books Father had bought at auction recently. Mother's role was to paste in the bookplates. As Father and I started talking, drawn together as if by a magnet, Mother rose abruptly and went upstairs.

Edith Nixon came down a few minutes later.

"Madam wants her knitting," she announced, "and is going to bed."

Father froze, then bolted upstairs. After twenty minutes, Edith brought Mother back in her dressing gown. On this and on other similar occasions, she managed Mother when Father could not.

The following morning Father told me, "Your mother is exhausting Edith. I plan to take Edith on as my secretary, to preserve her health. I know your mother will not understand the situation and will think I am trying to take Edith away from selfish motives."

The transition to personal secretary was no problem for Edith; she managed to remain the confidante of all three of us, flattering and cajoling both Mother and Father and advising me how to behave toward them. But I considered that notwithstanding Edith's blandishments, the situation was deteriorating. The bickering between Father and Mother disturbed me most of all:

"Cortlandt, you eat too much."

"Amy, you smoke too much."

They had always told me that well-bred people never quarrel before other people, certainly not before their children. Whenever I tried Mother's door, it was locked, and more than once I thought I heard her crying in her room. Father, I noticed, did not sleep in her room as he had always done, but kept to his own at the other end of the hall.

The circle of fire was breaking down completely. This must not be. I felt helpless — I needed advice from a professional.

≈ *14*

In 1925 "shrink" was not the popular byword it is today. A psychiatrist was only for crazy people. The mental-hygiene movement was just starting. My friend Mildred Thompson was among the first in the college world to recognize the needs of students for help in solving their emotional problems. She had organized a mental-hygiene service at Vassar, and I had helped her to obtain the services of Dr. Austen Riggs as consultant.

Dr. Riggs was Mother's cousin. I knew him only slightly, but his daughters were my schoolmates. Before World War I, he had established a sanatorium for the treatment of functional nervous diseases in Stockbridge. This institution is known today as the Austen Riggs Center.

When, on my first visit to Dr. Riggs's office, he looked at me with his deep-set dark eyes, I knew that he would understand and that I need not be afraid. We talked, and very gently he explained, "Although we are cousins, I never knew your mother very well. My mother, though, was brought up by your grandmother, Mrs. Bend, whom you call Angel. Mother agreed with everyone else that Amy was a great beauty, but said she was self-centered. Angel spoiled her.

"Even as a young girl Amy had strange ideas and felt that those who did not admire her were against her. In the course of time, people with a suspicious nature like your mother's may build up a system of delusions. Let me explain. If, for instance, your mother read in the paper that an Irishman has robbed a bank, for her it is a short step from there to thinking that all Irishmen are thieves and that one must beware of them and lock all the doors against them. If one accepts an initial premise, the delusional system is quite logical, and it is difficult not to be taken in.

"Your mother is building up a system of delusions about you, but I am afraid I cannot help. She would not listen to me, her cousin. You should consult another psychiatrist." He recommended Dr. Thomas Salmon.

It turned out that Dr. Salmon, who was one of the leaders in the mental-hygiene movement, had an office across the street from our house on Sixty-seventh Street. When I talked to him, he went further into an explanation of Mother's troubles.

"Your mother," he said, "has a thinking defect that we call paranoia. *This is not a moral issue, but a malady.*" (This phrase became a life preserver for me, and I have clung to it ever since that day.) "You are the subject of your mother's ideas. She believes that you are her rival for your father's affection, that you are conspiring with him against her. That is why she calls you an immoral girl. If you were to die tonight the hostility she is displaying against your father would disappear, but after a time she would build up a delusional system about someone else. It is important that your mother come to see me. Above all," he concluded, "the worst thing in the world is to suggest to her that she is insane."

Edith, I felt, would be the only person who could persuade Mother to visit Dr. Salmon. This she did. After Mother's visit, Dr. Salmon wrote Father requesting an appointment with him. Father showed the letter to Edith, who reported that Father was furious, exclaiming, "Impertinence! Cheek! I will discuss my wife with no one!"

"Mr. Bishop is quite right," Edith concluded, speaking to me, "and it was wrong of you to have gotten me to persuade Madam to see Dr. Salmon."

Confused and in pain, I retreated to Father's library. Mother's portrait over the mantelpiece dominated the room: the pink satin gown, the delicate tulle floating over the bare shoulders, the pearl necklace—each individual pearl selected by Father—the doll-like face, distant, unreal. In this room Father had gradually made me his companion.

I unlocked the bookcase where the Books of Hours were kept. The blue of Our Lady's robes and the miniature of the peasant felling the tree in the calendar for November were no less beautiful than they had always been. I read aloud to myself *Les Quinze Joies de Notre Dame*, but this was not enough. This kind of learning, though fascinating, did not help in understanding the present situation. I must learn about people.

My mind floated back to Grand-mère, who had died three years before.

Only last summer in Europe, when Grand-mère's name was mentioned, Mother, with tears of rage in her eyes, had once again vowed eternal hatred for her deceased mother-in-law. This, I realized now, was an example of paranoid thinking and not subject to reason.

As daylight faded, I returned the Book of Hours to its rightful place and kept thinking about Grand-mère. I loved her dearly.

Recently I had visited the seamen's mission that she had founded on Catherine Street. It was still operating, thanks to a legacy she had left them. The director, a Nova Scotian woman of Scotch descent, crafty, emotional, and capable, was quarreling with the Catholics across the street and giving out bread to solve marital troubles. Be that as it may, the people I met still spoke of Grand-mère's smile and the light in her brown eyes. The mission was dated, but Grand-mère's gift of herself was priceless and eternal.

Henry Street was very different but built on the same underlying base—love for one's fellowman. How could I follow Grand-mère's example in modern terms? Certainly not through my present job.

I was beginning to realize that my boss, Harold Rugg, knew nothing about history and was seeking to rewrite textbooks using a statistical approach, completely disregarding what I had been taught about the evaluation of evidence and the need to take into account the prejudices of previous authors. According to Rugg, an average of the number of pages devoted to a certain subject in older texts determined the amount of space to be devoted to that subject in the new book. "Estimating brains with a quart measure" was the comment of Prospero (Henry Osborn Taylor) when I went to him for advice. He summoned the veteran professor James Shotwell to my aid. Both gentlemen recommended that I resign. I did. Adolf also agreed, and wrote to me:

> I have been meditating the *coup d'etat* by which all things related to your "research" are to be eliminated and, as you say, it gives one a queer feeling, partly based on the consciousness of a coming vacuum in formerly filled hours and partly arising out of a wonder whether somehow or other this situation could have been used as a means of getting a result. I have a theory that these tragicomic periods are really the dying flickers of a childhood.
>
> This is a jolly coffee on account of the rain which pounds on the roof of the little restaurant. But the coffee has come to an end and so must this letter.

Then he gave me Lillian Wald's *The House on Henry Street*, the story of how she founded the Henry Street Settlement. I read every word of it. What courage it must have taken to start the settlement and to organize the Visiting Nurse

Service. Lillian Wald was not condescending, not pitying; she was realistic and firm but always idealistic. "Every human being, even the least lovely, merits respectful consideration of his rights and personality," she said. Her example pointed the way and was a determining factor in the plan I was evolving to become a professional social worker. Adolf was backing me at every turn and wrote a note introducing me to Walter Pettit, a former colleague of his at the Versailles Peace Conference, now a director of the New York School of Social Work. He characterized the profession I wanted to enter as "social engineering."

The Lady Julia, Prospero's wife and a member of the board of the Charity Organization Society (now merged with other private organizations under the name Community Service Society), was a bit more realistic.

"Remember," she cautioned with a sad smile, "organizations frequently forget about people and lose themselves in paperwork."

This did not dampen my enthusiasm. After registering at the School of Social Work I bought a red dress and a red hat. Oh, the joy of being alive!

Dr. Riggs and Dr. Salmon felt that the study of psychiatric social work would help me in understanding my own family situation. I presented the matter to Father, who was sympathetic to my plan. Not so Mother.

In the eyes of Mother's friends, social work was equated with socialism. These friends greatly pitied her — her daughter was a radical.

"Where shall I set a bomb?" I asked them.

Finally I forced Father to define his terms. Calling himself a liberal, he declared a radical to be one intent upon destroying existing institutions. I laughed and replied that his society was not interested in morality or ethics — the unpardonable sin was being "different."

Upon my entering the School of Social Work in February 1926, my first assignment was in the Yorkville office of the Charity Organization Society. Prospero wrote in characteristic fashion:

> You plunge into elemental humanity Monday morning — "Hamlet remember me" — and come in after your day's work on Monday if you choose, direct from the field of action — towel and soap await you. Also I can regale you with a letter from Henry Adams and my own remarks on religion.

Adolf had a comment too.

> Today will have been your first day. I hope it went well. It's not fun, but it's not bad when you get into it and it certainly shifts your outlook. Good fortune.

[79]

Climbing tenement stairs in Yorkville became for me a thrilling initiation into the mysteries of both life and death. The supervisor had a low opinion of my capabilities. I overheard her tell one of her staff, "Miss Bishop shouldn't have come here. I didn't want her. She doesn't even know the meaning of the word tonsillectomy."

I knew I was a greenhorn and probably a nuisance, but I wanted to learn. My fluency in Italian made communication with my Sicilian clients possible, and I marveled at the combined delicacy and earthiness of my first one, a blowsy mother of five who, while apologizing for discussing her marital and obstetrical problems with a "signorina," spared no details.

The Yorkville neighborhood (the Sixties to the Eighties, east of Third Avenue) was very friendly in the 1920s. I soon felt at home, especially after the Italian grocer gave me advice on how to find good spaghetti for twelve cents. It was not worth paying seventeen cents, he assured me—and when his little girl came running out of the store and threw her arms around me, I felt very happy.

Alas, the warmth and friendliness of Yorkville did not penetrate number 15 East Sixty-seventh Street! As soon as I crossed the threshold I felt as if I were entering a prison. Father's attitude toward Mother was changing—he had become most attentive and considerate of her feelings. But as I overheard a conversation on the stairs, she was telling him that I wished to put her away. This upset him greatly. Wishing to avoid a confrontation, I tried to explain in private Dr. Salmon's point of view, but Father rebuffed me, saying that he could handle the matter on his own.

Two days later, the situation had changed completely. Father asked me to give him my passport, since he was thinking of going to France in a few days. He did not wish to go alone and was not sure Mother would accompany him.

We were both going out at that moment, so I did not have time to reply. This is the time to make a stand, I said to myself. I marshaled my arguments. I wrote in my diary, "Social work is a profession for which I am being trained—a profession is necessary in this day and age. For me it is a matter of life and death. This is the decisive battle for the Americanization and emancipation of BBB." But histrionics turned out not to be necessary. The passport was not mentioned again.

The tables were turned—it was I, not Mother, Edith reported, who was in need of psychiatric treatment. Father and Mother had visited Dr. Riggs requesting that he take me under his care, since they felt I was deceitful, unstable, and indiscreet with men—and had an unpleasant laugh!

This seemed to me ridiculous—a bad joke. Naturally, I went to see Dr. Riggs, who reported that he and Dr. Salmon had seized the occasion of my parents' visit to see Father alone and to try to explain Mother's condition to him. "Your father," Dr. Riggs commented, "is like a child. He understands little about human emotions. It is hard for him to understand that paranoia is a persistent thinking disorder. I have tried to explain to him that your mother will continue to weave her entourage into her delusional system so that they all must accept her charges against you. Whoever does not do so is against her."

But it became obvious that Father had not understood Dr. Riggs. His attitude toward me changed completely. Was this Edith's doing? He hardly spoke to me and was no longer impatient with Mother. She appeared happy and affectionate with him. I felt that the circle of fire was closing again and I was outside.

When Adolf came to tea I wanted to talk to him about the family situation without going into details. Both his code and mine forbade the discussion of family affairs with comparative strangers. But our relationship was developing rapidly under rather special circumstances. We arranged to meet at the naturalization bureau, where Adolf helped me to straighten out the citizenship papers for one of my clients in the Charity Organization Society. In spite of the drab surroundings, I felt it was very romantic, our trying to work out a human problem together. It was only the first of a lifetime of such occasions. Two months before his death forty-five years later, Adolf appeared in court to defend one of my heroin-addict patients who was about to be sentenced in a case of mistaken identity.

On this first occasion, after taking care of the citizenship papers we walked swiftly down Broadway. Adolf took my arm and piloted me along the crowded sidewalk to Fraunces Tavern, where we had lunch. He did not look well. He had been up most of the night with a woman on Henry Street who had the flu. While Starlight straightened out the house, he had washed the woman's dishes. He wanted to talk to me about the Harvard Business School, where he was being offered a position. The administration wanted him — they considered that he had foresight and the ability to get a situation under control and that he was knowledgeable about business and legal affairs. But he was worried that he would become only an academician. What he hoped was that he could be both a professor and a practicing lawyer. He would start by giving just a few lectures; the final decision would be made later.

"Let's go on seeing each other," he declared, "but there will be no love affairs this spring. Until you come out of this [my problems with my parents], you are not worth marrying and the man who forced you would not be worth marrying either."

Then, speaking very quietly and taking my hand in his, he began, "To make it easier for you to speak to me, I'll tell my story. I've been through this also. My father was very angry with me and my sisters when we left home in order to set up our own apartment. We were all three over twenty-five and self-supporting."

"And now?" I asked anxiously.

"It's all over like a thunderstorm—he's forgotten all about it. But the hurt was very deep, especially in the case of Mother and the girls. But I always left the door open."

Three years before this, another man, angry and bitter, had said, "You are a sentimental adolescent. If you really cared for me, you would stand up to your family and fight. Either you would leave home or you would receive me no matter what they said."

At that time and now also I was not prepared to engage in a knock-down fight with my parents. I wanted to be independent, though the means by which I was to achieve this goal were not clear. I was determined to resolve the family conflict without bitterness.

"It is hate that kills," Adolf told me. I knew he was right. I was finding in this man a rare combination of sweetness and strength, intelligence, common sense, and idealism. I began to feel toward him as I had never felt toward anyone else.

But Father was still the cornerstone of my life. I felt sorry for him. Edith told me he felt sorry for me, since he had lost confidence in me, and considered me queer, abnormal, etc. How could I restore his faith in me? He must be suffering if he believed that all the good he had once thought of me was untrue. I decided to ask him directly to tell me what was wrong.

As I put the question, the surge of emotions within both of us was so great that we could not speak. I felt as if my heart would burst. Finally he pulled himself together and said that the trouble was all my fault. He had consulted Dr. Malcolm Goodridge, an internist, who said that Mother was quite well. He understood his wife perfectly and would tell me what to do. He did not go into particulars, and I did not ask.

What could I do? I wanted to maintain contact with Mother. She did not speak to me if she could possibly avoid it. She asked me not to call her *"carina"* (dear, in Italian, a language we spoke together), but I continued to go into her room to say good morning until the day she shouted at me, "Never come into my room again—I want nothing to do with you. You wanted me to disappear. Neither your grandmother, if she were conscious, nor your Aunt Beatrice will ever want to see you again. May you be cursed by your children if you ever have any."

I fled and was sick at my stomach. My Venere was gone from me forever. I

[82]

wanted to move out at once, but I realized that I should not be rushed into a decision, to use Father's own words. The month before, Dr. Riggs had recommended that I make independent summer plans.

With Mildred Thompson's approval and encouragement, I had applied to go as a volunteer teacher to Labrador in June—and had just been accepted.

Apparently a college degree was all that was required. I cannot imagine anyone less qualified than I was to teach small children. Dr. Wilfred Grenfell directed a privately supported medico-social organization devoted to the service of the people of Labrador and northern Newfoundland—it was an equivalent of a modern Peace Corps project. Medical students spent the summer in the base hospital at Saint Anthony, in Newfoundland. Scattered nursing stations were staffed by professionals on yearly contracts. The rest of the staff were summer volunteers.

This was to be a great adventure, but June was far away. In the meantime the atmosphere on Sixty-seventh Street was glacial. My attempt to talk with Father had come to nought. Edith reported that my parents had decreed that I was not to receive friends in the library but only in the reception room. She reiterated that Father had lost complete confidence in me and considered I was immoral (meaning what?). Adolf was a disreputable character; I should move out right away. Father was so incensed, she went on, that he was going to call Miss Thompson to tell her that deceitfulness and immorality were all I had learned at Vassar. Everyone was being told that I had conspired to put Mother away in an insane asylum. I could be "taken back"—those were Edith's words—if I gave up the tenements and my socialist friends.

The situation was becoming more and more bewildering and painful. In desperation I went to a pay telephone and called Adolf. His voice came to me reassuringly. "Your parents are driving themselves into a desert wilderness. There must be no bitterness on your part." In a letter following this call, he added, "I do not believe that all goldfish bowls require smashing. That is always possible as a last resort but there must be better ways and sometimes pure love conquers, as I think yours will in time. Meanwhile I am glad to be a safety valve or anything you choose until the stars come out once more, and the sailing is smooth toward the happy isles." Nevertheless, I was losing confidence in myself. I was not immoral. My physical contact with men had been limited to an occasional embrace. I was not deceitful, but was I perhaps crazy? To restore myself in my own eyes, as Easter was approaching I sent a plant to Adolf's mother, who replied graciously that she would take the azalea to plant in her own garden the next summer.

Then I followed Angel's custom and placed some roses on the Townsend graves in Trinity Cemetery. When I reported this to Angel, in the nursing home, a flicker of recognition and understanding seemed to pass over her face. The Easter Sunday communion service at Grace Church was most comforting—love must prevail.

But it was hard. Edith kept repeating the same story with additional details. I would be forbidden to visit Angel. Mother and Father would be sailing for Europe on Saturday. Edith would be going with them. The place in Lenox would be shut down, but I could stay in Sixty-seventh Street. This was Tuesday. The trunks were beginning to pile up in the front hall.

On Wednesday Father came back from Lenox, where he had been by himself, and visited Dr. Riggs on his own. This time Dr. Riggs had convinced him.

Father said to me, "Your mother believes you and I are conspiring against her. This isn't so. Dr. Riggs tells me that this is a fixed idea on her part—a delusion that is not amenable to reason. I don't understand the situation very well. I'll need your help.

"I approve of your plan to go to Labrador in June. Until then you can remain in Sixty-seventh Street, and go to Lenox when you wish. You can entertain your friends at home, but your mother does not wish Adolf Berle in the house. Personally I would not have imposed this condition, but remember, it is her house, and I don't want to cross her at this time. I can see that Adolf Berle is clever, perhaps unscrupulous."

In an effort to convince him and to assure him of my love and loyalty, I asked him to speak to Mrs. Murray Crane, the widow of the senator from Massachusetts and a lifelong friend of the Berle family. I obtained favorable reports on Adolf through the Bishop family lawyer and Dun & Bradstreet and showed them to Father. This didn't change his mind. So we left it that I would not invite Adolf to the house, but this did not mean that I would not see him on the outside. There the matter rested.

That evening at dinner I almost wept, because of an incident that made me recognize Father's dilemma. It was all over a piece of duck. He wanted a second helping. Mother said there was none, since "she," meaning me, had taken some. Actually, there was plenty of duck left. Father took a big piece and divided it with me. Mother made remarks about people who had smooth exteriors and were bad at heart. Father looked at her anxiously but said nothing. I became aware of how much courage and patience he would need and wished that I might always be standing by his side.

The following day was a day of contrasts. In the morning, in Yorkville I saw life through the eyes of a woman whose husband had been out of work for three weeks and who was a hundred dollars in debt. Both were in poor health. In the afternoon, I accompanied Father to a business meeting at which he was dealing in millions. I sat at his right hand. How naïve we both were not to realize that our relationship was the factual basis on which Mother built her delusional system. Her daughter had become a rival for her husband's attention and affection; the daughter must be eliminated. Those around her must rally to this end. Only with the greatest tact on the part of Father — tact and understanding that he did not possess — could equilibrium have been reached. We three could never rebuild the circle of fire together. The see-saw between Mother and Father must be kept in balance. Edith Nixon knew that as a superb manipulator, she stood in the middle, playing one against the other, each one certain that Edith was working for the good of all, while she was building up her own position.

When we got home, Edith reported that Mother was in a terrible state of mind, was refusing to come down to dinner, and was insisting she would not go abroad with Father. Finally Edith persuaded her to come down to dinner and was hoping to get her to sail on Saturday. Through the evening, Father appeared tired and depressed, like a pricked balloon.

Saturday came. Mother, Father, and Edith sailed for France. Mother made a point of refusing to say goodbye to me.

A letter from Father came, sent via the ship's pilot:

> My Dearest Child:
> It is a terrible thing for both of us — this separation at this moment when we have found each other again and when the need for the other is greater than it ever was.
> Yet it is a satisfaction to know that in parting we have got back to where we have always been until a short time ago. Now, however, we are both certain that the tie which has bound us can never be broken. I cannot tell you all that is in my heart. I know that you now realize what I have before me and that you can only help me in a passive way. You have many activities. I know that you are happy as you were not a week ago and though we shall be far apart in the immediate future, I know that in our hearts we are forever united.
> Lovingly and affectionately,
>
> Your Father

Two days later a radiogram arrived from the ship signed by Edith. "Write mother ask pardon." It struck a chill in my heart. What did this mean? I had no pardon to beg. I decided to disregard this message and wrote to Father frequently through the spring. He replied with chatty letters, reporting his activities in an impersonal way: The purchase of another book of hours; tuning up the Hispano for the next trip, consulting with the staff of the *Paris Times*, of which he was the owner and for which I had written articles the previous year. Only one personal note, on their arrival in Paris on April 20: "I hope you are happy and getting your life in shape as it should be. You know that your absence is particularly hard for me at this time. I know that I can trust you now and for always but it is a satisfaction to hear *viva voce* what you think and what you are doing."

Then a report written three days later on Mother's visit to Dr. Sicard, a prominent French neurologist, who declared that "your mother is very well indeed."

A letter from Edith was more explicit. "Madam saw Dr. Sicard and explained everything to him. Told him that she felt that if people kept thinking she ought to be sent to a home and if she lived in the atmosphere of such thoughts it was quite possible such a thing might come to pass. Dr. Sicard gave Madam a thorough examination and told Mr. Bishop that in all the years he has known Madam he never found her less nervous and in such good condition."

For good measure she added that my last letter to Mother had been a great disappointment—I should have said I was sorry for any errors I had made. Now "things are much worse and must be left to take care of themselves." Finally, she said that my sending Father a legal article on no-par stock by Adolf was a great mistake.

These letters filled me with dismay. Obviously the French neurologist, like the family physician whom I had consulted in New York, had not penetrated the paranoid system.

Once more doubts began to creep into my mind. What if Riggs and Salmon were wrong and I was deluded? But as events were developing, the correctness of the Riggs-Salmon diagnosis became more and more evident. Granted the premises, Mother's paranoid logic was perfect. Since I was evil and plotted to put her away, everyone close to her must be shielded from me and must rally to her defense. That was the reason why Edith had written that I was not to visit Angel. But Angel was senile, and although most of the time she did not recognize me, there were moments when she smiled and appeared glad to see me, so I continued to visit her. The visits must have been reported to Edith by her sister, the housekeeper; two weeks later the family physician called me to his office and showed me a cable signed by Mother and Father instructing me to discontinue my visits to Angel. Since I had consulted him before consulting Dr. Riggs and Dr. Salmon and he had denied the whole problem, his embarrassment was a source of great satisfaction to me. Since I was leaving soon for Labrador, I decided not to visit Angel again. She, poor darling, probably would not know the difference.

In Father's last letter, dated May 21, which arrived shortly before my sailing for Labrador, he advised me,

> Almost anything may happen before you return and I can well see that next October circumstances may be such that it will be better that you have an apartment of your own. If such shall be the case, I will provide an apartment for you. [Presumably in the Sixth Avenue building he had planned the previous winter. This offer was subsequently withdrawn.] In any event the decision must not be lightly made but only after most careful consideration of every point involved. This may be the last letter before you leave on your great adventure. Your father wishes you every success.

I was never to see Father again. He died in 1935, ten years later.

≈≈≈ 15

Fortunately family problems were not my only concern during that spring. Adolf, my playmate, was a source of great comfort and fun also. We were reaching a sufficient degree of intimacy and confidence in each other to permit us to discuss our respective family situations in greater detail. I told him the whole story as I saw it, including the fact that he was not to enter the house on Sixty-seventh Street. His reply, coming through the next mail, was characteristic.

> Playmate:
>
> As to cooperation, you are right as usual though that's not so easy either unless you are one of these super-men. I am not so enthusiastic about the young learning to wait. I've tried that—years of it—and the price which is precisely the glorious impact of first youth is an ungodly one. Understanding is different—that is necessary whatever happens. It is an individual question to be worked out by each scion of youth in turn, the experience of others being of little use save to demonstrate that there is possibility of high outcome in the end and that it is all bound up with establishing control of one's own soul in the passage.

Then, on a bus ride at sunset, Adolf told me more about his own experience and how his "revolt of youth," as he called it, had come about.

His father, a Congregational clergyman in Cambridge, Massachusetts, active in writing and in promoting educational projects, spent the winters in New

York after he retired. In 1923, the setting up by the young people of their own apartment, which Adolf had already mentioned, was only one of many events that infuriated Dr. Berle.

Dr. Berle's moods might have been compared to violent thunderstorms with thunder and lightning followed by torrential rain, clearing into bright sunshine, after which, according to the family expression, he would "forget what he did." These abrupt changes of mood were attributed to his having been cruelly and abusively treated by a Prussian stepfather; his own father had died when he was still a small boy. Protas, Adolf's grandfather, was said to have been a political refugee from the revolution of 1848 in Germany. After immigrating to Saint Louis he was naturalized an American citizen; he died as a result of wounds received during the Civil War.

Adolf's mother was the daughter of George Frederick Wright, a professor of geology and theology at Oberlin College in Ohio. In temperament she was very different from her husband. There was a serenity about her bearing that never ceased to impress me. On the surface it appeared effortless, but as I came to know her better, never ceasing to admire her and love her, I learned that this serenity came as a result of a deep faith in the providence of God. This faith maintains that there is an overall force for good in the world. Through that faith, and through the love of God and one's fellowman, come the strength and the courage to accept and to bear the inevitable and frequently apparently irrational tragedies of life.

"During the World War," Adolf explained further, "anti-German feeling ran high in Cambridge, where we lived then. We were thought of as German, and this meant that my sisters had little opportunity for normal social life. Some people, pretending to be friendly, urged us to change our name, which, of course, we would not do. As Americans, we were proud of our European heritage.

"In 1917 I had finished law school and was starting on my first job in Justice Brandeis's office, when I decided to enlist."

"If I had known you then," I interjected, "I suspect I would have been part of the anti-German crowd. In France, where I was brought up, the children were taught to be anti-German. The Boches, as they were called, were barbarians. Alsace-Lorraine, which they had seized from France during the war of 1870, had to be reconquered. Unfortunately this prejudice, from which I did not recover until I got to Vassar, prevented me from learning German. I was taught Italian and Spanish by private tutors, and I went to school both in France and in New York, but I refused to learn German."

"What a pity!" said Adolf. "At Harvard in spite of the war, I had the great privilege to read Goethe with Professor Kuno Francke."

We were not dead serious all the time—just some of the time. A happy note came in the mail one morning.

> Harvard Club Coffee-time.
> Playmate:
> Tuesday then. Unless otherwise instructed I will find you at that house on 67th St. at 7 or thereabout. Gilbert & Sullivan's *Iolanthe*, which I have just seen, will bear seeing again. I salute you over the coffee cups.
> A.A.B. Jr.
> P.S. I have been engaged since the play ended in the pleasing pursuit of reading editorials about myself in the *Boston Transcript* and *New York World*. But they say "all the wrong things." (Article in Law Review on no-par stock.)

On another occasion, Adolf took me to the Plaza. This we considered a great dissipation. We compared notes on our past as wallflowers. I told him about the dull days of my childhood when my governess walked me from Sixty-seventh Street to the dancing class on Ninety-first Street. And about the coming-out party given for my friends Sheila Burden and Adele Hammond: Even though my white satin dress with spangles had been made in Paris, no boys would dance with me.

"I haven't done much better, Playmate. I've been a chaperone at the Henry Street Settlement dances. Very dull. But tonight we'll dance together and have fun." We did.

Before taking me home, Adolf ordered the coffee he drank every night. While I was pouring it from the silver pot, he muttered to himself, "Never be afraid and you don't get hurt."

He is the most unusual man I have ever met, I thought to myself. Brilliant and quick-witted certainly, gentle and loving.

We reached Sixty-seventh Street by eleven o'clock, the curfew hour we had agreed on. He knew of my promise to Father not to receive him in the house, and he never pressed me. The redheaded Anna was hovering at the front door, no doubt taking notes to report to her sister Edith in Paris.

From time to time, acquaintances of my father's invited me to dinner. One of these introduced me to an older man, divorced, with two adolescent children.

He was being courted by a divorcée, but he fell in love with me in the twinkling of an eye. I was a damsel to be rescued immediately—none of that "working things out." He wanted to marry me right away. It was flattering to discover that at twenty-three I was no longer the wallflower of six years previously. I admitted to myself that I was infatuated, but fortunately, I kept my head.

A few days before I was to sail for Labrador, a very pleasant communication came from the Taylors. Prospero was to receive an honorary degree from Columbia University and I was to be their guest at the ceremony. The letter of invitation concluded with this paragraph:

> My dear Beatrice has so many problems to work out. You may be sure your life is not altogether easy or simple because of your many keys to Kensington [Kensington garden, where Peter Pan lived, was locked at night]. In fact, it may be more complicated and difficult. Years ago, I wrote a book on adjustments of the great ancients. I'll give you one some day but you have enough now. No more wisdom for the present.

Since Prospero and the Lady Julia had not been banned from Sixty-seventh Street, I was able to offer them a small dinner after the ceremony. The Lady Julia, from whom I learned a great deal (including the art of salad making), sent me a gracious acknowledgment:

> We enjoyed having you with us not only because you are very admirable in yourself but because you lend yourself to our pet theories of social intercourse as an art.

As the guests left, the clocks struck eleven, one by one; once again I was alone in the empty house.

Grenfell Summer, 1926 ≈

≈16

A few days later I sailed for Curling, Newfoundland, carrying a letter from Adolf as my talisman.

> Playmate:
>
> And now like the water baby, you are off for the shiny wall: and I hope there is all splendor of experience beyond. There is a certain satisfaction to one's soul in being very close to primitive things, when you travel not on the support of highly intricate social forms, but on the strength that the good Lord gives you, and on the elementary forces of earth and wind. I think any education ought to include at least one period when you face life pretty much alone and unsupported. It makes for sympathy and tolerant understanding in respect of the rest of the world and for appreciation of civilization and for a certain unafraidness in great hours, which last I have never quite compassed but hope to sometime. You'll be playing a lone hand, playing sometimes for a real stake perhaps; and, as a childhood goes, strength comes and compassion with it.

Arriving in Curling, I felt very alone indeed, neither romantic nor heroic. I wished I were with my parents in France, in Lenox riding my horse—anywhere but Curling. Whistling in the dark, I reasoned that the family tragedy was a good thing, that I need no longer fear becoming a parasitic Euro-American, and that my life on my own in the New World was beginning. That helped!

Adolf's first letter arrived the next day:

> All good fortune and golden adventure and add my greetings to your own when you face a strong west wind from the head of a Newfoundland promontory. There's more in life than philosophy or eco-

nomics and kingdoms are small things beside an open sweep of sunlit sea or the driving glorious rush of a northeast storm and there can be baptisms and forgivenesses and rebirths which need no confession of creed— Adolf.

From Curling the summer staff took another boat and were distributed to their various stations. Summer teachers were assigned to a small village, boarded with a family, and expected to teach the three R's, to conduct religious services, and to provide aspirin and small bandages when indicated. Emergency cases were taken by motorboat to the nearest medical post, which was staffed by a registered nurse who lived there the year round. The nursing station at Flower's Cove on the Straits of Belle Isle was nine miles by foot trail and about thirty minutes by motorboat from Pyne's Cove, the village to which I had been assigned.

Pyne's Cove consisted of ten houses. Aunt Jane was the matriarch there. Hers was the principal house, standing on a little knoll, prim and stark—an unpainted cube against the sky. I had a room in the house of a couple called Joe and Jessie. My bed had no springs; a humpy and bumpy chicken-feather mattress was laid over a criss-cross of ropes tied to the frame. A tin basin and a chair; a well-built privy outside—that was it. The schoolroom was in another house. There were about ten pupils, ages six to twelve.

In the morning I taught school, using reading primers, a blackboard, and coloring pencils. The afternoons were spent getting acquainted. When the cod were running, school was called off, since even the smallest children were expected to help, fetching and carrying as the fish were cleaned prior to salting.

The good people of Pyne's Cove were a marvel to me. Joe was always teasing and joking. They were poor. By our standards, they were not clean. The children cried, but more often they were laughing. They were not squabbling or bickering. What made this good humor possible? Perhaps they made the most of their lot, since they knew no other.

Adolf stated the problem and the challenge in his next letter:

> June 30: Now on the Straits of Belle Isle you are looking out for the fishermen's children, physically, mentally and morally. It sounds like a large order. I wonder would we dare to try such things without a tremendous underlying sense of our own superiority? But oddly enough, we do seem to make some progress whatever the basis and perhaps you and I, not being so convinced of being in a state of grace, get farther by simply endeavoring to put the resources we enjoy at the disposal of anyone able to make use of them.

Mail came irregularly by motorboat from Flower's Cove; by hand if someone was coming down the trail. I waited anxiously for a letter from Father. None came. It was the middle of July. I had been in Pyne's Cove more than six weeks. I was sick at heart and desperately lonely. It was not possible that Father's letters had gone astray. There were frequent communications from Adolf, from Prospero, and from my divorced friend.

I was having violent abdominal cramps, most unusual for me, and I imagined every known disease. "Bodily reaction to emotional stress," my chief at the New York Hospital twenty years later, Dr. Harold Wolff, would have said. The pain passed and quieted down after I made a decision.

I walked in the rain down to Flower's Cove, a fat commercial code book in hand, and cabled Father:

"No letter received from you since one dated May 21. Health very good. Love, Beatrice." I had written to him regularly and continued to do so.

That night I spent at the nursing station in Flower's Cove. It was a neat, comfortable frame house with hot water, beds with spring mattresses, electric lights, and armchairs. Miss Mahoney, the nurse, told of being called for by dogsled in the midst of a blizzard to deliver a woman living ten miles away. This sounded like a great adventure, which I, of course, could not have undertaken—I had no training. Still, lying luxuriously in the hot bath, I thought of getting a job somewhere, anywhere. It did not matter to anyone what I did. But that would be running away. I must go home, clarify the situation, be on hand to help Father.

In the morning it was no longer raining. I decided to make an early start for Pyne's Cove. At 6:00 A.M.., shivering and dabbing my fingers in a thimbleful of water, I thought: Is this Romance? Adventure? Hell, no! As I walked along the footpath winding through moss and lichen, the nine miles were quickly past, not a soul in sight.

I felt happy and lighthearted on coming into Pyne's Cove and recognizing the now so familiar houses. It was good to be back and to see Aunt Jane, Joe, and Jessie and the children through school. After that, some housecleaning and a sense that, with a table napkin and a few other accessories added, life could be quite comfortable and homelike. By then it was a glorious afternoon and time for a swim. Then sunset, sleep, and peace.

Two letters came from Adolf in the next mail. He had gone to Santo Domingo again and enclosed a snapshot of himself taken on top of a Dominican freight car running at full speed (ten miles an hour) from Santiago to Puerto Plata.

If there is only one coastwise boat running, your isolation must be fairly complete. I wonder if you will get to the stage (as I have done) where you get up at three in the morning to look at the lights of the one steamer which keeps the road to civilization open.... Your letter from Curling came in this morning's mail like a bit of northern air in the torrid atmosphere.... There is nothing like a frontier for that, even isolation and a little loneliness helps in taking a long estimate of the world in general and one's place in it.

Letters from the divorcé came in great numbers, voluble and passionate, but repetitive and inferior to Adolf's in style. Prospero was right in his comment: "You will never marry on a month's acquaintance, like your friend V. [a Vassar classmate who ran off with a Polish prince and lived dramatically and unhappily ever after]. You might have the impulse, but something in the back of your head, as Queen Elizabeth said, will pull you back or delay the matter."

The time was not ripe for marriage. When it came, I believed, I would have no doubts in my inmost heart, and my head would be working as well as my heart. First, as Adolf kept saying, I must stand firmly with both feet on the ground.

Three weeks had passed since the cable to Father. I had made a secret wish that I would receive an answer on my birthday, August 6. None came. Walking alone on the shore at sunset I read and reread one of his last letters, dated April 1:

> ...We are both certain that the tie which has bound us can never be broken.... I know that in our hearts we are forever united.
> Lovingly and affectionately,
>
> Your Father.

Why had he stopped writing? He had broken his pledge, a victim of Mother's hate and Edith's manipulation.

All the same I managed to have some fun. Swimming out to tag a floating iceberg in the Straits of Belle Isle, the whole population of Pyne's Cove watching in silence. Disapproval? Fear? Envy? Or saying to themselves, How foolish can this woman be? None of them knew how to swim or ever went into the icy water.

At other times, I went berry picking. The sun would be setting and all the sea burnished with red gold. In the gray rocks on the barrens, I found a delicate blue flower — its leaves were green tipped with gray. It was beautiful, perfect. I picked two sprigs and dropped them in a bottle, watching the sun set and the Labrador coast darken, while the clouds played around a slip of moon. "My peace I give unto you, not as the world giveth, give I unto you."

Joe and Jessie's brother John were sitting on the dock when I came back from one of these expeditions. They joshed me about the berries I hadn't picked. John offered to fix my shoe—a nail was coming through. "If you take it off, I would fix it at home, and you can wear one of my slippers in the meantime." A simple gift, freely given, freely accepted.

Over our cups of hot milk, Joe, Jessie, and I got to talking about children and school. Joe said he thought I had done better with the children than he had ever expected I would. I was thrilled.

I was learning what it means to share life with other people: Joe, Jessie, John, Aunt Jane, and their children. They did not have the experience to imagine what my life had been, but I could share theirs. They considered me as one of them. As I lived with them the direct human-to-human relationship I had read about in books became a reality.

On another occasion Jessie and I went "cruising" (walking along the shore looking for shells or wildflowers) together. It was a perfect summer day—warm sun tempered by freshness from the sea. On the way back we sat on the rocks by the sea.

"I'm three months gone," she confided. "I wonder why my babies are so small. I've lost three of them; one was so tiny that a woman put her wedding ring around its little wrist."

What a shocking waste, I thought. Nature uncontrolled, brutal—malnutrition, disease, and death. Jessie went on to tell me much about Aunt Jane, some of which I had already surmised.

"Three years ago, George, her eldest son, cursed her horribly and threatened to leave, then took a hatchet and smashed a basin with it. Every spring since then and into the summer, Aunt Jane becomes depressed. She worries and worries, and cries when George and Mary, Jane and Anthony, the grandchildren, are 'saucy' to her."

Parents and children, all over again. Aunt Jane spoiled her son to death, and she gets no consideration and no respect in her old age.

When we got home, Jessie was nauseated, so I packed the children off to bed and washed the dishes. The door was open to the starlit night. Then I went out and took a deep breath. I shall miss the open spaces, I thought.

Past mid-August, my sentence of exile arrived. The mailboat brought a registered letter from Morgat, Brittany, dated July 27. It was from Father, but Mother's seal was on the envelope. (She always enjoyed sealing letters with colored sealing wax.)

Dear Child:

I would like you to remove your goods and chattels and not to return to the place thereafter. Do it as quickly as possible. Your mother
may return at any time. Send me your address.

Affectionately, your father.

So that was it. A polite, affectionate, definitive dismissal with an ambiguous
threat. "Do it quickly; your mother may return." Why the big hurry. Did he
expect me to charter a speedboat, to hail a passing transatlantic liner? Didn't he
know I had an obligation to remain in Newfoundland through August? Freedom, independence, that is what I had longed for, but I had not reckoned the
price — an end to our life together, to Lenox, to the library at Sixty-seventh Street.
But there must not, could not be a complete break between us.

I wrote in my diary:

My darling father — life will be harder for him now than it has been,
for I know how close we were, living together day-by-day. Of course,
we must build another castle where we may meet and share in each
other's lives. But it will be hard to keep clear of the shadows. One thing
is certain, that we must each build up our own individual life and activity or perish. His loneliness will be greater than mine, and I shall not
be the only exile. A playboy, Dr. Riggs called him, but even a playboy
cannot escape the suffering of life.

In Mother's eyes, I am filthy and hateful, a loathsome creature.
She has cursed me as Lear cursed his daughters. "Let them anatomize
Regan, see what breeds about her heart. Is there any cause in nature
that makes these hard hearts." Paranoia is but a name. The workings of
the human heart are beyond our ken. Mother gave birth to me, unwill-
ingly it is true. She did what she considered her duty in bringing me up.
Her standards are those of a restricted world, but they are high, and
she did much for me. It is only a year ago that we laughed and played
together in Morgat and I used to put my arms around her and lift her
up in the water and hug her. When I was a child in New York, I remember calling over the banisters, "Papa, Maman," and they came up
to tuck me in. I knelt to say my prayers, and she kissed me good night.

Her cup of life has been full and beautiful, but she has only tasted
it at the edges; and now what she drinks must be thin and sour. She
has no friends but the faithful Edith [whose intrigues I did not understand until later] and Lupo, her dog. She is trying her husband to the
bounds of human endurance. His loyalty to her and compliance with
her wishes is indeed wonderful. She wanted jewels, and through the

years he built up a superb necklace pearl by pearl. Now he is casting out his darling child for her. But I fear there will be no peace for them. She will always want another moon, and whereas she has cursed me and cast me out, he still loves me, and my shadow and the memory of me will remain between them.

I thought about Adolf's experience. He and his sisters had moved to their own home. The first year following must have been very difficult for Mrs. Berle. Yet when I had met them the past winter, Dr. Berle was most cordial and no one could suspect from the outside that anything had been amiss.

Free at last, I had been set out in open ground to grow my own roots, to blossom and bear fruit. I could go to the ends of the earth and no one could gainsay me. The frontiers of my world would be those of my mind, always pushing further and further.

It had been a long struggle for emancipation from the parental world. Many of the values I accepted, not from authority now, nor from fear, but because they had passed the test of my judgment. My sentence of exile was the decisive stroke; I did not love Father less.

I would cultivate my inner soul, the oversoul, as Emerson calls it, which would grow strong and touch the Infinite on windy days in lone places as I developed *"la vie intérieure,"* as my beloved Mademoiselle Mulot had taught me to do. I did not want to run away and seek distraction, but to build a life with work and friends.

Thanks to Grand-mère's legacy, I was financially independent, like an endowed professor. The idea of having my own home was quite thrilling and a bit terrifying, too. Life in New York was overcomplicated; here in Flower's Cove a tin basin and a nail for a hook were sufficient. Aunt Jane was proprietor of the only darning needle and darning egg in the village. She lent them out, and they were always returned.

The only rocking chair in Jessie's house had been bought by her mother twenty-six years earlier for $4.25. The money had been earned by washing a sailor's shirt. Jessie, her brothers, and her children had all been rocked to sleep in that chair. As we were talking, little Allen, like a nice puppy dog, was licking the last crumb off his chipped plate. Jessie's mother rose to leave. "I must be home before dark and the spirits get out." This was a far cry from the elegant dinner parties of Sixty-seventh Street and Palazzo Rospigliosi, the American embassy in Rome at which Anti Bi provided pâté de foie gras, grilled shad, guinea hen, bombes glacées, Baccarat crystal, fine china, and six-foot flunkies.

There must be a middle ground between Sixty-seventh Street and Pyne's Cove, a place where elegance and good food were combined with warmth and sincerity. Perhaps I could find it. I wanted good conversation, too, such as I heard around the table at Henry Osborn Taylor's. The ladies who came to Sixty-seventh Street had no conversation. They, like Jessie, were afraid of the dark and had to be escorted to their cars by liveried footmen.

These reflections were interrupted by the sound of the rain on the roof. Joe and Jessie were sitting on the hen coop in the kitchen, and we shared a small nightcap of milk. After they retired, the cat curled up against the wall between the wood box and the stove. I did likewise and reread Adolf's latest letter by the light of one candle. The first part had to do with his legal work. He was proud that some of the ideas put forward in his article on no-par stock (the article I had sent Father) were being incorporated into the laws of Ohio.

But it was from Adolf the poet that my inspiration came:

> At Roger Baldwin's camp in New Jersey over the weekend; the hot weather broke in one smash of wind and thunder so that for a time I thought his little house would blow clean away . . . and then the cool west wind came up into a sapphire night and morning was crisp and cool and blue and grey with the air washed clean. I spent all day on the river watching muskrats and reading odd things. . . . Good fortune and high adventure, Playmate.
>
> A.A.B.

≈17

The end of August was approaching, when the summer workers went home. The date was not fixed exactly, communications and transportation being both uncertain and irregular. One day on the trail a man from Pyne's Cove met a man from Flower's Cove who reported that the steamer from Saint Anthony bound for Saint John, New Brunswick, was stopping at Flower's Cove two days later. It was time to leave.

The children gathered in the schoolroom to say goodbye, a silent line of them. I stood on one side, they on the other. It seemed as though there were a powerful electric current running through us all and then tearing us asunder. I took their pictures and told them to keep on washing their hands and brushing their teeth. Then home to Joe and Jessie's. Joe stretched out on the hen coop in the kitchen. We had cocoa and crackers and joked along as usual.

I went around to all the houses. Aunt Jane clung to my hand pathetically and said, "I watch for your going in the morning, for your singing out to me at dinner time. That's company, and I get lonesome when I'm like this."

Everyone—men, women, and children, about forty strong—came down to the wharf. I kissed the children and shook hands with everyone. When the boat shoved off, they fired a gun and waved till I could see them no more. I wept as I had not done in years—nor any time that I can remember. It seemed as if nothing mattered in the world but Pyne's Cove, and there I had left a part of myself.

On the following day the Grenfells arrived at Curling with a mob of people, so I had to be "civil." We had a buffet supper at the hospital, and the boys waited on the girls. We all appeared to be very matter-of-fact, just as though nothing unusual had happened in any of our lives. I left the group as soon as I could and went out into the sunset to watch the pink spray on the small waves splashing against the rocks. I felt that I had something very precious in my heart, and I wanted to keep it there—and make it grow. Man to man, human to human —that was the bond between me and the people of Pyne's Cove.

Since that time I have been blessed with many similar associations in human contacts: on the wards of Bellevue Hospital, in East Harlem, in Costa Rica, in Honduras, in the Santa Casa in Rio, and in northeastern Brazil. Sometimes we who have the temerity to go out as teachers, doctors, missionaries, or whatever to work among economically less fortunate people may perform important services, but always, provided we maintain an open mind and an open heart, it is we who are blessed.

Sitting on the barren gray rocks, I read my mail. A dear letter from Cousin Austen suggesting patience and understanding, adding, "Our home is your home." Prospero, worried that he had not heard from me:

> *Mea cella.* Dear Beatrice: Which means illustrious one, or rather, Beatrice dear, which means my heart is warm toward you. Prospero has been negotiating for a suit of horrid black but has not ordered it yet thinking he may hear from Portia by next week's boat mail. Prospero hopes all goes well with Portia which is a great matter. Otherwise we are all well.

From Adolf at Kinderhof, the Berle family's home in Boscawen, New Hampshire:

> At last via a round square table in Dartmouth with Professor Ripley and immediately into the mountains for five days on high trails, and back to civilization to find three letters from you. There's not space

to answer properly everything you touch on. But I can't let go your remark that contemplation of the universe leads to acute sorrow. I've quoted to you the passage from Goethe about the son of earth rebuilding his shattered world in his own soul. No, contemplation of the universe leads to faith and optimism, and to a certain appreciation of being a man in a man's time.

I was mulling all this in the mountains. We, Rudolf [Adolf's brother] and I, were four days above the timber line on the mountain crests in storm and fog, sometimes on barely visible trails. After hours of it, there would be a little sheltered place to bivouac and strike camp. The high winds and storms and rain made me clean again somehow as I've not been for a long time though the weather was villainous. We did have a moonrise as the clouds lifted a bit and it was like the opening of the gate of heaven.

I wondered about Adolf. It was he who had escorted me out of the paths of bitterness where other men had tried to drag me. He was my beacon on the way to growing up. Was he in love with me? Was I in love with him? What did being in love mean, anyway?

The next morning the summer workers left Curling. Going ashore in Bonne Bay, I almost fell on my knees to worship the nasturtiums, sweet Williams, and pansies. Also, the beets and carrots were more than one inch out of the ground! The rocky hills and lakes reminded me of Switzerland, and I was swept with a desire to be in Europe again with the family.

We sailed for Saint John, New Brunswick, and lay in the sun all day stretched out on the canvas cover of a lifeboat—content, without a desire in the world other than that the smoke from the stack should not blow across the sun. One of the boys and I sat up discussing "happiness" till 3:00 A.M. I can't remember what we said.

In Saint John, I drove up to the hotel in a taxi, the first time I had been in a motor car since June. It cost fifty cents. This hotel was very swank and modern — bellboys, newsstand, telegraph blanks, hundreds of rooms, all exactly alike, and hundreds of people. For three dollars I got a room with running water and toilet. It cost four dollars for one with a bath. Somehow it did not seem necessary to spend four dollars. I had not yet adjusted to the dollar; like the fishermen at Pyne's Cove, I thought in terms of quintals of fish. One quintal (a hundred kilograms) was several days' catch and brought four or five dollars, depending upon the market.

Still, the hotel was wonderful. The plumbing was glistening white. So were the sheets. The furniture was smooth and polished. I ran my fingers over the table top, the way the children in Pyne's Cove liked to finger my silk dress. I talked to an unseen person over the telephone and ordered milk and toast. It was like magic, except that the milk was slow in coming and the waiter spilled some on the white cloth. I laughed to myself. Here I was, twenty-four years old, and alone in a hotel for the first time, with six boys. No longer a *jeune fille*. The modern young woman has emerged. She must be without fear. Adolf believed she was:

> And as to the shedding of a garment of fear, I don't know that you had much to shed; however, if there were one thing I'd try to tell the world, it would be, "Never be afraid." The only way to get hurt is to get frightened and stop half-way. Perhaps this is the reason why we achieve that odd faith in God; we can't see but we know that there is light beyond darkness. It must be a fearful state to be without that irrational belief.

Alone in New York ≈

≈ *18*

I took the train for New York but decided suddenly to hop off at Hartford. One of my Grenfell companions drove me to Prospero's summer place in Connecticut. I could not face arriving at night alone in New York, with no place to go. Prospero and his lady received me with open arms. Walking through the garden I kissed the grass and beheld the flowers, the carrots, and the corn with joy and wonder. Most wonderful of all was the great oak tree on the terrace.

I reached Sixty-seventh Street the following day. Anna Nixon answered the doorbell. She kissed me but did not let me into the house. Standing on the steps, she read me a letter from Mother:

> When Miss Bishop comes back, do not let her sleep in my house. Do not let her take anything that is not hers. Otherwise we should not be able to get it back.

This letter was countersigned by Father.

Furious, I turned on my heel and went to the Women's University Club, where I found a room.

When I called on my Aunt Beatrice the following day, she accused me of wishing to put Mother away. "She is a brokenhearted woman, and so am I." I tried to explain that I considered Mother to be very nervous and in need of medical attention. She seemed to understand, and she concluded it was best that we not see each other. "Your mother needs me more than you do." And so all Mother's entourage was being drawn into the belief that I had masterminded a conspiracy to put her away and that people friendly to me were fellow conspirators and were therefore inimical to her.

There seemed nothing else to do but get started on my own independent life as soon as possible. Grand-mère's legacy meant that, though homeless, I was not penniless.

Homeless is not the right word—the Taylors, the Hammonds, and the Riggses all took me into their homes and made me feel as if I were their own daughter.

I went up to the Berkshires and stayed with the Riggses in order to dispose of my horse and say goodbye to the employees—and to the place that had been my home.

I loved the woods, the fields, the garden. I got on Cressed, the mare, and rode through the woods in the late afternoon. The trees were golden, the view of the lake superb, and as I cantered through the fields I could not help shouting for joy.

By the brook in the evening, I made a fire and fried eggs and bacon. I fed the dogs also, but a Pyne's Cove sense of values prevented me from giving them an egg. The paint on Jessie's kitchen floor had cost her five dozen eggs. I lay close to the dying fire, listening to the water running over the stones in the brook, watching the half moon through the trees. I was remembering cantering by the side of Mother, who rode sidesaddle, elegant in her custom-made habit, looking for all the world as if she were parading in the Bois de Boulogne.

I was remembering, too, Father when he declared his love for me eight years before. He was holding my hand as we walked through the pine woods. He wore leather wraparound puttees and carried a sturdy walking stick with a sharp enclosed point, the kind the Spanish *picadores* use to excite the bull in the ring. We were calling the dogs: Lupo, Mother's police dog; the two malamutes, Husky and Lasky; my cocker spaniel, Zut. When would I ever see Father again?

My feelings were a combination of exultation and sadness. I repeated the words of Alfred North Whitehead, whom I had met through Prospero: "Religion is what an individual does with his own solitariness."

Back to reality. As I was making arrangements for the sale of my horse, the superintendent of the estate informed me that he just been fired. One by one the Nixon sisters had managed to get all the old employees dismissed. I felt distressed and helpless, like a deflated balloon. This feeling increased on the train back to New York.

By the time I reached Grand Central Station, I did not care whether I lived or died. I thought of drowning my sorrows in drink...suicide—anything to get away from the pain of loneliness. Nonsense! I told myself. If I continued feeling this way I would be marrying someone, anyone. I had never felt lonely in Sixty-seventh Street, although I was alone. It was home, and I had the library.

On reaching the club, I found a note from my divorced friend inviting me to dinner. I accepted with alacrity. We dined and danced. I talked and talked like one inebriated, finding refuge in his arms as we danced. It was as if I were a needle and he a magnet and nothing could keep my hand away from his. But I knew I would not marry him. I could not conceive life in his company—his life was half-spent; mine was just beginning.

Vassar was another port of call. The academic milieu was very sympathetic, and I envied my former classmates who were teaching. Mildred Thompson, full of wisdom and understanding, urged me to get on with the study of social work and not to jump into marriage. We discussed Mother's paranoia at length. Nothing, I suppose, was ever going to persuade her that I was not conspiring to put her away. This was a fixed idea around which she organized her thinking, aided and abetted by the Nixon sisters, these clever schemers of whom I had been the complete dupe for so long. In this spider's web my beloved father had been caught, and my Aunt Beatrice had also been ensnared. "I'm surprised," Mildred commented. "I always thought she was an intelligent woman."

I was still trying to reestablish a contact with Father and consulted an Italian business friend of his. Yes, Mother had told him of the "conspiracy." Father declined to speak of me. *"Roba di matto"* (crazy), was the Italian's comment. "Were you pregnant? Is that why they threw you out?" Big laugh on my part!

Fortunately, classes at the School of Social Work were starting, and with Adolf's help I found an apartment at 5 Gramercy Park. My cousin Nancy Riggs joined me very soon. There was a housewarming attended by Mrs. Murray Crane and Alexis Carrel, Prospero, the Lady Julia, Adolf, and a number of my college classmates. It started at 3:00 P.M. and lasted until 9:30 P.M., with a young man ensconced in an armchair reading Henry Osborn Taylor's *The Freedom of the Mind in History.* Then the exiles' dinner party, attended by all those who had been forbidden to enter the house on Sixty-seventh Street! So 5 Gramercy Park became my home. I had created it. People drifted in and out; there was good talk, especially at teatime.

The course at the School of Social Work involved field work at the Bureau of Child Guidance. I greatly enjoyed the contact with patients. To come close to the intimate details of another's life, to preserve delicacy and consideration, and still not to be afraid to look at the facts is no passive role. It means giving of yourself; but the giving freshens and quickens the giver.

However, I had my doubts about the usefulness of riding out for an hour to New Lots, Brooklyn, to spend fifteen minutes with a child's teacher. Adolf also had expressed doubts in the following letter:

Joe, [a Henry Street boy whom Adolf had referred to the Bureau] came in this afternoon and we talked about diverse important matters. Ultimately he drifted to the subject of the Bureau of Child Guidance. "I had hoped," said he, "to find out something inside of myself which I didn't know before, or which might be useful for me to know. Anyhow I hoped to find out what kind of work I was best fitted to do. But if they found out, they didn't tell me. However," said he, his sense of tolerant justice coming healthily to the fore, "you have to give them credit for meaning well, and perhaps one ought to be grateful for their interest."

The lectures given by Dr. Marion Kenworthy also disturbed me. I found her monistic Freudian interpretation of life distasteful and incomplete. In fact, I had what the orthodox Freudians call resistance. I maintained in class that heredity, chance, physical environment, and factors other than egos and libidos played an important part in human affairs. Neither Adolf nor I was prepared to accept the unconscious as all-powerful, and we were not giving up the concept of the training of the will. Whimsically, Adolf said, "The behaviorists are convincing me we're all 'Predestined Baptists without a shadow of Free Will.' This leaves the world to worry along without effective help from you and me. But as long as we don't know it, we can play Chanticleer and make the sun rise; and it amuses us without seriously hurting the sun."

≈ *19*

At this point the family situation took a ridiculous turn. It became a case of the pot calling the kettle black. Mr. Buckingham, Father's secretary, appeared with a cable from Father ordering me to consult a prominent alienist concerning my mental condition and requested an immediate reply by wireless. Tongue in cheek, I called solemnly upon the obtuse family physician who had always denied that Mother was paranoid. He referred me to Dr. Menas Gregory, then director and chief alienist of the Psychopathic Department of Bellevue Hospital.

To my great amusement, Dr. Gregory declared that I was "sane and sound mentally, with no evidence of mental disease or disorder." I heard nothing more on this subject and hoped that Dr. Gregory obtained a large fee from Father. A few weeks later, Mr. Buckingham (who was soon to be fired and consequently forced to take his son out of college) appeared at my apartment to return the presents I had given Mother. They included jewelry of no great money value inherited from Grand-mère, a pink parasol, and the plaque of Saint Christopher that I had had made for my parents for their twenty-fifth wedding anniversary.

"Receipt of goods received to be signed before a notary," the messenger said. The pink parasol brought back the picture of "Mammina Mia" sitting on the balcony in Aix-les-Bains, a lovely, delicate creature in pink muslin frock, with a scarf and parasol I had given her. She was doing her tapestry. I was reading aloud to her.

This is a mirage, I said to myself. It never was real.

Still I never ceased trying to contact my parents. I called on Anti Bi once more. She had seen Mother and Father. "Your Mother has not changed. She is just as sane as she ever was. Unless you take back what you said about your mother's insanity you need never expect to see either of them again." I replied that I did not use the word *insane* but that Mother's behavior toward me the previous winter had led me to seek medical advice.

Today, sixty years later, when psychiatrists and psychologists have become the high priests of young and old, it is hard to understand the pre-mental-hygiene point of view. Nothing was going to break this barrier which held that only the insane, people who were raving maniacs, were treated by alienists and locked up in insane asylums. Therefore, Father, abetted by Edith Nixon, considered that his wife had been insulted by the suggestion that she needed psychiatric treatment.

Through the fall, I went to football games and saw a number of young men, thoroughly enjoying the freedom and the attention that I had been denied. Although a career in social work offered interesting possibilities, I was thinking a great deal about marriage, not as an escape, but as a complete lifelong relationship—physical, intellectual, spiritual, working together, playing together, talking together—not to be entered into lightly.

I had read extensively. The beautiful eighteenth-century colored illustrations, portraying in detail the love-making of Daphnis and Chloe, had been my delight as I had studied them in Father's library. Now I was studying Havelock Ellis, Krafft-Ebing, van de Velde, Marie Stopes. I came to realize that a strong physical attraction alone was not a guarantee of satisfaction in married life. Sexual compatability was made up of other elements as well.

Cousin Alice Riggs was full of wisdom. "How can you tell if you are really in love?" I asked her.

"The ultimate test," she replied, "is whether you feel that a share in creating that man's happiness is more important than anything else in the world. There is much to be said for the French conception of *mariage de convenance*," she continued, "where the mores of the two individuals are the same and there is no profound difference in questions of taste. Even with people of similar background, there are constant problems of adaptation when two adults live together, but these can be resolved when the man and the woman love each other deeply and are willing and able to discuss their differences."

I considered the possibility of a liaison with H. He was obviously an experienced lover, but over and over I said to myself, "That is beginning at the wrong end. Complete sexual intimacy comes later, when other matters have been settled." After an evening at the theater, H. and I had nothing to talk about. I felt that the desire of youth to reshape the world had died in him, and I could not imagine our having a life of common enterprise together. Neither could he. The physical attraction was strong, but that was not enough. When we parted, it seemed as if a crystal vase had been shattered on a marble floor and neither of us had bent down to pick up the pieces.

My next suitor was one who also had lost the sense of adventure as he was settling into a comfortable niche in the legal profession. He had charm and was a bon vivant. But my marriage, I knew, must be something splendid and complete.

By the new year, I had concluded that I probably would not marry anyone I knew. I wrote Adolf a dramatic letter, telling him I was not in love with him. He called me up and came to breakfast. We laughed, quite sincerely on both sides, I think, as the sun came pouring in the window.

I had forced an issue, he said, that he had decided some time ago was not to be forced. His had been a lone hand, and I was no different from the other people he had pulled out of a hole and who had then decided they needed him no more.

The following evening in front of the closed door of my apartment I found a package wrapped in white tissue paper and tied at each end with a small red ribbon. The package contained two Sheffield-copper candlesticks—a fee from a man on the Lower East Side whom Adolf had defended and saved from prison. These candlesticks took their place on the mantelpiece at 5 Gramercy.

They became and have remained our Lares and Penates, traveling with us to Washington and Brazil, and are now placed in the front hall in Nineteenth Street.

At this juncture Abram Hewitt, a mutual friend and a Gramercy Park neighbor, was very severe with me—rightly so, I think. "Adolf is falling in love with you in spite of himself," he said. "You are only playing with him. For him, this is serious: He is thirty years old—he has never been in love before. You must not hurt him, but stand on your own feet. He is a crusader, an adventurer of the spirit. You must never forget that. Never possess him—there are areas where you may not trespass."

So a platonic relationship was maintained, and my admiration for Adolf increased as he, Nancy Riggs, Abram, and I dined together, went to the theater, and discussed social problems, although Abram insisted that Adolf, Nancy, and I could not reason and had no brains, since we had not been to Oxford!

Occasionally Adolf took Nancy out *à deux*. As I looked out the window and watched them walking around the park, I repeated to myself Ronsard's sonnet:

> *Quand vous serez bien vieille, un soir, à la chandelle,*
> *Assise auprès du feu, dévidant et filant,*
> *Direz, chantant mes vers, et vous émerveillant*
> *Ronsard me célébrait du temps que j'étais belle.*
> ....
> *Je serai sous la terre, et, fantôme sans os,*
> *Par les ombres myrteux, je prendrai mon repos*
> *Vous serez au foyer, une vieille accroupie;*
> *Regrettant mon amour et votre fier dédain*
> *Vivez, si m'en croyez, n'attendez pas à demain*
> *Cueillez des aujourd'hui les roses de la vie.*
>
> *When you have grown old, in the evening, by candlelight*
> *sitting by the fire, carding and spinning*
> *as you recite my poems, in wonder, you will say,*
> *Ronsard praised me when I was beautiful.*
> ....
> *I will be underground, a ghost with no substance,*
> *resting under the shaded myrtle.*
> *You will be an old woman squatting by the hearth*
> *regretting my love and your scornful pride.*
> *Believe me, live now, do not wait for the morrow*
> *Pluck the roses of life today*
> *(Gather ye rosebuds while you may.)*

What is the matter with me? I asked myself. I am forever advancing and retreating, injuring myself and others in the process.

The resolution came at last, first gently, then like a breaking of a dam in a spring flood. It was Maundy Thursday. Adolf, Miriam, Adolf's younger sister, and Dr. Carrel came to dinner. We listened to Beethoven's *Moonlight* Sonata played on the Victrola and felt we were kindred spirits. Miriam wrote later:

> My heart began to sing on that evening, for something new had dawned in you, a shy loveliness which I knew Adolf loved. Since then

I have uttered more than one prayer to my own private saints for the serene and untroubled development of a thing so beautiful in and for you both.

The next day, Good Friday, Adolf took me to *Parsifal*. We were transported, exalted as I had never been before. We were as one, and it seemed as if all the reasonings and analyzings had been wiped out of existence.

Saturday afternoon, I went up to Vassar to stay with Miss Thompson. Miss Thompson had been a little reserved on first meeting Adolf but was now beginning to appreciate his great qualities. In fact, they became and remained devoted friends through the years. Adolf joined us that evening. He and I walked together in the April rain around the campus, laughing as we thought of the ten-o'clock curfew for undergraduates. We walked around the lake, and the delicious smell of wet earth and the pattern of the trees in flower, mirrored in the water through the lamplight, were suddenly obliterated as Adolf took me in his arms and murmured, *"Cras amet qui numquam amavit"* (May he love tomorrow who has never loved before). I thanked God that he had come.

On Sunday, we went for a picnic with Nancy Riggs and Lina Ware, a college mate of mine, cooking steak with spring onions and fried tomatoes. Then we walked barefoot along the bank — one must feel spring through the soles of one's feet to really appreciate it. The mud was oozy, and we looked into the pink-etched hearts of spring beauties. Before taking the train, we walked together in the pines behind the chapel. It was a beautiful weekend — God given. We agreed not to talk too much, to let things take care of themselves. Up to this point, we had plotted out so many rules and regulations that our feelings had been crushed.

The pact was not to be sealed for another four weeks. I wanted my adoptive families — the Riggses, Prospero and the Lady Julia, the Hammonds — to know Adolf. I did not want to capsize the world I had built so carefully. I wanted the Berles to accept me. I could not afford to be ostracized by either Adolf's world or mine. Everyone admired Adolf for his brains, though some thought him sententious. He had faced the world too young, with too many responsibilities, and he had elbowed himself into recognition through his superior intellectual powers. I knew that the funny little corners would wear down. He had never belonged to the sporty, rich Harvard crowd. He was an intellectual. So was I.

Marriage ≈

≈ *20*

Almost two years after our first meeting under the Washington Arch, in mid-May, Adolf and I became engaged. On this May morning a scarlet tanager was flying through Gramercy Park between showers. What better omen could there be?

Over the following months we explored our bodies as we had been exploring our minds, step by step, but we were mindful of Havelock Ellis's remarks on chastity in his book *Sex in Relation to Society*:

> It is a virtue because it is a discipline in self-control, because it helps to fortify the character and will, and because it is directly favorable to the cultivation of the most beautiful, exalted, and effective sexual life....
>
> Full satisfaction can only be attained by placing impediments in the way of the swift and direct gratification of sexual desire, by compelling it to increase its force, to take long circuits, to charge the whole orgasm so highly that the final climax of gratified love is not the trivial detumescence of a petty desire but the immense consummation of a longing in which the whole soul as well as the whole body has its part.

Deliberately we chose to delay the consummation of our marriage until our wedding night, expecting to reach the climax during our honeymoon. We were not disappointed in our expectations and continued to be lovers for more than forty years.

We believed that marriage was for life, that our love would sustain us through the days of joy, through sorrow and tribulation, that we would raise a family together but also would each have independent careers. This was our ideal, and looking back over our forty-three years together, I feel that we came close to achieving it.

In June I returned to visit Prospero and the Lady Julia in Connecticut. Sitting under the oak tree where I had come in pain and distress the previous fall, I was now full of joy.

I wrote in my diary:

> There came a day about a month ago when quite naturally I learned to say "we" instead of "I." Those things vaguely felt grew into a certainty, and I knew. We came to an understanding so thoroughgoing, so comprehensive, as I had not thought possible. It's the same old story: People will tell you, "You *know* when you're in love" — well, you do.
>
> Adolf is the man with whom I would share life — from the secrets of my soul to those of my body. Together we shall live a long life in work and in play, and together we shall rear children. Here is a great human soul that moves one to tears — to tenderness and passion. For him, it is worthwhile to live life and to lay it down.
>
> We are not afraid. We come to each other in pain and in joy and find comfort one in the other. This, our relationship, is something we have wrought with our own hands which shall grow to the end of our lives. Nor will we forget what the poet Gibran said, 'Let there be spaces in your togetherness.'

While I was philosophizing in Connecticut, Adolf was writing from Roger Baldwin's camp along the Hackensack River. Roger Baldwin (who died recently at the age of ninety-four) was a friend of Adolf's father, and he extended his friendship to Adolf, to me, and to our children. Roger was a founder of the American Civil Liberties Union, which he ran for many years. But best of all, Roger was a naturalist.

Adolf wrote,

> Midnight coffee.
> Dearest and Playmate:
> The others have at length turned in, leaving [me] a quiet hour to drink the distilled moonlight which flutters down the leaves and to think of a dear picture. I wish you were here. Prospero's garden must be lovely but for concentrated beauty, it would be hard to match this leaf-enclosed place tonight, save only that grace and beauty seem to follow you. Also, it is the hour of prayer when hope and thought lift to the gates of heaven. I hope to return to some slight measure of accomplishment in time to come; for the best of strength or beauty or

hope, or achievement or of whatever may be good in this life or the next, lies in sharing it; and as my own horizon, thanks to you, widens and grows, there comes a great desire to join you in contributing to the everlasting growth of things — that perhaps is what marriage can be at its greatest — and it subtracts not a hair's weight from the tenderest of it, and I have rendered thanks that we sought each other in strength and not as a refuge, meeting pain with erect heads, demanding everything of love without fear — so that the fragrance of your hair and the warmth of your eyes was no less sweet than the glory of your mind and soul. My guttering candle tells me it is time to stop — good night, dear heart; I send my love on the wings of the moonlight, hoping only that it may brush your cheek, and that you may smile in your sleep.

Later in June, before Dr. Riggs and his family left for Dark Harbor, Adolf spent his first weekend with me in their home in Stockbridge. Mrs. Riggs, Cousin Alice, wrote to a friend, "I have a real confidence that Adolf Berle has the kind of chivalry and fidelity which will make Beatrice always safe and happy."

I continued writing in my diary:

> The joy and peace that are ours is beyond belief. Our life has begun and its foundations are solid. He has been taken in by Ohmie [Dr. Riggs's mother, a formidable old lady], Cousin Alice and my Riggs "sisters," Nancy, Marjorie and Alice. And I know that he is happy and at peace even as I am.
>
> We have been out in the woods together and kissed as we stood on a stone, the brook all around us. Together we have been where so often I walked alone.

Adolf's family also approved of our engagement.
Lina wrote:

> Seeing you and Adolf together, I am sure as one can humanly be of your combined future. Not that I ever had any doubts! But now I shall be able to identify you and him — indissolubly as not before, and I am glad of it. I don't know whether you and he altogether want to be "identified" as used to be considered in the older ideal of marriage. At its worst, it was a tragic thing; but at its best, it represented something which has never been surpassed, and that, I think, you can attain.

Each of Adolf's parents responded in characteristic vein.
Mrs. Berle:

> I know that in the intimacy and friendship which marriage brings,

[113]

the truest happiness is to be found in the mutual sharing of joys and sorrows, anxieties and responsibilities; and in the wholehearted cooperation in outside interests as well as personal ambitions, each attains their highest development.

Dr. Berle:

> I can only say that the affection and anxiety and interest which I have all these years given to my own children will also be yours. I think I can promise you the strong affection of the clan as a mighty fortress. We are pretty vigorous individualists but as a family we back members against the world.

We were also trying to keep the record straight by writing to my parents, now in Rome. "I have been casting and recasting a certain letter," Adolf said, "which will after more revisions go to Rome. But we are looking forward and not back. Our lives and the love in us will be something new, demanding, I think, very little of what has gone before."

I also wrote my parents asking for their blessing. No answer came. A few of their friends tried to put in a word but were rebuffed. The only direct communication I received from Father was the following cable: "I sent you no message whatsoever." This came in reply to a letter I sent him after a childhood friend of his who had seen him in Paris reported that he had asked for me. So we went about our business, letting three months elapse before making an announcement of our engagement in the press. The *New York Times* for September 9, 1927, carried the following item:

> There was announced yesterday in Lenox, Massachusetts, and New York the engagement of Beatrice Bend Bishop and Adolf A. Berle, Jr.

We were not planning to marry until the winter. I still had another term of field work before obtaining a degree from the School of Social Work. For this summer period I was assigned to the Riggs clinic in Pittsfield, Massachusetts, under the direction of the social worker Anna King, whom I introduced to Adolf over a weekend in the Berkshires. In his next letter he characterized her accurately.

> She has such a sane human view of things and such a common sense approach that one instinctively trusts her judgment almost beyond reason. To be competent without egoism, and kindly without condescension, and realist without cynicism—these are great gifts, all of which she has.

The entire staff was much more human than that in the Bureau of Child Guidance in New York, where natural expressions of human interest on the part of staff vis-à-vis clients were considered unprofessional.

During this time I lived in the Riggs house in Stockbridge. Dr. and Mrs. Riggs were not there; they took their summer holiday in Maine. Adolf came up on the train Fridays (rarely) or on Saturdays, returning to New York on Sunday. The interval between Sunday evening and the next Saturday afternoon was very long indeed but there were always letters to be read, reread, and preserved to this day.

> Dearest and Playmate:
>
> I have been counting the over-full hours, with an overwhelming gladness that another day lets me come back to you, and with a sort of fierce joy that the hours with you have to be taken from the teeth of swift-moving work and life. Great happenings should not come too easily!
>
> I saved your letter for a quiet moment, as a child saves his one permitted sweetmeat, reading it at early morning as a bit of glory with which to start the day. You are beyond measure kind: there was a fragrance of princes' gardens blown by your own sweeter breath which caught my heart. I prayed for you once in a far-away chapel by a tropical sea: for strength, growth, hope and sweetness and in that moment a drift of jasmine scent came down the sunrise like an answer from Our Lady, the Beautiful Mother herself. But we have a knowledge all our own. We made our love with our own hands and hearts out of pain and travail, honorably and worthily, choosing that rather than easier or less splendid alchemy. For we both have sought stars, and have found them; and with them have laid hold of the stuff of new life and new worlds. In a moment you gave me what I had never had before—the serenity of feeling in rhythm with the pulse of things. You suspect but will never know, the sudden, relieving glory of it.
>
> Adolf

I pondered over the phrase "the serenity of feeling in rhythm." This we had given to each other, and this I knew would smooth out what the world called Adolf's "intellectual arrogance." Little did those who used that phrase know the sensitive, loving human being below surface. His concern for individuals never flagged, as the following letter shows:

> Six hours interlude here and crowded to the limit. Triumph for the day: The youngster in jail got out when the Grand Jury refused to indict. There is some use in knowing how to play the bazaar in the lower

East Side. Dear heart, this is an interesting world to explore in all phases, good and bad.

The above refers to the defense of an eighteen-year-old boy, resident of the Lower East Side, who was arraigned on the charge of holding up a store. Adolf was able to get together the evidence for a perfectly beautiful, truthful alibi.

But a couple of weeks in the Tombs is no place for an eighteen-year-old. And I'm still feeling unhappy about it all.... One ought to get used to untangling knots of that sort with quiet serenity but I don't seem to.

The postscript to the letter concludes:

Johnny Lee's relatives have just been in. They offer to pay something. They say it can be done because the boys ran a raffle to help get "Johnny out of trouble" — and chipped in ten percent of each crap game they went into!!!

Nancy and I took advantage of the Fourth of July holiday to visit Adolf's family. We drove up to Boscawen, New Hampshire, where Adolf met us. Clergymen, like diplomats and corporation executives today, are nomads, frequently against their will. In 1903, on his return from Chicago, where Mrs. Berle had contracted diphtheria and had been desperately sick, Dr. Berle resolved to purchase a permanent home for the family. He bought a house in the country. There Dr. Berle spent the greater part of his later years, until his death in 1960.

As we drove into the yard, we found Dr. Berle waiting for us impatiently, Mrs. Berle with him. He took us immediately for a tour of the house—books, books everywhere, in the study, in the two parlors, in the dining room, in the halls upstairs and downstairs, in the bedrooms. Dr. Berle was telling us about the Berle Summer Home School in which all members of the family had participated as teachers. Reaching for a catalogue lying on his large roller-top desk, he read, "the aim of this school being to instruct a small number of superior children in such a way as will make them natural companions of knowledge." Easy access to books was the key. All kinds of books. "Never be out of reach of a good book," he chuckled, pointing out Goethe in German and the Bible in Hebrew and in Greek, and picking up Lewis Carroll's *Sylvie and Bruno*, a little-known work full of delightful nonsense.

"Do you know about the railway ghosts?" he asked in a serious tone of voice.

"No," we replied respectfully.

Laughing, he went on, "Railway ghosts welter—it has to be in something thick. They welter in bread sauce." And then he chortled as he read:

He thought he saw a Banker's Clerk
Descending from the bus.
He looked again and found it was a hippopotamus.
"If they should stay to dine," he said,
"There won't be much for us."

Adolf walked in at this point, apologizing for not being there to receive us. "I went out with Lina in the Tin Lizzie [Model-T Ford] to get the ice. If you'll excuse me for a minute, I must hose the sawdust off the ice before putting it in the ice chest." Nancy and I volunteered to help.

The kitchen, with its Crawford coal range, was the most popular room. I noted especially a large coffee grinder, and a frying-pan clock on the wall, ticking loudly.

Mrs. Berle pulled the last loaf of her bread out of the oven. "There is never any left for toast," Lina laughed. "Father sees to that—and so does the rest of the family."

After the ice was put away, Adolf took me on a tour through the barn. He pointed to a corner full of tools with nails, screws, old locks, wire... (I would not have dared use the word *junk*). "Father loves to fix things," he remarked. In the loft of the barn were wood panels of scenes from *Alice in Wonderland* and Thackeray's *The Rose and the Ring*—scenery painted by the four Berle children for home dramatics.

"The one winter that we spent here, I was only eight years old," Adolf said. "Rudolf was two. Lina, Miriam, and I walked to school. It was my job to carry in the wood and keep the stoves going, so I learned to split wood at an early age. Once, we made a great snow fort out there on the lawn."

The house, a well-proportioned frame building shaded by great elm trees, fronted on the main road. It had been the home of Daniel Webster. General John Dix, of Civil War fame, was born here, and on the bronze plaque sunk into a glacial boulder were inscribed his words: "If anyone attempts to haul down the American flag, shoot him on the spot."

"When I came home from the war in 1919," Adolf was saying, "I was mowing hay with a scythe in the field by the house. A lady stopped her car and asked the way to the next town. I gave her directions.

"'Young man, you speak so well, you should not waste your time cutting grass. You should go to college.' I smiled but did not go into my past history. Come now, let us go in for supper."

We sat around the dining-room table enjoying fresh peas and new-baked bread. Although Dr. Berle was inclined to monopolize the conversation, the rest of the family had plenty to say. The story goes that Justice Frankfurter, then a professor at the Harvard Law School, was invited to a meal at the Berles' and, finding that he was not the only star in the firmament, commented, "Conversation at the Berle table is a marathon."

When it came time to retire, Dr. Berle went to the upright piano and played Brahms' Lullaby, which he had sung to the children when they were small. *"Guten Abend, gute Nacht, mit Röslein bedeckt...."* It was a lovely evening. Nancy and I shared the guest room in the front of the house—two iron bedsteads, white coverlets, simple painted dressers and straight chairs, the sort of thing being sold today as "antiques" in second-hand-furniture shops along the roads.

Adolf's room, which he shared with Rudolf, was at the back of the house over the barn. It contained two army cots with iron springs, brown army blankets—Spartan simplicity.

The following day, Adolf took me on the Merrimac River in a canoe and showed me the coves where he caught pickerel. In the afternoon, Lina drove us in the Ford on the back roads. Walking down to the edge of a brook, Adolf pointed out clumps of cardinals, which unfortunately would not show their brilliant scarlet flowers until August. Cardinals were among the first flowers we were to plant by our own brook in the Berkshires. Best of all was watching Mrs. Berle in her garden tending her delphinium, a variety called Blue Sky. She promised to give us some seeds when we started our own garden. "Remember," she said, "a garden starts the year before last."

The time passed all too quickly. Nancy and I drove back to Stockbridge, and Adolf took the night train to New York. His father was firm in his recommendation that I must take care of Adolf—see that he got more rest and sleep. "I will try," was my reply, but I was doubtful of success and surprised when his letter came.

> Harvard Club, July 5.
>
> Your injunction was strictly obeyed and a night's sleep was duly had on the train, which miraculously was on time, whereby it comes about that there is time for these lines between breakfast and work. It was a good three days, the longest time we have had together—where in fact we are never far absent from each other whatever maps may say and railroads may do.
>
> As usual, I remain lost in admiration of your ability to traverse many worlds gracefully, always at home and always beautiful. No won-

der all gates are open and all personalities at your command but how do you do it in these flashing groups? Perhaps you have that singular instinct for universal rhythm which finds a common beat with every mind and heart.

All love, dear heart, may the sunlight always find you.

Our next excursion was to Dark Harbor, Maine, where the Riggs family kept a small sailing yacht. It was my twenty-fifth birthday. Adolf presented me with an engagement ring that he had designed and had made for me, a moonstone engraved with a bee surrounded with a circle of oak leaves, set in a golden ring of oak leaves. *"Fortis et dulcis"* (strong and sweet) was the motto inscribed within the ring.

According to an unverified legend (probably invented by Dr. Berle), the bee, the oak leaves, and the motto form the exiles' crest adopted by the younger sons who left the castle of Berleburg in Germany to seek adventure. It was also claimed that this was the bee Napoleon appropriated for himself when he became emperor.

Whether based on fact or more probably on fiction, the heraldic emblem *"Fortis et dulcis"* was a most appropriate characterization of Adolf. Later I had a similar ring engraved for him by the same Austrian craftsman.

In Maine, we went sailing with the family, but best of all, we walked together in the spruce woods where Adolf introduced me to chanterelle mushrooms while Lord Jim, the Riggs's German shepherd, leaped ahead.

Back in Stockbridge, we decided to spend our weekends looking for a house. A friend of Adolf's commented, "Those two look more like two seventeen-year-olds buying milk and honey than like grown-up people buying a home."

Adolf replied in a letter to me,

> But it occurs to me that both you and I have been grown up and in difficult situations far earlier than many people. Now, perhaps for the first time we recapture the full splendour of youth, which after all is a matter of heart. I like the idea of building a home for years to come and I value the walk through the hills at moonrise and the silent contemplation of your friendly pines, which speak to you out of the years. They will be waiting for you when all questions are answered. They stand as straight symbols that all loves and loyalties endure even through darkness. My love to you, star of many seas, sleep sweetly and waken to sunny days.

On the last Sunday before returning to the city, we found the house of our dreams—forty acres of land, pine trees, a mill pond, price fourteen thousand dollars, plus another thousand for additional woodland. "What would either of our childhoods have been," Adolf wrote, "if we had not made good friends with some trees and we should, I think, want our children to feel the same kinship with unspoiled forest and trees."

The cost was divided evenly between us. The deed stands in the name of Adolf A. Berle and Beatrice B. Bishop, tenants in the entirety. According to Massachusetts law, this meant that both of us owned every bit of land together, making division impossible. What would have happened if Adolf and Beatrice had not married? we used to ask each other, laughing.

Konkapot Farm, as we called our land, naming it after an Indian chief, was our home through the forty-three years of our life together.

New York was home also, and after the summer's apprenticeship I returned to 5 Gramercy Park with a certain satisfaction. This was my kingdom, which I had created. There Adolf and I became engaged, and soon we would be living there as man and wife. Ours would be a rich and full life.

In October I started as a psychiatric social worker in the Cornell Clinic at First Avenue and Twenty-seventh Street, at a salary of eighteen hundred dollars a year. Adolf was pleased about this and as serious about it as I was, expecting of me professional interests and standards equal to his own. He was active in many fields. The intensity of his activities and their diversity are perhaps best characterized in a letter he had written the previous summer.

> Dearest and Playmate:
>
> There is a certain intoxication in taking on from time to time as much work as seems possible and whipping it without losing control of the many tendril threads.
>
> Just a line in the middle of a swift moving day. There are cables to Haiti, telephone calls from Cuba, a man going south to Puerto Rico, another coming north from Santo Domingo; the whole Caribbean web is vibrating just now, and I confess to enjoying the swiftness of the motion and the broadness of the sweep. I wonder was it the same in the Roman offices when the Alexandrian triremes brought in the Egyptian cotton and grain or the Tyrian sailboats went out to collect the working of Hispanian mines? And still more I wonder what will be said of us a few thousand years hence: that we gave birth to a Virgil or Horace, barely known in our own time, or set up a code of law for the world to follow? This web of economic empire must be

merely a background for something else. It simply cannot be an end in itself.

We decided to be married in December, in Grace Church, where I had been christened and confirmed and where members of my family on both sides had been among the founders.

═══ *21*

On our wedding day, I walked unattended down the long central aisle of Grace Church, where I had walked alone behind Grand-mère's coffin five years before. Now I was a woman, a bride, ready to give myself unreservedly to Adolf, to make life fruitful for this extraordinarily gifted, dearest and sweetest of men and to realize those advantages of breeding, position, and education that had been bestowed on me.

The small company of fifty were gathered in front of a screen of evergreens extending across the center aisle at the eighth pew. We had chosen the Wedding March from Mendelssohn's *A Midsummer Night's Dream* to be played between the formal betrothal ceremony and the marriage. Bishop Charles Slattery, former rector of Grace Church, a close friend of Grand-mère's who had officiated at her funeral and Dr. Berle's classmate at Harvard, came down from Boston to assist the rector, Dr. Russell Bowie.

Rudolf Berle was best man. Abram Hewitt, G. D., Ed Wright, and Horace Gilbert (colleagues of Adolf's at the business school) were ushers. In the sacristy, they had been warned to expect trouble. Father had written the bishop in November,

> You should know that neither my wife nor myself will be present at Beatrice's wedding — and that neither of us have given consent to the marriage.

A second letter was delivered to the bishop that morning. It read:

> I have not as yet determined whether or not I shall be present at the marriage [of my daughter] and make a public statement, as provided by the Book of Common Prayer, or whether I shall place the entire responsibility upon you.

After the words "If any man know any lawful impediment why this man and this woman should not be joined in holy matrimony, speak now or forever hold your peace," the moment of pause must have seemed eternal to the groom and the phalanx of ushers ready for action. Nothing happened, and I was blissfully ignorant of the whole matter until Adolf told me several days later.

The wedding breakfast was the occasion for a lively theological discussion between Dr. Carrel and Dr. Berle. It took place at the home of my mother's cousin Marie, Mrs. Morris Kellogg. My godmother "Coco," Mrs. Breck Trowbridge, had given me a beautiful wedding dress—ivory satin, short in front, waist at hip level, long train, in the fashion. The lace veil had been Grand-mère's.

Both Coco and Cousin Marie had stood by us, risking their relationship not only with Mother but also with Anti Bi, who maintained that I had "accused" my mother of being "insane." Indeed, Anti Bi did not appear at the wedding, nor did we ever see her again. She sent us a scrap basket for a wedding present.

Our honeymoon was spent under our own roof at Konkapot Farm, coping with the New England winter, thawing out freezing pipes by applying old-fashioned flatirons heated on the kitchen stove, and keeping the wood fires burning.

The release of passion so long contained brought joy and contentment beyond our dreams. I wrote in my diary,

> We were friends before we were lovers. Our spiritual and intellectual marriage was made long before we stood at the altar. The physical came last, and has swept over us like a great wave. I would not have thought that either of us could be so passionate. I am glad we are. And through the exploring and the marriage of our bodies, we reach states of bliss and ecstasy previously unimaginable. It is as when man discovered fire! We may not only worship it and possess it but must also learn to use it as the goldsmith does."

Then came a state of relaxation and deep contentment.

> It is as if the river which is our life had found its bed and were beginning to run deep and straight. Our hearth fire is burning and we can sink back luxuriously and dream of long years together, living a full and complete life.

The two weeks passed all too quickly. On the way back in the train, I was in tears, relieved only by a ridiculous happening—maple syrup leaking out of the suitcase! Adolf was not sympathetic with my tears, though I told him he should be flattered. Sniveling females were not for him!

I forgot that there is not only us, but there is Adolf and there is Beatrice also. I wanted to lose myself entirely in him, to possess him absolutely, his body, his mind, his every moment. It seems as if I had been forever looking for something to fill my whole life and being and had found it in Adolf.

But I remonstrated with myself:

AAB is a great and free spirit. It is your inestimable privilege to love, honor and cherish him, but never possess him. For this you must keep on cultivating your own garden for in this way only you will have more to give him and may love him wisely. All our resources were mobilized and organized to get married as fittingly as possible. Now we will make our marriage a work of art — hand wrought and sublime.

So we went home to 5 Gramercy, where I had lived alone and where we were establishing a way of life together. Adolf worked in his office and lectured once a week at the Harvard Business School (two midnight trains between New York and Boston!) while I continued at the Cornell Clinic. There were two evening clinics a week, and on rainy evenings Adolf called for me in a taxi. I can see him now, sprinting up the long stairway, his little Dominican cane tucked under one arm, a bunch of roses in his hand.

Of course, Adolf then and always worked too hard, too many hours. I was trying to persuade him to give up the midnight train to Boston, which he did finally after starting to teach corporation finance, "of which," according to his diary, "I knew little and the students even less," at the Columbia Law School. His association with Columbia was most satisfying and continued up to his seventieth birthday. In spite of our many activities, we managed a couple of weekends at Konkapot in below-zero weather and later saw the snowdrops coming up by the Riggs house in Stockbridge, not having any of our own yet.

Our life in New York was enriched by evenings at Mrs. Murray Crane's, where Padraic Colum read his poetry, and music at Mrs. Reginald de Khoven's. It seemed that the older ladies who belonged to my parents' social circle were making a special point of being kind to us.

Adolf was a man of intense intellectual activity; he could think faster and further than anyone else. This meant that he was very productive, and his concentration on a given subject at a given moment would be to the exclusion of everything else.

I was mindful of Abram's advice before we were married: Adolf is a free spirit; you must never try to possess him. Still, this meant moments of loneliness and anxiety. I remember a particular evening in February. The clock struck nine, and I had not heard from him. I sat on the windowsill; the lights had long since come on in the street and in apartment houses across the park. Had there been an accident? I called his office—no answer. I called his partner at home, who replied that Adolf had still been in the office when he left at five (this was a methodical, unimaginative, nine-to-five man). Finally at almost nine-thirty, I heard the key in the lock. I threw my arms around him. "What happened?"

"Why, nothing. I was working in the bar-association library."

"Why didn't you telephone? I was so worried."

"There was nothing to worry about." The business of not letting anyone know where you are or when you may be expected—is it an expression of independence, or is it irresponsibility? At any rate, it is most annoying, as every woman knows.

But when we finally settled down to dinner that evening, Adolf told me about his studies in corporation law and finance, through which he was trying to frame laws ensuring a greater degree of responsibility on the part of corporation executives toward stockholders. This was not my field, and though as our daughter Beatrice commented, "Daddy always explains complicated subjects in simple terms we can understand," I never became sufficiently proficient in economics to be more than an interested listener. This satisfied us both.

≈22

The work at the Cornell Clinic was not altogether satisfying—too many long subway rides to New Lots, Brooklyn, the end of the line. "It is somehow like throwing stones into the sea and I feel little can be done unless one has a controlled environment. What is the use of telling parents and teachers what to do when you know they are unable for various reasons to follow your advice?" I wrote. I was tired and developed a series of boils and sties. Adolf was tired too.

My supervisor was leaving to organize a department of psychiatric social work at the Psychiatric Institute. She invited me to join her, and I was also offered her previous position as director of the Cornell Neurological/Psychiatric clinics, with fifteen attending physicians and two social workers. Both of these were interesting professional opportunities for a young woman one year out of school. But it would have meant longer hours, greater responsibilities, and only two weeks' vacation. I resigned from the job I held and also declined both positions. We went to the country and started our garden. For me Adolf came first, then and always. He did not pressure me.

This choice, like similar choices I made through the years, did not mean that I gave up my career. It meant that I established a system of priorities, which I followed through the years. Adolf came first. The children came next. The career was third, but a very important third, enriching and supplementing the other two.

With these considerations in mind I looked for a situation that would give me more time with Adolf. This came in the form of a job as a student adviser and teacher of a course called History of the Family at the newly organized College of Sarah Lawrence in Bronxville.

Teaching at Sarah Lawrence proved interesting. Among other things, it brought me into contact with Helen Lynd, the co-author with her husband of *Middletown*, the first original socioeconomic study of an American manufacturing town. Unfortunately, the administration of this new college ran into difficulties so that a number of us, myself included, did not return the second year.

At the same time, Adolf and I were deciding to embark on the great adventure of having a child. Conditioned as I was by my mother's disgust with all matters female, including pregnancy and childbirth, I was very apprehensive. How would her attitude affect me? How would the intrusion of a child affect Adolf's and my relationship? Fortunately, thanks to Adolf's understanding love and my general good health, the pregnancy was uneventful, and I completed the academic year teaching at Sarah Lawrence.

The baby was due in early October 1929. Anxious to put down roots in the city as well as in the country, we bought a townhouse in the Gramercy Park neighborhood. Payments on the first and second mortgages were to be met by renting two floors. We moved in on October 1. Two days later while Adolf, Abram, and I were unpacking books, my labor started.

We walked over to the Lying-in Hospital at Seventeenth Street and Stuyvesant Square (now the Beth Israel Medical Center). Immediately upon arrival we were separated. The men were shown into a waiting room decorated with a wall painting of a stag at bay. I was whisked into an elevator. The 1929 fashion for the management of labor, delivery, and postpartum care was not concerned with bringing mother, father, and child together. Asepsis, not "togetherness," was the most important consideration. In my room, alone except for the monitoring of labor pains by impersonal nurses and house staff, I read aloud to myself *La Chanson de Roland* until the pains became unbearable, when I was taken to the delivery room and anesthetized. After a few minutes I was unconscious, and I did not even know when Alice was born.

Coming out of anesthesia I was calling for Adolf. Through the night he had been wandering about between the hospital and the house, and now he was allowed to see me for only a few minutes before I was given another hypodermic.

I cannot say that Alice made much of an impression on me when she was brought in the following day. Still in a daze, I was dreaming of looking for wildflowers in the woods with Adolf and longing for Mammina (my mother) to feed and cuddle me. It was a full week before I realized that we had a daughter. My diary entry for October 11 reads:

> Alice weighed 6 lbs. 2 oz. at birth and she passed her birth weight today [October 11]. She is petite and beautifully made. She seems thoroughly sound and takes her bottle as she should. I did not breast feed her nor was I encouraged to do so by the hospital staff. [In 1929, formula and sterilized bottles and nipples were the order of the day.] Her head is beautifully shaped, her fingers are quite long, her mouth expressive. I feel very tender and loving toward her and love to hold her in my arms. I love to see her in Adolf's arms and dream of what she will become. Every so often a feeling of exaltation comes over me.
>
> Adolf, Alice and I. We should be great human beings for the Lord has been good.
>
> Of course, whether one should thank the Lord is a question. There is no doubt we three should be thankful deeply though, to the Lord or some outside power, as we are the darlings of the gods on whom every joy and blessing has been bestowed—but when you consider all those who through no fault of their own are unfortunate, the mercy of the Lord becomes a questionable hypothesis.

At the end of three weeks, Alice and I went home. I sat in the autumn sun. I had a baby—it was true! I wept for joy. Alice in the clothes basket, all covered with pink blankets, with her wee head sticking out, stirred me beyond words. A Scottish nurse, who remained with us for two years, took care of formulas, bottle feeding, diaper washing, and hanging the diapers in the yard to dry.

Shocking in the light of 1980 ideas! But Alice survived, and I doubt that her continuous exposure to my fears and impatience would have been good for either of us. Adolf and I both enjoyed playing with her, and as the years went by our relationship developed into a powerful emotional tie based on mutual respect and affection.

1930 was the year when we attempted to bring together our past experiences. Adolf was to find out more about the French girl Béatrice, and Béatrice was to learn about Adolf's "mistress," the Caribbean.

Charles Taussig (later a member of Franklin Roosevelt's Brain Trust), Adolf's closest friend and client, was going to Cuba for the new year on sugar business. Mrs. Taussig and I were also invited.

Charles Taussig was a lovely man. He and Adolf had much in common; both combined the practical with the romantic, both belonging to the confraternity of what are euphemistically called sugar tramps. As in all agricultural businesses, when the crop comes in, haste is of the essence. The cane must be cut and piled on a train in the field in order to reach the mill within the day, for the sugar content decreases with every passing hour. A breakdown of the mill or sabotage will ruin the crop. Cutting cane is brutal business, and the exploitation of the laborer has been the subject of more than one revolution. Mechanical cutting, as practiced in Hawaii, is expensive.

I was unaware of all this; I was thoroughly enjoying the brilliant sunshine and the Malecón and orchids hanging in the gardens. This was my first experience of the tropics and the then ultraluxurious life in Havana, in which I was suddenly included. It had been a good year for sugar. As one of the Cuban ladies said to me, "This year we have pearls and orchids and Paris gowns; next year if the crop is poor we will have nothing. That is life." I shall never forget the brilliant display the ladies made, with their jewels and satin ball gowns in pastel shades, walking down the long staircase in the Vedado country club by moonlight. While Adolf and Charles worked, Ruth Taussig and I loafed on the beach. It was a curious sensation being just Adolf's wife—and I was not sure I liked it. Adolf had always gone alone to the Caribbean.

Havana was not like Haiti or Santo Domingo. The gay life and the luxury without a secure economic base were distressing to Adolf.

I recalled one of his early letters to me:

> The night's work is over and it has been one evening. I have been starting off a new administrator to Central Teresa in Puerto Rico, giving the usual farewell dinner and the talk, aside from business, has been of our southern ports of call, Santo Domingo, Haiti, Puerto Rico, Oriente and Santa Clara provinces in Cuba; of the native lords of the hills, the great South American liners making call at Port-au-Prince, the little insular craft which plies across the passages from island to island, taking more time across the Archipelago than you take to cross the Atlantic; of Donna Blanca and her friendly inn in Puerto Plata; and of sugar and cane and sugar again, and the men that make it and the mills that grind it. Politics—and of the secret request of the Cuban President that Cuba be annexed to the United States with note of why the little folk in the hills wanted it; and then of cane and sugar again.

That is how the Caribbean work is done, Playmate, and sometime I hope we'll have a chance to see it together.

In an attempt to recapture the atmosphere of Adolf's previous visits to the Caribbean, we watched the sunset from the Morro Castle, returning by moonlight in a rowboat.

On our return from Cuba in February, I learned that Angel had died. Fortunately she had been unaware of her surroundings for some time, but still, I sent a telegram to my parents expressing sympathy and requesting information about funeral arrangements. The reply came: "Your presence at Mrs. Bend's funeral not desired. Signed, Cortlandt F. Bishop." Adolf and I walked down to Grace Church together and sat quietly in the pew where I had spent so many Sundays of my childhood with Angel. She had had a sweet and gentle spirit.

Perhaps, had she been a little stronger, a little more intelligent, a little more critical, many things would not have happened. It was she who made the "beautiful Amy Bend"; she enjoyed describing Mother's getting her first ball dress from Worth in Paris, white fluffy tulle with pink roses. But I suppose spoiling a beautiful child is *de natura rerum*. It would have taken more than human wisdom to foresee the resultant state of affairs, and I am glad she never knew of it. I wish she had known Adolf; she would have loved him.

When summer came, we left little Alice in the charge of the registered nurse who had been with me at the Lying-in Hospital, and sailed for France tourist third class on the *Olympic*. Quite a contrast to the French Line! Indifferent food, crowded quarters, but great poker games with fellow passengers.

In Paris, Adolf took me first to "Tanta" Eva's, 21, rue de Tournon. While assigned to the American Commission to Negotiate Peace at Versailles in 1919, he had stayed with her as a paying guest. The association had developed into a continuing friendship through the years, and now she had invited us to stay in her apartment while we were in Paris.

The apartment was on the top floor, four flights up. The stairs were lighted by the *"minuterie,"* a gadget typifying the French sense of economy. On entering the building, one presses a button that lights the stairs just long enough to permit the swift of foot and strong of heart to reach the top before the light goes out. The sluggish and the arthritic are caught in the dark halfway up and must fumble for another button. We made it to the top in one sprint.

"So my little lieutenant got married," Tanta Eva said in greeting.

"Yes," Adolf replied. "My wife was raised in France. She has a baccalauréat from the Sorbonne."

On the mantelpiece were several photographs of French officers. Tanta Eva belonged to a traditional army family in which the men were professional soldiers from generation to generation and believed in honor, patriotism, and the church. My classmates at Saint-Germain had been of similar background.

Tanta Eva led us into the dining room, where we sat around a fine old walnut table eating pâté de foie gras and drinking Vouvray wine while she and Adolf exchanged family news. Tanta Eva inquired first about Miriam Berle, who had spent a year at the Sorbonne after the war and stayed with her.

"How is Odette?" Adolf inquired, in turn.

"She is supporting herself and her son by working in a government office. It is hard, but one carries on."

Odette, Adolf told me, was the widow of an officer killed at the Battle of the Marne in Sept. 1914. Her son was born after the father's death. Adolf recalled a family dinner to which he had been invited when Tanta Eva was incensed over the fact that Odette was no longer wearing a crepe veil.

"You must always wear mourning for your husband," she remonstrated.

Tanta Eva's brother, a general, disagreed vigorously. "She is a young woman. She must marry again."

Alas, Odette, like many French widows of World War I, struggled alone to the end of her life.

When it came my turn to reminisce, I took Adolf to the little "lake" in the Tuileries Gardens. We watched the children still wearing black aprons over school uniforms and poking their little sailboats with long poles. *"Mon petit bateau a-t il des jambes?"* I hummed. *"Mais oui, mon gros bêta; sans cela, il ne marcherait pas."* (Does my little boat have legs? Of course, dumb bunny; otherwise, he could not walk.) It seemed that we must recapitulate our individual experiences, interpret them to each other so that our separate memories, even of inconsequential things, were being woven like threads of gold into the fabric of our life.

On the Place de la Concorde, we stood together looking at the statue representing Alsace-Lorraine. When I was a child, Alsace-Lorraine had always been decked with black crepe, I recalled. In 1919, the region had been restored to France, and from then on her statue was always decorated with garlands and flowers.

"My office was over there," Adolf told me, pointing to a window on the second floor of the Hôtel Crillon. "From there I watched Wilson's triumphal entry. He was the messiah, the people's hero. Peace without victory. Open covenants openly arrived at. The self-determination of people."

"Reading about this in high school, I was thrilled too," I told him.

"Then came the terrible disillusionment," Adolf went on, "the many secret deals. The French exacting from Germany reparations that could never be paid, demanding control over the Ruhr and the Saar; the Allies supporting the White Russians under Kolchak, who had already been defeated; the League of Nations — not a true league, but a replica of old alliances. At that point I was on the way to becoming a destructive revolutionary. A number of young people on the peace-conference staff who called themselves the *"jeunesse radicale"* resigned in protest. I was in the army, so I could not resign. I asked to be relieved, risking court-martial. I felt neither the interests of the United States nor those of world peace were being served. My request was refused at first, but after a few months, I received an honorable discharge."

I could hardly wait to take Adolf to Saint-Germain-en-Laye, outside Paris, where I had gone to school while my parents traveled.

Going along the rue Voltaire in Saint-Germain, we came to the massive door, surmounted by a heavy stone cross: a door I had always suspected had not been opened since the days of the dukes of Rohan. I yanked the crooked jointed wire by the little side door. In response to the faint tinkle, a black-capped, wrinkled face peered through the grate and asked our business.

"We have come to see Mademoiselle Mulot," I said. A little suspicious on seeing a man, she opened the door reluctantly and let us into the courtyard filled with nasturtiums, then disappeared.

I led Adolf through the *cour d'honneur*, lined with pollard linden trees, into the garden. Catching sight of Armandine, the old cook, through the kitchen window, I almost shouted: "Where is Mademoiselle Mulot?"

"La petite Béatrice!" Armandine exclaimed, dropping her spoon into one of the enormous vats on the stove.

"La petite Béatrice no longer. I am a married woman, and this is my husband."

Mademoiselle Mulot was coming toward us, a lithe figure dressed in black, her dark hair wound in a simple chignon that emphasized her high forehead. She turned toward Adolf, her deep gray eyes alive with interest. *"Bonjour, monsieur,"* she said softly, bowing her head slightly while extending her hand, that expressive hand I had always admired and still do, the long index finger extended at a wide angle from the thumb, the other fingers partly flexed.

I asked if I might show Adolf the *parc*, as the garden was called. It was summertime. The children were on vacation, and the tall windows opening into the old ducal salons, now transformed into classrooms, were closed.

Going down the *grande allée* shaded with beech trees, the three of us, arm in arm, Mademoiselle between us, came to the little wooden bench where she and I had sat so often after the official lessons were over and she had spoken to me of meditation and prayer.

"Béatrice was a lonely child," she said, turning to Adolf.

"I understand," he replied. "I am doing my best to make up for that. I have come here to thank you for the manner in which you educated this girl so that she grew up to be a woman."

"We used to have long talks about that," she smiled. "I believe a woman should develop her intellectual and spiritual faculties to the utmost so that she can become the lifelong companion of a fine man, who in turn must have been educated to be worthy of her."

When it came time to leave, she walked with us to the entrance. The chapel door was open. The three of us knelt in prayer for a few moments. As we rose, she kissed me on the forehead—"the noblest part," as she always called it.

Turning to Adolf, she said, "I prayed that Béatrice might make a good marriage, not just in the wordly sense, but a relationship complete in all respects. I can see, monsieur, that together you will achieve this ideal."

There were other pieces of France we had to see together. The Comédie-Française: Adolf preferred Victor Hugo; I preferred Corneille. We had both read Henry Adams's *Mont Saint-Michel and Chartres*, so we went to pay our respects to the superb stained glass of the Grande Verrière.

Before we sailed for home, Adolf took me to dinner at Foyot's—one of the finest restaurants of the time, of which Father had spoken frequently but to which I had never been. It is no longer in existence. Adolf chose the menu. I still have it. *Caneton à la Nanteuse, Crêpes Suzette.* I chose the wine as Father had taught me. We had come around full circle.

Although our experiences and our political views were different, we knew that we both loved France and French people. It was as if two X rays of the same subject taken at different times were superimposed and the differences accounted for.

≈≈ 23

Back home, we found Alice in good health. A sturdy child, independent of mind and spirit, then and always.

Our second child, Beatrice Van Cortlandt, was born on November 24, 1931 — my father's birthday. Gradually I was losing my fear of handling the babies, but I was happy to keep a nurse for the children, and so was Adolf. Vivacious, charming, and loquacious from birth — that was Beatrice. I insisted that she was born speaking four-syllable words! She was not as sturdy as Alice and as a child suffered from asthma — a condition prevalent in my mother's family — but she has grown up to be a fine, healthy woman.

My own career was not making much progress at this time. I was doing some freelance marriage and family counseling for a church in Brooklyn. In the summer I taught the history of the family to a group of young adults at Vassar College. I was exploring the field of marriage counseling, which was being developed by Emily Mudd, a sociologist, and Robert Latou Dickinson, a remarkable gynecologist and artist whose contributions to the study of sexuality have been hailed by Masters and Johnson as the first modern scientific treatment of the subject.

The study of drawings and pelvic models in Dr. Dickinson's studio at the Academy of Medicine, and conversations with Alexis Carrel were leading me to a realization that a knowledge of physiology and medicine was essential to a better understanding of people. One thing led to another, and I decided to enter medical school.

I had majored in history and English at Vassar and had a master's degree in history from Columbia. As a result I was deficient in chemistry, a pre-medical-school requirement. Adolf and his client Charles Taussig, president of the American Molasses Company, were most helpful. In order that I should not lose another year or more by taking college courses in chemistry, they provided a tutor, a Turk who was an industrial chemist employed by Charles. With his instruction I was able to pass an examination satisfactorily — which shows how limited were the requirements in the thirties.

Although my qualifications were now in order, medical schools would not take me. "Ridiculous! Why waste an expensive medical education on a married woman of thirty with two children!" exclaimed the deans of Cornell and New York University medical schools. Finally I was admitted to Columbia University Medical School, whose Dean, Dr. Rappleye, believed in taking a chance on a maverick. I was to enter the College of Physicians and Surgeons in the fall of 1933. I have never ceased to be grateful to Dr. Rappleye.

For Adolf also, the thirties were a crucial period.

As the Depression deepened and the rate of unemployment rose, he became more and more concerned. On a spring morning in 1932, we walked together along an old woods road on Beartown mountain behind our property. It was one of those rare spring days in New England with a little patch of snow glistening on the brown leaves, the maple trees in tiny leaf, yellow-chartreuse, a warming sun, and a profusion of wild violets along a damp bank. Adolf was talking to himself most of the time.

As we continued our walk, we thought of the countless young men with no jobs and imagined how they might benefit from a chance to work and earn money. This germ of an idea was realized through the organization of the Civilian Conservation Corps, in which Charles Taussig took an important part and which was dear to the heart of Mrs. Roosevelt. One year later trucks spun in the mud of the country road and half-chopped saplings bore the marks of repeated assaults by neophyte woodsmen. Barracks were built on the site of an old farm on Beartown. Now, fifty years later, all trace of the camp has disappeared but for one chimney.

CETA, recently eliminated by the Reagan administration, may be considered the modern equivalent of the CCC.

That same spring (1932) Adolf and his friend Louis Falkner, a young economist of the Security Research Department of the Bank of New York & Trust Company, completed a memorandum entitled *The Nature of the Difficulty*, in which social, economic, and financial problems were discussed and a number of remedial measures were suggested.

The Modern Corporation and Private Property was published in 1932. In this book, which has become a basic text for students of economics, Adolf analyzed the revolution in the nature of property as it shifted from tangible lands and goods controlled by the owner to stocks and bonds, where the control passed to the corporation manager and the owner had only a passive role. The implications of this change in the nature of property and the consequent growth of the corporation formed the base of Adolf's continuing lifelong study.

Adolf and I knew that ideas, in order to become political reality, needed a sponsor—"a prince," I said laughingly. The aide to the prince turned up in the guise of Professor Raymond Moley, who presented Adolf to Governor Franklin D. Roosevelt. The group who gathered around Roosevelt included Raymond Moley, Rexford Guy Tugwell, and Samuel Rosenman. A newspaperman dubbed them the Brain Trust. Charles Taussig, Professor James Angell, Marc Lowenthal, Hugh Johnson, Louis Howe, and others were part of this company at different times.

Adolf knew also that a "prince" alone was not enough—the ideas must be translated into legislative terms that Congress must then approve. Between Roosevelt's election to the presidency in November 1932 and his taking office in

March 1933, the new government was at the mercy of a lame-duck congress. Congressman Fiorello La Guardia proved to be the savior of the situation. Thanks to his help, important legislation was passed creating the keystones of the New Deal — old-age, sickness, and unemployment insurance and the Securities and Exchange Commission.

La Guardia was brought to Nineteenth Street by one of Adolf's former law students. Unfortunately, details of this meeting are not recorded in either Adolf's or my diary. I remember only that both of us were impressed with Fiorello's dynamism. The attraction was mutual; we three became and remained friends until Fiorello's death in 1947.

During the summer of 1932, Adolf was called to Hyde Park frequently. I drove him over and hung around while he worked with the other Brain Trusters or with Governor Roosevelt. Sometimes we were invited to stay for lunch. About ten people assembled in the dining room and Roosevelt was wheeled in. I fell under his charm immediately and was impressed with how completely he had overcome his handicap, adjusting his braces while we chatted as naturally as another man might have put on his rubbers.

Eleanor appeared to be only a visitor in her mother-in-law's house. Even after Eleanor became the first lady, Sara Delano sat at the head of the table opposite her son, saying to Eleanor, "Just sit anywhere." Unfortunately, I never had more than a superficial contact with Eleanor, although Adolf had the privilege of working with her on a number of occasions. Sara Delano, on the other hand, took me under her wing. She soon discovered that she had known both my grandmothers and could trace their lineage as far back as her own.

Turning to Adolf she said, "I am glad Franklin has at least one gentleman working for him. Are you very radical?"

I retorted instantly "Now, Mrs. Roosevelt, what do you mean by radical?"

She paid no attention and went on, "I do hope you are not. I am an old conservative."

With a twinkle in his eye, Adolf gallantly replied, "If only there were more like you."

As the tempo of the campaign quickened, Adolf became more and more involved. He was writing speeches upon speeches. In Roosevelt he was finding a man who was interested in his ideas. "Ideas are more important than men," Adolf told me, "and we can be the masterminds directing a political campaign as we supply the ideas to a candidate for president."

The speech delivered by FDR at the Commonwealth Club in San Francisco on September 19, 1932, was the most significant of the campaign pronouncements. Adolf and I wrote it together, sitting side by side at the long table at the farm. The original manuscript in both our handwritings is now in the Roosevelt Library at Hyde Park.

In this speech, Adolf discussed the role of government as the country changed from an agricultural to an industrial economy:

> Every man has a right to life; and this means that he also has a right to make a living. . . . Every man has a right to his own property which means to be assured, to the fullest extent attainable, in the safety of his savings.

> Further, in this set up: "business men have undertaken to be not business men, but princes — princes of property. I am very clear that they must fearlessly and competently assume the responsibility which goes with power.

(*Princes of property* was our pet phrase and quoted prominently in the press, to our mutual delight.)

Anticipating the environmentalist by three decades, we concluded:

> Clearly, all this calls for a reappraisal of values. A mere builder of more industrial plants . . . is as likely to be a danger as a help. Our task now . . . is the soberer, less dramatic business of administering resources and plants already in hand . . . of distributing wealth and products equitably; of adapting existing economic organizations to the service of the people.

We went down to Washington for the inauguration and stayed at the Carleton Hotel, where the sickly green-yellow of the halls reflected exactly my state of mind.

What would Adolf's next assignment be? Would he become a member of the government? In what capacity? How could he continue to be an independent consultant? At breakfast we discussed the various possibilities. In a grandiloquent manner, Adolf declared, "Pulling out from the government now may be declining a place in history. Shall I be Alexander Hamilton?"

William Woodin, the incoming secretary of the treasury, with whom Adolf had worked closely, offered him a position on his staff. I never knew exactly what the position was. The idea of pulling up roots and moving to Washington frightened both of us. What would have happened to my plans for entering medical school? Neither of us was ready for it at this time — certainly, I was not — nor could we afford it financially. There were no doubts about my feelings, as the following diary entry indicates:

March 5, 1933

Home after the inauguration and never have I been so glad to get home.

It was a continuous standing in line going from one place to another and no place worth going to. And as for it being a good show, there was no show. We have lost all color and all sense of pomp and ceremony; probably there never was any in this country. There was no thrill in the crowd, only idle curiosity.

We heard Roosevelt's speech pushing through the Capitol grounds as the other half of the population was pushing away, bored. It was a great speech and with all the banks closed a few hours before—most timely and dramatic though the crowd showed no indication it thought so.

It may be, too, that the people as well as I have lost the capacity for that fine frenzy of enthusiasm for any cause. A. is the one person who has not lost it and whose romantic sense is getting plenty of nourishment. But playing god is not all beer and skittles—it's d———d hard work.

I have not spent an evening with him for a week and the only quiet time we have had was yesterday morning. I have not spent an evening with him for a week? a month? A refrain familiar to the wife of any politician.

Being in public life does mean that your time is not your own and that your personal life is to a large extent drafted. Neither he nor I wish to make that sacrifice, but what must be must be, and emergencies, I suppose, do not last forever.

As I took the train for New York, Adolf went to the Treasury preparing for the reopening of the banks on the following day. Eventually he came home and decided to accept a part-time position as special assistant to the Reconstruction Finance Corporation. This gave him a stance in Washington and permitted him to continue with his multiple activities in the capital, to teach at the Columbia Law School, and to organize the Fusion campaign for the election of Fiorello La Guardia as mayor of New York in 1934.

I took no active part in the mayoral campaign or in any other campaign. I remained an interested observer.

In the fall of 1933 Adolf was sent to Cuba as a special financial advisor to the American ambassador, Sumner Welles. Wives were not included on that assignment. I was registering at the College of Physicians and Surgeons of Columbia University, buoyed by Adolf's encouragement. Once again a letter from him was my talisman, as it had been on the way to Newfoundland.

There could be nothing sweeter in life than watching you go from triumph to triumph. I shall be beyond measure glad if I can parallel your upward course in my own fields, and the great joy will come in the alliance of two strengths contributing to the human values of each. Not for us the philosophy of a towering tree and a clinging vine. Have you ever seen two eagles in the spring? Meeting, circling and then flashing upwards in a great spiral until both reach heights which neither would explore alone? I have watched them in the mountains and have admired them in the spring sunlight — each rises with his own strength but the mating of the two gives the impulse to seek the sky and the joy of finding the upper air. On what would be a lonely course for either alone becomes a glorious journey towards the sun.

But I was not as sure of myself as he was! From my diary:

Education has always been a most satisfactory experience for me; it has meant the opening of many doors and a measure of achievement. But now, clearly living is more important than learning. Will I be able to be with Adolf and the children and follow what is considered one of the stiffest academic programs? The possibility of academic failure must be seriously considered, as I cannot fail at home. In the event of failure, I will go back to the study of languages, literature and writing. I cannot conceive going on in my work of marriage and family counseling without additional training — and I will not be a committee woman.

The prospect of the study of medicine delights me.

≈ 24

In the winter of 1935, we learned that Father was seriously ill. Although nine years had passed since he banished me, I had never lost hope that someday we would meet again and that he would know Adolf and his granddaughters. This was not to be.

Adolf and I called at the family home in Lenox.

From my diary:

March 26, 1935

Father is dying. It will not be more than a few days now. I have been talking to Dr. Ira Dixson. The night nurse told him that Father had spoken of his "baby" — had asked for his daughter, wanted to see me. This was last week before the cloud went over.

When I went to the house with Adolf February 22 — Mother came down the stairs looking like an old hag with eyes that were not there. "There is the front door," she said—"both of you get out. Your father does not want to see you alive or dead—we asked him."

I suppose they did ask him and he said so, but deep down he wanted me. They kept me from him. I suppose there is nothing so unremitting as Mother's hate. She terrorized my father with it in regard to my grandmother for 25 years, and there is no greater tragedy than his—he who so loved life, who could so enjoy it, denied it. And on his last days his wife hired a Holmes man to keep his daughter from him.

It hurts. I have lived now for nine years without seeing him. I have made a home and a full life and in back of my mind I have always felt that some day I would see him again; that some day he would come to know Adolf and be proud and happy about his daughter.

It is true that had we seen each other again, it would have been painful, but we would have had fun too.

In the meantime I go about trying to fulfill my destiny, which I suppose is the realization of my father's dreams which I have made my own. I suppose that is the way the world goes on and I shall die with those dreams unfulfilled. But I shall not have denied life—I shall have done more than skim the surface. I shall not have been afraid of my own soul and I shall have gone into the depths and heights of other lives not my own.

Father died two weeks later. The funeral was private. Later I paid my third visit to the family plot in Greenwood Cemetery. First it had been Uncle David, then Grand-mère, now Father. But this time, I was not alone—Adolf was with me.

Father left that part of his estate over which he had complete control to Mother and to Edith Nixon with the proviso that in order to benefit from the legacy Edith must reside with Mother. This she did until Mother died in 1957 at the age of eighty-seven. Left alone, the Irish intriguer lived on in a nursing home until her death some years later, befriended only by the Episcopal minister.

The remainder of my father's estate went to Columbia University. It had been my father's intention to disinherit me completely, but Adolf and other lawyers were able to prove that part of the trusts established by the will of my grandfather, who died in 1900, must revert to his descendants—that is, to me and my daughters.

This meant that we were independently wealthy, and it freed Adolf from the necessity of practicing law primarily for financial gain. He could afford to work for the government or to be a full-time professor if he chose to do so.

We were in complete agreement that whereas we might disapprove of inherited wealth, we were not prepared to organize a revolution and that as long as the capitalist system existed, we considered wealth a sacred trust to be used as intelligently as possible for the well-being of ourselves, our children, and those individuals or causes that we would like to help. We were anxious that wherever possible, gifts to individuals should be made through institutions, schools, colleges, and small foundations managed by friends, for we wished to maintain a personal relationship with the beneficiaries unencumbered by a sense of personal gratitude or obligation on their part. Similarly, gifts made to institutions were listed as anonymous. We had no say in the management of the grant or the gift— the recipient was entirely free. There were no strings attached.

Alice was the first beneficiary of the trust fund that was established after my father's death. We took her with us to the inter-American conference in Buenos Aires in November 1936. She was seven years old. Unfortunately, we could not take Beatrice. She was only five, and her asthma precluded such a long trip.

I obtained a trimester's leave of absence from the medical school. Adolf, Alice, a French maid, and I, plus two large wardrobe trunks and several valises packed with finery suitable for diplomatic ceremonies, joined the party on S.S. *The American Legion*. With us were Secretary of State Cordell Hull, Undersecretary of State Sumner Welles, their wives, and a number of ambassadors and delegates from Mexico, Central America, and the Caribbean. The purpose of the conference was to determine how the maintenance of peace among the American republics might be safeguarded. The round trip to Buenos Aires took fourteen days each way.

President Roosevelt joined the delegation in Rio, going on to Buenos Aires, spending about nine days at sea on the warship *Indianapolis*. This took place less than fifty years ago. Can one imagine the secretary of state spending twenty-eight days on a ship at sea in 1983!

On shipboard there were work sessions every morning—endless, tiresome drafting and redrafting of conference proposals by the staff until, as Adolf put it, a speech to be delivered by Secretary Hull became "your personal enemy." But what leisure, compared to the pace of today. There was time for shuffleboard and walks around the deck. Alice became quite a favorite of Jean Paul Sannon, a fine historian from Haiti. She also charmed Sumner Welles. "Sumner Welles has redeemed himself in my eyes by presenting Alice a horrible tin pan with rattles on it. By his order this is to be shaken in Mummy's ears when Mummy makes Alice do arithmetic on Sunday, and by my order, it is to be shaken in Sumner's ears when he looks too solemn. All this to his great amusement!"

In Buenos Aires while the conference was going on, Alice attended a French school. "The children were not very friendly," she complained. "They stole all my marbles." Visiting a lady's pet penguin was more fun. For my part, I visited medical facilities, notably a maternity hospital where newborn infants were placed in a crib at the mother's bedside and not in a sterilized nursery. When I reported this practice to my American colleagues, they were horrified — the unhygienic backward custom exposed infants to germs! It took another twenty-five years for Americans to promote "living in" of infants with their mothers.

"The most recent papal encyclical has reinforced the ban on artificial contraception," I reported. "Some women I spoke to were convinced birth control was a sin, while many did not think so. Since the quality of condoms is poor and the pessary is unknown both to the laity and to the profession, the abortion rate is high."

When President Roosevelt arrived in Buenos Aires, Adolf and Sumner were very busy putting together the speech that was to be delivered at the state banquet. It was agreed that out of courtesy to Mr. Roosevelt, in a wheelchair, the Argentine president would also remain seated while he delivered his welcoming address. Apparently President Augustín Justo forgot and rose to speak. When Mr. Roosevelt came to reply, there was no one at his side to help him get to his feet. Undaunted he grabbed the arms of the chair, turned his back to the audience, and pushed himself onto his feet. This courageous maneuver was met with thunderous applause.

When I related this to Alice, she insisted, "I want to see Mr. Roosevelt too." This was arranged on the day he was sailing for home on the *Indianapolis*. We were given a pass to stand on a covered dock, from which we could see the president going up the gangplank. There were very few people, so it was easy for the president to pick us out. He waved to me, and I pointed to Alice. He waved again to her and smiled. Alice's reaction was immediate, "Now I know he is my friend."

The trip home was leisurely and gave us the opportunity to make friends with several Latin American diplomats, notably Blanca Espinosa de los Monteros, pretty wife of the Mexican delegate who became ambassador to the United States when Truman was president, and the Nicaraguan Luis Manuel Debayle, an old fashioned liberal in spite of being the brother-in-law of Nicaraguan President Anastasio Somoza.

Walking up and down on the deck we discussed our children's education.

Through our contacts with the Roosevelts, we were constantly aware of the pitfalls surrounding children whose parents were in politics. We felt we had some important things to transmit to our offspring. We believed in book learning and in trying to develop a strong intellectual curiosity. Our children must be prepared to meet different kinds of people in different situations. In that respect, we felt that form was important — to know the form in a particular situation and to be able to fall in step. For instance, they should be able to walk into a drawing room filled with older people with the same equanimity and dexterity as they would show in helping their hostess with the furnace, washing dishes, or baby tending; in other words, to meet a social situation in terms of the other fellow. Discipline was essential — but not discipline for discipline's sake, but with an end in view: the ability to be tolerant and understanding of different people's points of view while preserving one's own sense of values. This sense of values, based on individual integrity and public service, must be maintained in a changing world. Then the children must acquire skills that would make earning a living possible. Perhaps more important, they must come to realize that living is becoming, that things do not just happen, that there are relationships and connections, that the world is not static.

Two children seemed enough, but Adolf, a dynast like his father, really wanted a son. So we decided to take another chance — a decision we never regretted. I became pregnant again, and Peter Adolf Augustus was born December 8, 1937.

After Peter was born I returned to medical school for the spring trimester and finished my clinical clerkship at the New York University division at Bellevue Hospital, only twelve minutes' walk from our home on Nineteenth Street.

Although the physical facilities were poor — the hospital was overcrowded, with beds in the hall, and elevators out of order — the practice of medicine at Bellevue was superior. The professors of the three New York City medical schools, Columbia, Cornell, and New York University, all spent some time teaching students and caring for patients. I learned a great deal — among other things, the effects of extreme fatigue: my shameful feeling of great relief when a woman with a septic abortion died before the time for her next scheduled blood count. The clinical clerks at that time were required to do blood counts every six hours on seriously ill patients.

When we had returned from Buenos Aires, Adolf had been busy at Columbia and working with Mayor La Guardia, but the pressure for him to take a position in the State Department was increasing. In February of 1938, he was named assistant secretary of state.

This appointment was the subject of much debate in the family. Rudolf, Adolf's brother, was against it, saying that being imprisoned in the State Department would not increase Adolf's opportunities for direct access to the president and would curtail his free-ranging activities in other fields. Huger Jervey, a dear friend and Alice's godfather, was against it, saying I was no diplomat's wife and would ruin Adolf's career by expressing my opinions too freely. This naturally hurt my feelings, and I vowed to remain silent and discreet when circumstances required it.

But the problem was more fundamental. It was an example of Adolf's ambivalence—the conflict between the thinker and the man of action. Really, he wanted to be both, but on his own terms, preserving his independence. Most of the time he succeeded. On the one hand, he did not heed Carrel's advice: "Let others act; it is Adolf's ideas that count." On the other hand, brushing aside the counsel of those who urged him to run for public office, he accepted the State Department position.

Adolf rented a furnished apartment at the Anchorage in Washington, a comfortable residence for foreign-service officers in transit. We met on weekends, either in New York or in Washington. The girls visited during spring vacation. Seated in the deep dark leather chairs of Adolf's State Department office, little Beatrice, age seven, printed on official stationery, "I like Washington—The End." Prophetic indeed!

In June 1938, I received my medical degree from New York University. How to continue my medical education was a real problem. Perhaps the medical deans who had turned me down had been right after all. Columbia helped me out once more. I was appointed as an extern on the First Medical Division—the Columbia division—at Bellevue Hospital beginning January 1939. The hospital, as I have noted before, was only twelve minutes from home, and in 1939, walking from Nineteenth Street to Twenty-sixth Street at night was not dangerous.

This arrangement made it possible for me to accompany Adolf on the next inter-American conference scheduled to take place in November 1938 in Lima, Peru.

Our departure was somewhat dramatic. We had managed to get up to the Berkshires for Thanksgiving—the children, a nurse, and ourselves. On Thanksgiving night it started to snow, and by morning we were snowed in. There was no choice but to ski a mile out to the main road, using the tops of fences as guideposts. The main road was sufficiently plowed that we could be driven to the dock in New York, where our ship with Cordell Hull and the rest of the delegation was waiting for us. Once again, the State Department spent twelve days going and twelve days coming—a total of twenty-four days at sea.

The American delegation was intended to be representative of the country and included Alfred Landon, the unsuccessful Republican candidate for president in 1936, and Dan Tracy, president of the American Federation of Labor, a tough customer. I wrote in my diary:

> It must be said that I have prejudices in regard to labor. I still believe that an employer is responsible for providing the best conditions possible, that he must be fair and just always—but also I know that he is not. Therefore, labor needs a dedicated champion. Romantically, I believe in a man who will deny himself and work for his people unselfishly and to the limit of his endurance. David Dubinsky was such a man and I held him in great respect. Tracy and Alexander Whitney of the BA conference are just politicians. As Adolf says, they're not in business for their health. They're paid a d——d good salary in order to see that the union member gets a share, a good share of the pie, not because he's more useful or a better member of society but because he belongs to that particular group regardless of the merits of the case.

But fortunately the labor leaders were not my responsibility. Adolf defined my role clearly—I was expected to entertain Alfred Landon, a very pleasant assignment. I found him a kindly, nice, home-folks sort of man, better informed and more fair-minded than I had expected.

In Peru we visited Inca ruins and private collections of antiques. We enjoyed the social functions, and Landon cooperated in the work of the United States delegation in a manner that ensured its political success and impressed our southern friends.

As in Buenos Aires, I was filled with dreams of the possibilities for the development of a nonindustrialized country.

> Here are all the modern techniques and all the mistakes of modern civilizations to choose from. Would it be possible to choose the techniques and avoid the mistakes?
>
> The Indians who work in the Serra de Pasco mines work only 20 out of 30 days. The other ten are devoted to their own affairs—their "cosecha"—so they never starve. Neither, of course, do they wash often or own an automobile, but how necessary are those things to the welfare of mankind? Could not their nutrition and health be improved, their

social structures preserved without creating an immoderate desire for the gadgets of modern technology? Is it essential to be able to choose between a pink and a yellow toothbrush?

≈ *25*
_____

After the occupation of Czechoslovakia in 1939, it became obvious that Adolf could not leave the State Department. We decided that a divided family was intolerable, and we rented a house in Washington for that summer. "Woodley" was the property of Henry Stimson. It was a superb house with large grounds situated in the cathedral section of Washington. There we moved with the girls, Peter, his nurse Hagie, the German couple who took care of the house (Hermann, the husband, was a veteran of World War I), and a French lady to teach the girls French. At last we were all together in one place.

In September 1939 came the invasion of Poland. The news was brought to us in a trembling voice by Hermann, who was the first to hear it over the radio. Adolf rushed to the State Department, and we knew then that our stay in Washington would be prolonged indefinitely.

The girls were enrolled in the Potomac School.

Adolf assisted me in establishing a connection with the George Washington Medical School and Gallinger Hospital. "You may get a foot in the door through my political connections," was his comment, "but after that you have to make good on your own." Over the five years in Washington, I managed to accumulate the required number of residencies and fellowships to become eligible for examination for the specialty of internal medicine.

Gallinger was not Bellevue. It was a poorly run hospital, with a budget subject to the whims of Congress and an attending staff that lacked the vigor and the quality of the Columbia-Cornell–New York University faculties. Still, I learned a great deal. The white and the "colored" patients occupied separate wards. On rounds, when the staff entered a room where three "colored" patients had been chatting together, dead silence fell and I felt as if an impenetrable curtain had been drawn. In the emergency room at night, I found it terrifying to deal with screaming black girls writhing in pain with septic abortions and black men cursing and groaning with chest wounds caused by a well-placed ice pick (the favorite weapon at the time) thrust under their ribs, or children dying of pneumonia or an infection of the bloodstream (no antibiotics then). Not until we went to Brazil did I learn to communicate naturally with black people.

Sometimes the nights were very quiet, and rather than lie in a stuffy room on a bed set against a hot wall with the sterilizers on the other side, I sat by a window reading *The Three Musketeers* or *The Count of Monte Cristo*, waiting for the dawn, when flocks of white heron flew over the Anacostia River. It was a relief to return to the shade of the great oaks at Woodley to be with Adolf and the children.

In February 1940, Adolf's mother died in Oberlin, Ohio, of a massive cerebral hemorrhage. His father, Lina, Miriam, Rudolf, and he gathered together at her bedside. He wrote:

> Following the family custom and Mother's wish, we did not have any great funeral; merely a prayer and the Twenty-third Psalm.... Home on the evening train. I took Father with us.[1]

I was waiting for Adolf and his father in Washington. The old gentleman was deeply shocked. He remained with us for a brief period, after which he returned to the Harvard Club in New York for the winter. He spent the summer at Boscawen, always jealous of his independence. Adolf wrote to friends in answer to their letters:

> Mother's death was a shock and a grief—the passing of one of the few thoroughly practising Christians I have ever known. Hers was a quiet and entirely unostentatious influence, which carried very far indeed. She declined to assume any of the trappings about which people make such a stir; insisted that hatred and ill-feeling was wrong, for its own sake. She died as she had lived, simply the work done, in quiet and without pain.... It was a great comfort to all of us that she died in the shadow of Oberlin where she had been reared and was married; so that in a sense the cycle was complete and she went swiftly home.[2]

Adolf and I managed a few moments alone together to talk about this remarkable woman. As Adolf said, the fact that she recognized her father's and her husband's authority and remained loyal to both her husband and her children through storm and stress, did not mean that she did not have ideas of her own. She never argued, but kept her own counsel and acted upon it. In 1920, Eugene Victor Debs, confined to jail for opposing the First World War, was running

[1]Beatrice Bishop Berle and T. B. Jacobs, eds., *Navigating the Rapids* (New York: Harcourt Brace Jovanovich, 1973), pp. 289–90.
[2]Ibid., p. 290.

for president of the United States on the Socialist ticket. A single vote for him was cast in the town of Boscawen. That ballot was cast by Adolf's mother. Needless to say, the voter's identity was never revealed!

"Do you remember the story of the fairy and the fringed gentian?" Adolf asked the children.

"Of course we do. You showed us the fringed gentian in the wet field below the house. You told us that the gentians earned their fringes because they allowed a passing fairy to seek shelter inside. But the closed gentian, the bottle gentian, remains closed always and can never open to the sun, for he refused to take the fairy in out of the rain."

"That is right," Adolf said gently. "It is the story my mother told me; it is the story you can tell your children as you walk across the field of gentians after your mother and I are gone."

At Gallinger Hospital, the day of the garden party we had been ordered by the White House to give in honor of a scientific congress, I had been struggling with a young patient. John was a boy of nineteen who was dying of acute rheumatic fever complicated by an infection of the heart valves. Before the discovery of penicillin, this was a fatal disease.

As the boy lay in bed, weak and pale, we heard the circus band playing on the hospital grounds below. I looked out of the window and saw patients in wheelchairs and others in bathrobes watching the tightrope walker. "Can't I go?" John murmured feebly.

I rushed for a wheelchair but, the chief resident said, "NO." The patient might die on the way down in the elevator. What if he had? To die on the way to the circus would have been a happier ending than any we could provide. But the chief resident's word was law, and I drove home to dress for the party.

While I was putting on a white chiffon dress and red shoes, I could see a few guests strolling down the meadow. Albert Einstein was among these, distinguished by a shock of white hair. Tables with refreshments were scattered over the lawn. When I took my place on the receiving line, the orchestra from the Shoreham was playing. Rudolf was standing in for Adolf until the latter arrived.

As the twilight deepened, the guests moved over to the lighted tennis court, some to watch, others to dance. It turned out to be a great party after all. Adolf and I waltzed together. Was this Becky Sharp's ball the night before the battle of Waterloo? I wondered. When the party was over I found I had lost a little teardrop-moonstone earring, a special gift from Adolf. I almost cried, but the next morning we found it on the tennis court where we had danced together. One good omen after all.

A few days later, Adolf went to Boston to deliver the Ware lecture from the pulpit of the Unitarian church, and to visit Anna Brock, who had been his friend and the friend of his parents since she taught him in the third grade. In the midst of turmoil, the lecture was his way of affirming his mother's faith and renewing his strength. I could only stand by in admiration as I read his concluding remark:

> To the old statesman [Samuel], there was but one foundation which was real; and that lay not in the pride and strength of any ruler, nor in the successes of any individual, but in faith which alone made possible the individual lives, the social achievements, the national life, the universal hope, in which his nation could find continuing life.

The fall of France in June 1940 was, for me, the severest blow of all. I felt desolate and helpless. Adolf reacted by taking me, the children, and Piglet (Beatrice's little bulldog) on a picnic. He wrote of the occasion in his diary:

> We canoed up the Potomac and got gorgeously drenched in a thunder shower. I never thought of anything all day. It was just as well, since my head had stopped really working. I wish there were more chance to do this, for I found myself getting entangled in strange and unpleasant thoughts. Obviously the struggle is moving along in Europe and I have a terrible feeling that the Germans are going to wind up masters of the situation... and yet I do not believe that what I see is going to last for ever.

At the end of the day, we declared to each other, "Playmates we were and must continue to be, and we as a family and as a nation must survive."

≈ 26

Soon after this we were to continue our partnership in international affairs in a more active and more personal way. Adolf had been devising measures that would permit South American countries to make up differences in trade caused by their being cut off from the Nazi market. An inter-American conference was called in Havana in July 1940, to work out these plans. Outside the conference room, Adolf and I arranged to bring together members from different countries who were as much strangers to each other as they were to North American delegates. Salazar, a sophisticated Guatemalan, a well-traveled diplomat of the old school, listened for the first time to the Schnekes—members of the Socialist party from Chile, who had never been out of their country before and were burning with indignation over their people's plight.

On another evening we were in the midst of a passionate discussion between Ramos, defense minister of Cuba, and López de Mesa, minister of foreign affairs of Colombia. Ramos was denouncing the concept of equality among men and calling for a pure race. In a position of power he would have been distinctly dangerous, but we understood that in spite of his title, he was not very influential.

To his turbulent tirade on white supremacy, López de Mesa replied in measured and perfect Castilian, demolishing Ramos's premises one by one.

The Cuban admitted he had met his match and applauded: *"Muy bien, muy bien."*

López de Mesa, historian and anthropologist, was a solitary man, but when Adolf and I had broken down the barrier, he became a fast friend. His compatriots spoke of him as *un hombre muy raro*, an eccentric. To us, he was particularly dear because he insisted on a pluralistic view of history, a concept Adolf and I had formulated at our first meeting. "Mono-ideology," López de Mesa said, "is the most persistent intellectual sin of man."

Admittedly, this kind of discussion did not necessarily lead to concrete results, but it served as a means of personal communication between an American official and Latin Americans for whom discussion of ideas was important.

While the conference was going on, Adolf's former sugar clients, whom we had not seen since our last visit to Cuba in the early thirties, were anxious to communicate with him. The wealthy Aspuru family, later exiled to Spain by Castro, were still in control of Central Toledo, one of the most important sugar mills on the island, situated a few miles outside of Havana. On the night that we were invited to dine with them, Adolf was delayed as usual. I went out alone, a solitary figure dressed in black chiffon dress (the fashion at the time), seated on the white leather cushions of the Aspuru limousine. Speeding through the hot tropical night, I could see the small lights flickering on both sides of the road through the open doors of the cane workers' huts. It was July, and the sugar cane was not very tall yet. At the end of the dark road, a closed gate with a lighted sign: Central Toledo *Es prohibido pasar*—entry prohibited. Beyond, a lighted veranda. A white coated servant opening the car door. Manuel Aspuru, thickset, blue-eyed, dark haired, courteously kissing my hand, led me into a drawing room where the men were standing on one side, the women on the other.

It was Adolf they wanted—the economic royalists were all there, prepared to wait for the prophet all night. Small talk petered out—even Maria Antonia Aspuru, an accomplished worldly lady who enjoyed orchids and pearls in the rich sugar years and later in exile learned to earn her living, ran out of steam. About 10:00 P.M. I persuaded everyone to go in to dinner. Adolf arrived after eleven and was surrounded immediately by all the gentlemen and Maria Antonia. While Adolf was trying to explain the expanded role of the Inter-American Bank as it applied to the sugar growers, I overheard Logarte, the president of the Cuban Stock Exchange: "The United States should take a strong stand. You are our father to whom we look up." Times have changed!

The conference came to a successful close a few days later with the passing of the Act of Havana, which recognized "the right of any American nation to take steps to protect the peace and security of itself or of the continent in respect of any of these colonies"—which in practice meant a blanket authority to the United States to seize any of the islands if there were any threatened change of sovereignty, or if there were some kind of indirect control amounting to the same thing, or if they became a menace to the continental peace. Adolf and I celebrated by spending the day at the beach together. I had not seen him so gay in many months. Little did we think that twenty years later the Act of Havana would become a scrap of paper as Soviet arms invaded the hemisphere.

On our return home in August, we got off to the Berkshires for a few days and took the children on a camping trip. In fact, there were two: little Beatrice's first night out on a small mountain "haystack," alone with her father and the visiting porcupines, which chewed her boots; and a threesome canoeing trip to Lake Umbagog that included Adolf, Alice, and me.

Camping equipment was less sophisticated in 1940 than it is now, but under the direction of the master camper, Adolf, it was quite efficient. A supply of shoelaces was indispensable for holding up tents and tying together blanket rolls, fishing rods, food parcels, and, on this expedition, Alice's pigtails. We had threatened to leave the pigtails behind—to cut them off—but Alice would not hear of it. She had spent the last year growing them and would not be parted therefrom. Another essential was Adolf's brown fishing hat, which he used to keep the sun off his nose, the rain out of his neck, to flatten his curls—and to catch frogs.

Returning to Washington, we continued to enjoy watching Mr. Hull play croquet. This was one of the perquisites of living at Woodley. The secretary came every afternoon, weather and international affairs permitting. He planned his game like a political campaign, winning nine out of ten times. Adolf rarely found time to attend, but the girls, whispering their comments on the game and the corpulence of certain members of the State Department, were keen and quiet observers, until the silence was broken one afternoon by piercing shrieks from little Beatrice, who had sat on a bee's nest while climbing a nearby apple tree.

We had no formal lease with Henry Stimson, the owner of Woodley. It was understood that we could leave on thirty days' notice—this is what Adolf expected would happen—or that Stimson could occupy his house on thirty days' notice were he to receive a Washington appointment. "Most unlikely," said Adolf in June 1939—but the unlikely became a reality. Mr. Stimson was appointed secretary of war in 1940. We moved next door on Cathedral Avenue, and then that house was sold; in 1941 we moved to a house on Nebraska Avenue, now the Japanese embassy, and lived there until we went as ambassadors to Brazil in January 1945. It was a comfortable family house with a garden in which Henry Wallace planted some of his special hybrid corn with the children.

All was serene at home, but Adolf's position in the State Department was far from secure.

> November, 1940. The election is over but that apparently does not end one's personal uncertainties. There seems to be some question in Mr. Hull's mind as to whether he wants to stay—Bullitt is around making intrigues and God knows what Sumner is thinking about. I agree entirely with Charles Taussig that it is important for the country that the Hull-Welles-Berle Trinity continue. However, should any shifts occur by which someone came into the Department from the outside over Adolf, he would have to leave. I would regard this as very unfortunate, as the U.S. has been spending several years in making Adolf into a first-rate public servant, and we the people voted for Mr. Roosevelt in order to continue the foreign policy of Mr. Hull.

Two months later the situation had not changed.

> About a week ago it looked as if we might all be going back to New York in a hurry. One of those absurd things happened which I suppose are of the essence of political life. The President (apparently) tried to slip a politician over on the Department in the place of old Judge Moore. Someone (the Secretary or Sumner) proposed Breck Long instead. It has now been agreed to return to the *status quo ante*: Moore with no counselor and all assistant secretaries. But (1) Grady has resigned and

not yet been replaced; (2) Long is sick; (3) Moore has been out for months: ergo, A. is doing the work of four men. What is the sense of that???

Still Adolf continued to labor in the vineyard in spite of all obstacles.

≈≈≈ 27

In the meantime, my medical career took an interesting turn. Dr. Thomas Parran, surgeon general of the United States Public Health Service, offered me a commission in the Public Health Service with the rank of major.

At the time there were only two or three other women in the Public Health Service. Naturally, Dr. Parran did not expect a married woman of forty with three children to join the coast guard. He wanted me to organize an employee health service for clerical government workers. I objected strenuously to becoming an administrator. Though the employees of the War Production Board and of the Office of War Information became my chief responsibility, I managed to continue making rounds at Gallinger three times a week. On hot, humid days, with the chief of personnel, a gruff, practical man, I made the rounds of the temporary buildings and picked out those employees whom I knew to be cardiacs and sent them home, leaving the healthy to sweat and broil. Before the war all government offices automatically closed when the thermometer reached ninety degrees Fahrenheit, but it would have been considered unpatriotic to close when GIs were fighting for our country all over the world.

We carried out a mass screening program for tuberculosis, finding a number of primary lesions among young clerical workers. Of course, there were many personality problems, particularly alcoholism, and I learned to appreciate and work closely with Alcoholics Anonymous.

Most interesting, however, were the recruits for the Office of War Information. By hypothesis candidates were to be either women, men over forty, or men declared unfit for military service. All, however, were supposed to be fit to go under fire. My assistant was very authoritarian, while still exercising good medical judgment. She would declare that so-and-so had an enlarged heart and was unfit for overseas duty. The management of OWI insisted that the qualifications of this individual were unique, that no one else could be found to take his place. I would go quietly to Elmer Davis, explain the risks involved, and say that we were not making policy and that it was management's responsibility, not ours, to decide whether the cost and the risks incurred in the possible or probable breakdown of this individual were worth their sending him or her overseas. Of course, we were not always right — the man with the enlarged heart came back triumphantly from North Africa thumbing his nose at us, whereas a diabetic had the breakdown we had feared and predicted, causing great difficulties for all concerned.

The amount of clerical work involved in government service appalled me. Although I did not have to do much of it myself, I could not help feeling that the effect on those who spent their lives doing it was deadening. Therefore, two separate offers I received to join the office of private practitioners of internal medicine were very tempting. But this would have meant answering night calls and keeping irregular hours incompatible with family and diplomatic life! Still, I did take on a few private consultations for women in the diplomatic corps. A female physician who spoke their language — Spanish — inspired their confidence. As Castillo Najera, the brilliant poet-physician Mexican ambassador, speaking of physicians in public life, used to say, "If you do not trust your physician, whom are you going to trust?"

International crises notwithstanding, the tension and the rivalry between Cordell Hull and Sumner Welles was ever present and never ending. Adolf was the buffer. In August 1943, the Kentucky feudist got his man. According to the story Adolf told me in strict confidence, two affidavits came into the possession of the Foreign Relations Committee of the Senate. These affidavits were made by two employees of the Pullman Railroad Car Company, claiming that Mr. Welles had made homosexual advances to one of them on the occasion of a train journey to Senator Harrison's funeral several years before. This material was circulated by Bullitt all over Washington, forcing the president to ask for Mr. Welles's resignation.

I maintained a discreet silence and did not talk the matter over with anyone. When Mrs. Hull brought the matter of the undersecretary's sexual perversion into the conversation on the occasion of the annual call the wife of an assistant secretary was required to make on the wife of the secretary of state, I was shocked and disgusted. Pleading ignorance, I changed the subject. The situation reached a climax on Sunday afternoon, August 22. Sumner informed Adolf that he was taking the night train to Bar Harbor and that Adolf was to take charge until Mr. Hull's return from Quebec three days later.

Adolf pleaded with Sumner to remain until Mr. Hull's return, urging him to take a mission to the Soviet Union, so that a graceful exit would be possible and everyone's face could be saved. Sumner refused, claiming he would have no political support, but insisted that his departure be kept secret. Adolf was left acting secretary for sixty hours and succeeded in keeping this cat in the bag until Drew Pearson leaked the news on Tuesday. We heard on Tuesday that Sumner had spent Saturday evening with Drew Pearson. I often wondered about the relationship between the diplomat and the journalist. Did Pearson have the power of blackmail over Welles?

Mr. Hull returned on Thursday and proposed two men, both over seventy, for the position of undersecretary. The president turned them both down. He was furious with Hull and with Bullitt—the latter was never received at the White House again.

One month later, on a Saturday evening, the news of the appointment of Ed Stettinius as undersecretary came over the radio. Adolf heard that Mr. Hull was going out of town on Sunday and asked him about the appointment of Stettinius. "I hardly know him," was the reply. This was at 7:00 P.M.; the official announcement was made at nine. Mr. Hull did not call Adolf and presumably would not have called him had they not met in the hall. He just slipped away, leaving Adolf acting secretary once more with no instructions.

I was incensed. A plague on both their houses! A third-class intern in a third-class hospital would not behave in such an irresponsible manner. Thinking as a physician, it seemed to me that the question of possible homosexuality was irrelevant to the conduct of foreign affairs—but I realized that people's prejudices and passions on this subject were so violent that a rumor, whether true or false, was damning to the reputation of the subject and furnished an occasion for blackmail. I realized also that Sumner's pose of the haughty, imperturbable diplomat who never removed his coat either mentally or physically meant that if he broke form, he could only collapse. Adolf had told me of occasions when Sumner had invited him for a drink and, after several shots of whiskey, become quite incoherent, so that Adolf was obliged to lead him by hand to his chauffeur.

It did not seem right that Adolf should work for an unscrupulous and ungrateful man like Sumner or keep patching up a selfish, diffident old man like Mr. Hull who trusted no one and was overjealous of his reputation.

Still, Adolf maintained his equanimity. Commenting on Sumner's resignation, he sighed, "It is a top-rank personal tragedy of Greek proportions."

In order to relieve the tension, from time to time Adolf brought out the Dinosaur.

The Dinosaur, as everyone knew, lived in the Smithsonian. At times, Adolf explained to me and to the children, the poor creature became seized with a desire to see the world. Out he would come, scattering glass everywhere.

He walked down Pennsylvania Avenue lifting his feet carefully to avoid injuring anyone. He was not malicious—just mischievous, enjoying his little jokes.

The fountain in front of the Federal Reserve Building was his favorite resting-place. As Harold Ickes came through the door reviling an unfortunate guard because Ickes had been stuck in the elevator, the Dinosaur picked him up, gently, ever so gently, by the seat of his trousers and dunked him in the fountain. A few minutes later, Bill Bullitt came along in a black limousine. As he stepped out, the Dinosaur picked him up also, and into the fountain he went. As Bullitt and Ickes spluttered, the personnel of the Federal Reserve Bank crowded the windows trying to suppress fits of giggles behind expressions of appropriate consternation. The Dinosaur rose to a standing position and walked quietly back to the Smithsonian.

There were other victims also—Felix Frankfurter, Dean Acheson...

Through the winter and spring of 1944, the greater part of Adolf's energies was concentrated on preparations for the civil-aviation conference. At this time there were two dramatic incidents for me: D-Day and the visit of Count Sforza.

The family, of course, knew nothing about the preparations for the invasion of France. Adolf told me later that since these had been primarily military plans, he had tried not to become involved, so as not to be a recipient of information concerning troop movements.

On June 6, 1944, when the announcement of the landing in France came over the radio, the children and I were quietly shelling peas from the garden. We were thrilled, overcome with the drama, the daring of this great adventure. How remote it seemed. Yet as in olden times we, the women and the children behind the lines, were the conservers of land and food for the morrow.

The meeting with Sforza came about because Adolf insisted that the Italian people had the right to make their own decision about the type of government they wanted and Sforza should make his case in his own country. This view was in opposition to Winston Churchill's romantic dream of reestablishing the Italian monarchy and the State Department's hesitation to take sides.

When Adolf's view prevailed, Sforza, before leaving, spent an evening alone with us. In the cellar, I discovered a bottle of Lachrima Christi, an Italian wine, which he greatly appreciated. I found him to be a fine gentleman, full of vigor and clearheaded. A brilliant conversationalist, he claimed that Winston Churchill was not intelligent. Whereupon I asked him to define intelligence. "Intelligence," said he, "consists of an imaginative and sensitive appreciation of the future." (According to that, Adolf ought to be the most intelligent man in the world.)

Sforza said Winston Churchill was not intelligent because he still thought of the British Empire as the center of the universe, not as the British Commonwealth.

Wine was a subject for conversation on another occasion at a dinner given by the Soviet delegation at the time of the preparations for the civil-aviation conference. Since, alas, I do not speak Russian, I struggled to find a subject for small talk. It was a hot August evening, and the Russians were serving sweet Crimean wine. "There are, I suppose, many kinds of wine grown around the Black Sea," I said innocently. "Dry ones also?"

"Of course, of course."

Whereupon an unfortunate junior officer was sent off to fetch a bottle of "dry Crimean wine." He reappeared an hour later with a bottle of wine even sweeter than the first. What could I say? Just smile a wan smile.

Adolf did better—he beat one of the Russian officers at a chess game.

At the last minute, the Russians withdrew their delegation.

The conference opened in Chicago in November 1944. Adolf was chairman. The negotiations were particularly difficult. Pan American Airways and British Overseas Air Company were fighting to divide the world between them, excluding all other nations and smaller companies. Senator Brewster, although a member of the United States delegation, was lobbying for Pan American Airways, undermining the position of the United States delegates.

I remained in Washington, taking the mail plane every four or five days to spend twenty-four hours with Adolf. It was a long, dreary flight and an uncomfortable stay. The wind around the Stevens Hotel blew icy gusts. We knew no one in Chicago. Occasionally, when I could pry Adolf loose, we went to the art museum. The Picassos were our only consolation.

Agreement on a compromise, offered by Canada, appeared within reach, when the news came that Hull had resigned and Stettinius had been appointed secretary of state. Adolf, in the reorganization of the department, was abandoned, left in midair with no position, no authority. FDR was in Warm Springs.

The British cabinet met on November 30, intending to accept the Canadian compromise; they were informed by Lord Swinton, the chairman of the British delegation, that the conference had adjourned. For three days, Adolf continued on his nerve, sustained by the resolve of his brother Rudolf, the tender and loving care of Fiorello, and my presence. A letter over the president's signature finally arrived, dated December 4 and stating that Adolf was still chairman of the conference.

In the closing plenary session Adolf summarized the measures that the members of the convention had agreed upon and that ensured freedom of the air. (They continued in effect until the rash of hijackings began.) My eyes were filled with tears as Adolf concluded, "If I take the wings of the morning, and dwell in the uttermost parts of the sea; Even there shall thy hand lead me, and thy right hand shall hold me" (Psalm 139:9–10).

When Adolf returned to Washington, he was sick at heart as I had never seen him. He felt betrayed. During the final days of the Chicago conference, the president had offered to appoint him our ambassador to Brazil, but he had declined, feeling he could not accept at gunpoint.

Being the man he was, however, he did not allow himself to become embittered; he accepted encouragement from both the president and Nelson Rockefeller, who said that one cannot refuse to serve in wartime and that the embassy in Brazil, in spite of the manner in which the offer had been made, could be an important channel for furthering inter-American cooperation — as indeed it proved to be.

Adolf and I always talked things over, but we had great respect for each other's individual decisions, unilaterally made but cooperatively executed. All through the New York–Washington shuttle in 1938, I had listened and tried to adjust our family life to Adolf's desire to be in two places at once and to undertake too many responsibilities, until we both finally agreed to move me and the family to Washington. But this time I took a more active part. I urged Adolf to accept the ambassadorship, feeling that a change of scene was essential and that this would be a situation in which we could work together in pursuing our country's interest in the hemisphere. So it turned out to be.

Brazil, 1945 ~

≈≈≈*28*

There was a little more than a month between the time Adolf decided to accept the assignment to Brazil and our departure. There was a great deal to be done. First of all, we were determined to learn a little Portuguese before landing. We were not going to limp along speaking a bastard hybrid tongue, interlarding an occasional Portuguese word into Spanish, which we both knew quite well. The navy provided us with a fine teacher, from whom we took ten lessons amid packing cases and last minute State Department business.

According to State Department regulars, 1945 was still the era of ceremonial diplomacy. Ambassadors were expected to ship their belongings by boat and to possess a vast amount of silverware and linens. The "post" report recommended silver tureens, platters, candelabra, place settings for forty, etc.; bed and table linen; pictures; and china and glassware for everyday use. The department had recently purchased some china and glassware for official parties.

As I was dismantling 4000 Nebraska Avenue, where we had been living, it was obvious that in spite of four years of official entertaining in Washington, our "ambassadorial equipment" was deficient. I contemplated taking some place settings from Great Barrington. Adolf was adamant! "This is a short-range assignment. We have a return ticket as soon as the war is over. Not one spoon is to be removed from Konkapot. That is our refuge, and it remains intact."

So I settled the knife-and-fork problem by purchasing some discarded metalware from the Cosmopolitan Club in New York. I did take a number of books, bibelots, family portraits, and the like, since we were informed that the embassy was a vast caravanserai, never before inhabited by a family. Indeed, our predecessor, Jefferson Caffrey, was a bachelor, and so was *his* predecessor, Mr. Morgan, but we were going as an American family.

The girls were to stay with friends in Washington until the end of the school year. They were excited at the prospect of going to Brazil after Daddy showed us pictures of the great falls of Iguaçú, greater than Niagara. (Actually, we never did get to the falls until later trips south many years later.) Peter and Miss Hagen, a nurse and a friend, would join us when Daddy returned to Washington for consultation within a month or two.

As the time of departure approached, I became overwhelmed. Since the air force was sending us down on a C-54, we could take a lot of things, but they all had to be packed in cartons. Adolf was too busy to help and, of course, still unhappy about the Chicago betrayal. The government at the time did not provide packers. Finally my boss, Thomas Parran, surgeon general of the Public Health Service, came to my rescue. "I have had a lot of experience—we regulars, like diplomats, move every two years." He was most efficient; by Inauguration Day all was ready.

Adolf took us to Franklin Roosevelt's fourth inauguration—Alice, Beatrice, Dean Mildred Thompson of Vassar College, and myself. We were among the few admitted to the White House grounds for the ceremony, and we stood on a canvas sheet stretched over the wet grass under the portico. Bishop Dunn gave a beautiful prayer. Henry Wallace swore Truman in as vice-president with a loud, clear voice. Supreme Court Justice Harlan Stone swore the president in.

There had been a great deal of talk about the president's health. Although in the campaign speeches, which I had heard over the radio, his voice seemed to have lost none of its vigor, today, he *looked sick*. His speech was not a very good one—I found my mind wandering. I did not feel that I was compelled to listen, as I always had before. When FDR shook hands with Truman, his face broke into a smile, but I could not feel the vigor and the warmth of other days. Was this merely weariness? Was there a disease process going on? Was he in pain? He seemed to get up on his feet with more difficulty than I had remembered.

It was going to be a grim period—but how could it be otherwise? He was the symbol of so much to so many of the world's peoples—no one else had been able to take his place. The president had had, and we hoped still had, the capacity to be a very great leader—we could not have elected a man like Dewey, a man who never would, never could, have that depth and vision. Adolf did not comment on the ceremony except to say we must put together the spare parts of a faith in the American tradition.

After a brief cup of tea in the White House, not wishing to intrude further on the president, we went over to the State Department, where Adolf, with our three children present, was sworn in as ambassador by Justice Bob Jackson.

Two days later, Adolf, the American ambassador to Brazil, his wife, and his secretary, Miss Louella Livengood, boarded an Air Transport Command C-54 with their goods and chattels.

This turn of events amused me very much when I realized that here I was the wife of an ambassador, entering just the life for which my mother, in her foolish way, had brought me up. I suppose no experience is wasted, and having seen this life close at hand, I had no illusions about the glamour. There is plenty of hard work, and one gets d——d tired of being on parade all the time. However, at that moment in the world's history, Adolf and I seemed to be cast for that part, and we would, I thought, play it to the best of our ability. It is true that we fitted the part in the sense that we would provide for the Brazilians an example of American family and intellectual life.

Our first stop was the air-force base at Borinquén, on the western tip of Puerto Rico, one of the stops on the southern route. About a hundred planes were there overnight, and most of them went roaring out before dawn. We came on the field at 7:00 A.M., just as the sun was breaking through a pink cloud on the horizon. Two planes went out, flying together, their wings tilted, circling like great birds, dark against the light clouds. I was thrilled, thinking that thanks to Adolf's work at the Chicago conference, flying for peaceful purposes would now become available to all peoples.

The following day we flew over a lot of water and came upon the swamps of Guiana. Here the earth is void and without form—the part of the world the Lord forgot. Devil's Island consists of three small islands with some barracks about seven miles from shore. One hates to think of what men could do to other men—and no doubt *do* do—in a set up of this kind.

The second night was spent at the American airbase at Atkinson Field in British Guiana.

As we were getting farther away, the snake-pit aspect of life in Washington began to recede, and we spoke of many warm personal friends. I knew that many people loved Adolf and me, and I tried to assure him that he had not cast his bread upon the waters in vain.

The third day we came upon the mouth of the Amazon at sunset. It took an hour to cross the main branch of the river, the boundary of which melted into clouds in the west—a seemingly infinite expanse of water. There was a glorious pink cloud shaped like a gigantic Benvenuto Cellini cup in the sky, and all around us were ever-changing mountains of clouds, which we flew through or around. We felt like the lords of creation, and at the same time, before the immensity of space, we could but echo the psalmist, "O Lord, what is man that thou art mindful of him?"

That evening we hit the tropics with a thump, like stepping into a hot-house. Everyone sat in a continuous drip. But the night was comfortable for sleeping. The American airbase at Belém (Pará) had about 670 men. It was in the middle of a swamp; the barracks were made of concrete and were screened. The young consul in charge, a Bostonian named Kidder, had attended one of our parties for young foreign-service officers in Washington. His wife was joining him soon, and I heard later that they did a fine job.

On the fourth day out of Washington we arrived in Santa Cruz, the army airport for Rio. It was a luminous, brilliant day. There, no platform or landing stairs being available for the C-54, the sergeant finally put down his little rickety ladder ("Since you insist, ma'am"). Did he think I could jump down six feet or more to the ground? We descended in front of any number of gold-braided officers and spoke words of greetings in Portuguese. Fortunately, neither of us was timorous and the wind did not blow my skirts over my head. We were conveyed to a small plane and brilliantly piloted to the city by Luis Sampaio. It seemed as if every Brazilian we ever knew was at Santos Dumont, the Rio commercial airport, and they all broke into applause as we stepped down from the plane (on a proper gangplank this time!).

Adolf's view of ceremonies in general was different from mine; his principal desire was to hide. I loved this ceremony, especially the tremendous spray of orchids I received from the minister of protocol. We were whisked off in his car and arrived at the embassy residence—"a majestic pile," Adolf called it, "which would do credit to a *nouveau riche*." It was larger and more desolate than I had anticipated. Carleton and Elizabeth Smith, who had made a brilliant career first as fellows of a private Brazilian foundation and later as cultural attachés for the United States government, came for dinner. Their presence was the only relief from the tomblike atmosphere created by former Ambassador Caffrey's housekeeper—an Irish woman who never moved an inch without locking the door behind her, explaining that Brazilians stole everything from silver to blotting papers. She was dead wrong, of course!

The morning following our arrival we found that the house's new reservoir, installed by American engineers, was dry. The Rio fire department promptly appeared, hauling a couple of tanks up the mountain, and dumped water into the reservoir, observing that they had warned the engineers that the spring they had planned to depend on was not reliable!

Adolf would have sold the whole show for fifteen cents on the dollar and a ticket home, as he put it, but I felt sure that things would turn out all right. He went down to the chancery, and I started getting our cartons unpacked and putting a few family photographs around. In the late afternoon, we went to an antique shop and purchased an eighteenth-century-colonial polychrome figure of Saint Anne holding little Mary's hand. The colors were faded, and they have faded even more through the years, but the feeling of Anne, the loving teacher, remains. We placed her on the mantelpiece of the embassy library (she later came back to New York with us). Then we went to the beach and stood hand in hand against the pounding surf.

The following evening we were invited to dine at the home of the distinguished jurist Saboia de Medeiros, whose son was a Jesuit priest who had been our guest in Washington. He became a great friend, and Adolf helped him with the organization of a technical school in São Paulo.

The Saboias had a beautiful apartment overlooking the bay. Law books bound in rich leathers lined the walls up to the ceiling. As we were leaving after dinner a tremendous thunderstorm broke out, the water coming down in sheets. Power went out, and on reaching the embassy we found the dragon housekeeper stuck in the elevator between floors. What a joke! The staff and I could hardly refrain from giggling. Served her right. She left the next day.

The second evening was spent at the home of Assis de Chateaubriand, a peripatetic journalist we had met in Washington. The banker Drault Ernani and Austregesilo de Atheiyde, the chief editor of *O'Jornal*, a Rio newspaper, did the honors until Chateaubriand arrived an hour later. The house was one of the few remaining private houses on Copacabana Beach, already crowded with high-rise apartments. It was dark — the fine Portinari paintings on the wall were almost invisible. Chateaubriand arrived at last, volubly recommending in Portuguese, incomprehensible French, and pidgin English that we read his newspaper, *O'Jornal.* This I did every morning at breakfast, and it improved my vocabulary no end. Chateau, as he was called, and we found ourselves mutually very *simpatico*, and he became and remained a powerful, staunch friend of the American ambassador.

This meeting encouraged Adolf to carry out his plan of holding a press conference — an unprecedented "happening," which was well received in Rio. Jefferson Caffrey, an able career diplomat, had accomplished a great deal for the United States by diverting President Vargas and the powerful Brazilian generals away from the Axis; they became our allies and sent a Brazilian expeditionary force overseas. But he enveloped himself in a pile of bricks, entertaining formally and ostentatiously, extending a limp hand to those who looked for an *abraço*, the traditional embrace, and a friendly smile.

Adolf and I were determined to communicate directly with people. The Irish-dragon housekeeper was replaced by Dona Maria, a Portuguese, who had been housekeeper to Mr. Morgan, Caffrey's predecessor. Here we were picking up an old tradition; Mr. Morgan had been a beloved American ambassador who had been warm and friendly to the Brazilians for twenty-five years and was buried in the Rio cemetery. Fortunately, Dona Maria spoke French; it took some time for me to become fluent in Portuguese. Together we managed fourteen servants and made what Adolf called this "Atlantic City hotel off-season" into a home where people liked to come.

On the first weekend, Adolf and I drove through the Forest of Tijuca, following a little brook, where a stone table and stone stools for picnickers suggested a perfect setting for gnomes. Alone together and very happy, we climbed a winding path through the shade to the rock of Tijuca and at the end of it went up the stone steps the Brazilians had cut into the rock for the benefit of Alfred, king of the Belgians, whose reputation as an Alpinist was much insulted by this attention. But we, the *"povo"* (people), were grateful to come so easily upon the glorious view of Rio and all its surroundings. I know now where Satan tempted Our Lord—I suspect he must have climbed every peak around Rio!

We had sent the car back and were expecting to take the *bonde*, the trolley, at the foot of the hill. But as we were waiting, the car of General Hayes Kroner, the military attaché, appeared, and we were driven home. At that time, riding on the *bonde* without a jacket was forbidden. An ambassador in shirt sleeves would have been refused a ride! How embarrassing for all concerned!!

The second weekend provided a different kind of adventure. We were invited to spend the night in La Casa de Pedras, the house of Drault and Miriam Ernani. This was like taking a deep plunge into cold water. The other guests were all *Nortistas* (from the north of Brazil), all talking as fast and furiously as Chateaubriand. We clung to Dona Miriam, whose French helped us through. In true Brazilian style, we were given the master bedroom. Rudyard Kipling's book *Brazilian Sketches* was on the night table. Had our hosts read the book?, I wondered. They knew no English, but Kipling's remarks about Brazilians were to the point:

> For the Brazilian has not yet reached the impersonality of ideal business! If he likes you as an individual, he will do more than anything for you. If he doesn't he will do less than nothing. If he knows little about you, but perceives that you have manners and a few trifles of that sort, he will wait and see and he has heaps of leisure.[1]

[1] Rudyard Kipling, *Brazilian Sketches* (New York: Doubleday, Doran & Co., 1940).

[164]

After this we tried to settle down in the embassy, but at the end of three weeks we were to be off again—Adolf was a delegate to the inter-American conference at Chapultepec near Mexico City, and I was going to see the children in Washington. Still, I felt that we had made a good start. American prestige was at its height. Brazilians respect intellectuals. They knew Adolf by reputation and were prepared to like him. This gave him a chance to be himself and to reach out to them. They were also prepared to like me because I had a French education and was an American professional woman. So it turned out that both of us were the right people at the right moment.

We left just after Mardi Gras. In 1945, Mardi Gras was a really happy, nonviolent festival in which alcohol played only a small part. People danced the samba in the streets in costumes that they might have been preparing over the past year. The laundry at the embassy was filled with billowing skirts that our laundress had assembled. I remember particularly a man trying to board a *bonde* without paying the fare and the joking parley between him and the conductor going on for two blocks as he ran along beside the car. He finally desisted. Everyone along the sidewalk was laughing good-naturedly.

≈ 29

We flew north in an army plane. En route, we spent one night at the base in Dutch Guiana. It was pouring rain and the Dutch ladies who had come to a party at the base in evening dress, *très correctes* and very stiff, were having a hard time puddle jumping, or at least trying to. In the morning I thought I heard an oriole as we were off for Panama. Crossing the Orinoco, Adolf went up into the cockpit, trying to picture Sir Walter Raleigh's journey on that great river three hundred years earlier.

Stopping at Curaçao, we drove around the town. Every little corrugated hut along the road is painted once a year, by law. A physician told me, however, that in spite of their attention to cleanliness, the Dutch there shut their eyes to venereal disease.

The oil refinery is tremendous. The army people and Adolf spent their time trying unsuccessfully to figure out why the Germans had not knocked it out at the beginning of the war. Adolf had been instrumental in getting some troops on the island previous to obtaining the Netherlands and Venezuelan governments' consent when German submarines were spotted nearby.

We flew on to Panama, coming into sight of land on the exact minute when our pilot, Captain Mathieson, had planned that we should. Since Panama was his home base, this was a matter of professional pride.

The next morning I was Cinderella; my private plane turned into a pumpkin as Adolf flew off to Mexico without me. But I managed to hitchhike on another plane to Miami, where Charlie Sprooks, the chief of protocol, had a train reservation for me. Certainly being a VIP, a darling of the Air Transport Command, thanks to Adolf, was the most wonderful way to travel in wartime, bumbling along on an international scale! Which map shall we slide off today?

In Washington, I saw Alice and Beatrice, who were staying with a friend, and collected Peter for the return journey to Brazil with Adolf, who had come to Washington with the Brazilian foreign minister to consult with the president. Again we traveled in style, courtesy of the Air Transport Command.

On this trip, coming into Atkinson field, Peter, now seven, and I went into the nose to watch the landing. I was buckled into the little swivel seat, and Peter sat on my lap. It was just at dusk. As the darkness closed in, all was gray. We were like a point in space—indeed, exactly that: We had position only as evidenced by the calculations the navigator was concluding.

As it grew darker, we were able to see the stars and the first-quarter moon through the skylight above our heads. Soon we saw a ribbon of water and were told that seventeen miles beyond that lay the field. Peter was thrilled. "Hold on tight, Ma." We reminded ourselves that we had sat this way when we cantered on Apollo, my horse, when Peter was a wee boy.

Adolf was leaning over the radio operator's table touching us. I thought of the Virgin of Chartres with the child on her lap. Here we were, all three together flying through the firmament, very close to God, it seemed to me. We strained our eyes through space. Peter saw a little light below us—people do live in scattered spots in the jungle. After about fifteen minutes, we saw a glow over the horizon, and in another few seconds, the control tower flashed. Peter and I counted—one, two, three, four, five. We were on the way to earth, to things concrete and defined.

We all relaxed a bit—man cannot endure the contemplation of the infinite very long. In a few minutes, there would be people, new to us, individuals carrying on routine daily tasks. We would wash, eat, and sleep.

We crossed another narrow ribbon of water and saw the runway, long and straight, all lighted up like Fifth Avenue. We circled over the barracks and the planes on the ground, coming back to the runway, gliding down with great precision and smoothness, with just a little bump as the big ship touched the ground.

Putt-putting along, we met "Follow Me"—the ridiculous little jeep that guided the big bird, now so clumsy, to its stopping place on the ground.

We were met, had a shower, ate a good steak. The base colonel suggested a murder movie, but fortunately, we were too late for it. We had a little Donald Duck in the outdoor theater. People laughed at the film, but this was of no concern to me. I had been in the spacious firmament on high, and I was going back tomorrow.

It was mid-March when we got back to the embassy. We were both busy trying to communicate with Brazilians on all levels. To our dismay we found that a number of embassy secretaries had been in Brazil more than a year and still spoke no Portuguese, nor had they made an effort to learn. We were continuing our studies with a private tutor, who came for lunch at the embassy every day, conversing with Adolf if he had the time, with me, and with the girls when they arrived. Adolf recommended to his staff that they follow his example. Being of a mean disposition, I arranged the seating at diplomatic dinner parties so that our non-Portuguese-speaking staff people were exposed to Brazilians whose English was nonexistent!

When the news came to us of President Roosevelt's death, we had been in Brazil a bare three months. For us, Adolf especially, this represented not just the loss of a world leader, but a deeply felt personal loss. We grieved, but we were not alone. Those Brazilians with whom we had established a personal relationship came to the residence, mourning the man whom they also had considered their personal friend. Many of them had seen him passing through Rio in 1936. University students carrying a black flag marched silently up to the embassy, and people came in droves to sign the chancery register—those who could not write made a cross.

Adolf organized a memorial service in the embassy garden. I spent the morning getting the chairs and the microphone set up. Suddenly, I heard *plop, plop, plop!* It was breadfruit crashing out of the tree, spreading a gelatinous mess over the driveway. Suppose this should happen in the middle of the service! Swiftly the gardener clambered up the tree, machete in hand, hacking off the ripe fruit, while another man picked up the mess in a wheelbarrow.

The service began with the Protestant minister saying a prayer and the reading of passages from the Bible. The Brazilian army band played. Adolf recited: "I will lift up mine eyes unto the hills from whence cometh my help—my help cometh from the Lord who made heaven and earth." Weeping, we turned our eyes to the Christ on the Corcovado, mindful of the artist Portinari's little maid who cried out, "If only God had taken me instead of Roosevelt!"

Alice and Beatrice did not reach Brazil until early June; Adolf brought them down from Washington, where he had been called back for a brief consultation. Then the embassy became a family concern in which we each had a role. Peter attended the American school; we thought a Brazilian school would require too great an adjustment for him. His Portuguese was limited but enthusiastic—"*Vamos a praya agora,*" shouted from the top balcony to the garage below when it was time to go to the beach, or "*Joga bola encima,*"to the gardener if his ball dropped over on the other side. Sometimes a couple of two- to three-foot *jacara* (alligators), gift of the director of the new motor company, appeared in the dining room—Peter's contribution to a diplomatic lunch party.

Beatrice, now fourteen, attended Miss Bennett's school, a bilingual Brazilian school started by the Methodist missionaries and attended by Brazilian girls. She also joined the Girl Guides, where she made friends whom she sees to this day. Alice, now sixteen, had the great good fortune to be invited by Portinari to his studio, where she spent the mornings not only learning to draw—he was insistent that technique was an essential preliminary to creation—but listening to endless political discussions between Portinari and "the Barão Tamandare," a jovial cartoonist and satiric writer.

I was most anxious to participate in Brazilian medicine. After visiting various hospitals, I applied to the Santa Casa, a combination of hospital and asylum for the aged or abandoned. There was one in every Portuguese colony, established by the Infantas, daughters of the Portuguese kings. The one in Rio is a beautiful old building whose corridors are lined with eighteenth-century blue tiles, all of different designs. The Sisters of Saint Vincent de Paul, many of them French, their kind faces framed by their large white "cornettes," are in charge. The twenty-bed wards did not allow for privacy, but the large windows open to the tropical gardens and to the street gave good cross-ventilation.

Unfortunately, many wards were under the jurisdiction of individual professors of medicine who paid little attention to each other and sometimes left the service in the hands of incompetent aides. I was fortunate in being assigned to a medical ward run by a young man, Murillo Belchior (a good friend to this day), who had recently returned from a medical residency in the university hospital in Ann Arbor, Michigan. I worked on the ward every morning when we were in town, learning a great deal of medicine and coming to know and love Brazilians in all walks of life.

Paulo Cesar de Andrade, my mentor at the Santa Casa, represented the best in his generation—a devoted and skillful surgeon, gay, charming, a brilliant conversationalist. French trained, he knew that the American era had come and must be adapted to Brazilian needs, that Brazilians had to scale down their ideas and spend less money on equipment until they learned how to use it. He had organized a modern surgical service within the Santa Casa, staffed by three of the few available trained nurses, staffed by competent surgeons of his generation and ready to receive young men returning from a residency in the United States. This service also organized refresher courses for graduate physicians. I asked a number of physicians to prepare lectures on public-health problems in Brazil and included one by a United States public-health sanitarist on the building of privies. The series of lectures, including a chapter on the use of penicillin that I wrote (a new subject in 1945), was published and distributed to physicians in the interior.

On a wet August morning, as he was driving along Praia Flamengo, Paulo Cesar's car skidded into a lamp post; he suffered multiple fractures and was never to come out of coma. Along the corridors of the Santa Casa, leaning against the portraits of former *dignissimo provedor* (trustees), men and women wept: Guillerme Guinle, banker and millionaire; Assis Chateaubriand; Carmen Saavedra, beautiful and brilliant; scores of "notables"; scores of poor people; all sorts and conditions of men and women on whom he had operated, for whom he had cared with skill, and to whom he had given of himself without stint.

August is winter in Rio—damp and rainy, the temperature dropping below sixty degrees. There was a fireplace in the embassy library, which we did not need to use but which delighted the mother superior of the Santa Casa, a Bretonne, when she came to tea. But for infants living in the *favelas* (slum areas), a wet August afternoon could be very cold indeed. On such an afternoon, Miss Hagen, a pediatric nurse who had taken care of Beatrice and Peter and who had come to Brazil as our guest, came in from the small private pediatric clinic in a poor neighborhood where she had been working. She rushed into the library in a state of righteous indignation. "These poor children are shivering with cold!"

The following day I asked Dona Geronima to come for tea. Dona Geronima was an older, unmarried lady who belonged to one of the aristocratic families of Rio and was known for her good works and organizing ability. She brought her niece by marriage, Elisa Lynch. Miss Hagen explained that infants needed blankets, shirts, and diapers. Following this little meeting, Elisa Lynch organized a group of ladies who came to the embassy ballroom once a week and made lay-ettes. Adolf laughed gently, "You're doing what my mother did in the parson-age. This is the ladies' sewing circle."

So it turned out to be. The women got donations of materials and sewing machines. The embassy provided a small collation—*cafezinho* and a few cookies. The whirring of the sewing machines carried through the open windows down to the pool, where Peter was teasing the *jacara* to come up on land. Other am-bassadresses came, apparently all proficient in the use of sewing machines, while the Baroneza de Bonfim and I sewed by hand. This was to be a Brazilian show, and I only put in a brief appearance from time to time.

The volunteer as we know her in the United States is not indigenous to Latin America. People predicted that the group would dissolve after our departure. They were dead wrong. Thanks to the energy and dedication of Elisa Lynch, they became the Organizacacaõ das Voluntarias, which persists to this day with chap-ters in all the major cities of Brazil, providing garments and layettes for the needy and hospital linen—in some cases also branching out into vocational training.

An unexpected dividend from the sewing circle came in the form of an in-vitation to a special mass at the church of Nosa Senhora da Gloria on August 15—the feast of the Assumption. Nosa Senhora de Gloria is the small baroque church perched on an elevation commanding the bay. I sat with Dona Geronima in the gallery. Right above the altar in the chancel were the prince and the princess, descendants of the former emperor of Brazil, along the aisle, the Irmandade, members of a religious society, with swords and velvet cloaks, each carrying a big candle. Next to them pressed the people—a black man gazing at the altar and a woman of pure Portuguese descent with sculptured features and a tower-ing coiffure.

Working in the Santa Casa was not my only medical activity. From time to time I received calls I could not refuse, although, of course, I was not licensed to practice medicine in Brazil. One call I remember particularly—a youth about fif-teen years old came to the embassy gate saying that his father had sent him to beg me to see the boy's sister, who was very sick. I followed him for several blocks to an old one-story building on a side street. A young girl opened the door. The father and the mother, both light-olive-skinned, sat by a bed where a dying black girl was lying. Alas, she had tuberculosis meningitis, and there was noth-ing I or any doctor could do. But not yet accustomed to Brazilian ways and fresh from life in Washington, I was impressed by the fact that this girl was indeed the daughter of the house and that her skin color was immaterial.

On another occasion, at about nine o'clock one evening, when Adolf was away, the guard at the gate called. Did I want to receive two young men? Who were they? Dr. Niemeyer (the neurologist who had taken care of Paulo Cesar) and another physician.

They came up to the library, and we discussed the possibility of operating on an infant with pyloric stenosis. The infant was the son of one of their colleagues. Was surgery possible on one so young? I was able to reassure them that this was not only possible, but a well-established procedure in the United States, and I joined them the next morning in the operating room, where a successful operation was performed.

As I extended my medical associations, Adolf used his teaching skills with profit and enjoyment. The press conference, the first of which had been an unprecedented event, became a custom sponsored by the dean of the press corps, Herbert Moses, who was able to extricate Adolf from a Portuguese sentence when necessary, although by August both of us had become able to participate in most conversations.

These meetings with the press came to be called *sabatinis* (seminars) and were enjoyed by both the newspapermen and Adolf. Other *sabatinis* that were genuinely seminars took place at the residence, where a group of about ten young men gathered at weekly intervals to discuss economics and political science. One of these, Paulo Egidio Martins, president of the students' union at the time, was elected governor of the state of São Paulo in the 1970s.

≈ 30

We wanted to know all Brazil—not just Rio. The only one of our colleagues who had traveled was the Canadian ambassador, Jean Desey. Travel was not easy —there were few roads and few trains. We were lucky—the United States Air Force and the Civil Aviation Board each had a four-seater Beechcraft, which could be used by the ambassador for official business.

We flew to the interior of Goiás, to Minas Gerais, to the falls of Paulo Afonso, to the Amazon, and to the south. I would go along on most of the trips; sometimes Adolf would take one of the girls in my place. Each trip increased our knowledge of the country and showed us further possibilities for United States assistance to Brazil.

Life in Brazil was much simpler in 1945 than it is in 1980 and depended a great deal on personal relations. Apolonio Sales, the minister of agriculture, was a frequent visitor at the embassy. He had straight, coarse hair like an Indian, negroid features, olive skin, and burning dark eyes. He was a *caboclo*, as people of mixed blood are called in Brazil. He had a dream, an impossible dream, which he communicated to the American ambassador. The São Francisco River in northern Brazil pursues a tortuous course, the waters dropping over a great fall in a desert land — an unused potential for electric power. Adolf, taking Alice and the minister along, flew to this remote area, called Lapa, inhabited by a few Indians and a few missionaries. On his return Adolf was convinced of the feasibility of harnessing the river for power, and he was able to obtain funds through direct contact with Washington for the building of a Brazilian "TVA," furnishing light and power to the northeast of Brazil (including Maceió, where I served as Project Hope physician twenty-nine years later).

Another expedition took us to Anápolis in Goiás. Walking around Rio, Adolf had noticed that the price of rice was going up and people were complaining that it was in short supply. The rice grown in Goiás, we were told, could not reach Rio owing to a shortage of gasoline for trucks. We flew to Anápolis, which is a small town in that territory. As we circled the airfield, crowds of people came running out, so unusual was the appearance of an airplane. (Today there is a daily service between Anápolis and São Paulo.) While Adolf was ascertaining that indeed there was an abundant crop of rice for which no transportation was available, I visited a small, well-run hospital founded by a group of Protestant medical missionaries. We spent the night with a dear friend, an American journalist named Virginia Prewett, who was farming in Goiás.

Virginia's house was made of bricks, red bricks. Red mud was all around; inside the house an open brick firebox, waist high, for heating and cooking. As we snuggled in bed to keep warm at night, a full moon lighting a large expanse of desert land, the silence was broken by the barking of coyotes in the distance. It made us feel as if we were part of a surrealist painting.

When we returned to Rio two days later, Adolf managed to get some gasoline for the trucks, so that rice moved again into the big cities.

Our greatest adventure was the trip to the Amazon. No American ambassador had ever been to the Amazon; in fact, Desey, the Canadian, was probably the only ambassador who had ever ventured so far from Rio. Before the war, few Brazilians traveled within Brazil; there were no roads, and coastwise vessels were few.

The expedition to the Amazon included several members of the embassy staff. Santarém was our first stop on the way up the Amazon coming from Belém.

It is a beautiful little town on an elevation at the bend of the river. We met a fine bunch of young health visitors from SESP (Serviceo Especial de Saude Publica, the government public-health service) who were giving a six-month course to young girls from the interior, teaching them routine sanitary and health care: boiling the water before drinking it, cleanliness, building privies—all good missionary work!

In the afternoon we flew on to Belterra, the Ford plantation for the growth and cultivation of rubber trees, where we spent the night. Rubber trees grow wild in the jungle and are tapped by workers called *seringueros*, much as we tap sugar maples, but the yield is uncertain. Since the supply of rubber from the Far East had been cut off by the war, the Rubber Development Company, a United States government enterprise, had sponsored the Ford Motor Company in running a rubber plantation in the Amazon jungle.

Coming upon it from the air, we saw a neatly squared-off area of perhaps a square mile or two planted with single trees, where much of the vegetation had been cut down. As we landed, a factory whistle blew, indicating the end of the working day. Not that set times for work meant much to the Indians employed there, who came and went along intricate waterways in their canoes as they chose, disappearing as soon as they had earned a little money. They were the despair of the Ford manager, who had been with the company for many years and lived with his wife and other American personnel in suburban style, looking forward to his vacation home next year and unable to understand why Indians kept on disappearing into the malaria-ridden jungle notwithstanding good wages. There were perfect hybrid trees (Brazilian jungle root, East Indian trunk and foliage) planted in rows on cleared ground. There was a small hospital in an antiquated building, run by an American doctor, where the chief malady, tropical skin ulcers, was treated in a casual fashion.

Manaus was our next stop. The governor's palace, on a slight elevation, is screened, a necessary but unusual feature. Until recently the building had been the headquarters of a German firm, and it contained a modern bathroom fitted out with German fixtures. The authorities were very cordial, particularly the chief of police, a jolly mulatto with a blond, blue-eyed wife of northern-Italian descent. In fact, many of the people we met were of Italian descent and had been to Italy—but not to Rio! Before the war, a fleet of Italian steamers ran a regular service between Manaus and Mediterranean ports.

Our vice-consul, until recently a member of the Romance-language department of the University of Minnesota, joined us, and we were pleased to note his interest in Brazil and in his progress in learning Portuguese. We visited the charming opera house built in the late nineteenth century—*très précieux*, ornate and quite charming. The *salon de promenade* is painted Italian style, with scenes from the life of Guarani, the Amazonian Hiawatha.

In the evening we were taken to the country fair, said to be the first of its kind in the Amazon. After being officially received, Adolf went outside and shook hands and chatted with as many people as he could reach while I was being conducted around the exhibits. I admired a hammock on display, and to my great embarrassment, it was taken down and given to me as a present!

From Manaus, we flew to Pôrto Velho, in the territory of Guaporé, where the governor, a remarkable man, Aluizio Ferreira, had transformed the remains of an old construction camp into government offices, barracks, and a school. There we observed him holding court, trying to solve people's problems, both great and small, organizing young draftees to build roads and sanitation facilities. Our stay was celebrated with a parade—in clouds of brick-red dust shifting to saffron, sapphire, lemon yellow, emerald in the rays of the setting sun, several road tractors, a few cavalrymen with drawn swords, army draftees in blue jeans, and school children led by a couple of French nuns paraded past Governor Aluizio, the American ambassador, and his wife.

We spoke to some of the draftees later, particularly those who served at the banquet later, and to the French nuns—the teachers—"the real heroines of the frontier," as Adolf said. Was this where my beloved mademoiselle Mulot might have been, had her superiors permitted her to become a foreign missionary instead of a missionary at home? I wondered.

On that day we had been taken for a ride on the Madeira-Mamoré railroad, a one-track railroad circumventing the falls that divided the Madeira River in order to connect the Mamoré and the Beni Rivers, which come together to form the Madeira. The little engines were of 1890 vintage, shiny and freshly painted museum pieces, their parts hand-wrought in the railroad shops. We rode on a gasoline car the whole length of the track, from Pôrto Velho to Mamoré, stopping as people hailed the train to talk to Aluizio. It was hot—very hot—along the track. We were offered large chunks of juicy pineapple; never before or since have I tasted better pineapples.

We also stopped at an agricultural station, where a young *agronomo* was trying to grow rubber, his workers living in a communal building, sectioned off until such time as there were enough workers to make individual houses. Each person is provided with a mosquito net for his hammock, and Aluizio spent some time insisting to several individuals that they use them! The colony was also having dysentery trouble, so we arranged to have the SESP come up from Guaraja Mirim to give some help.

In order to try to understand what it was like to gather rubber in the jungle, we were fitted out with mosquito nets, anointed with insect repellent, and taken for a short walk along a *seringueros'* trail. It was dark, and after we stumbled for a few yards in the thick underbrush, amid clouds of insects, we were thankful to return to the open space. The rubber tapped from the trees is made into balls weighing about one hundred pounds each and rolled onto railroad cars for transportation to the Amazon. We were given a small ball about the size of a basketball, inscribed, "Nosa Senhora de Nazareth"; this was a native offering, which had been picked up from the river.

Arriving in Guaraja Mirim, we were billeted in the stationmaster's home, a modern building, one of six in a row with showers and toilets. There we were entertained at a most remarkable dinner party in the railroad station, where Aluizio's office was, up one flight of steep stairs. There were about twenty-four in our group: the pilots, the mayor, RDC personnel, the United States representative from Bolivia, and Aluizio. The dinner was cooked in one of the small houses across the way, under the supervision of the prefect's wife and carried across the hundred yards and up the stairs by the land guard, in spotless uniform. The menu included palmito soup, delicious Bolivian beef, rice of course, and a very fine cake with bright green icing, decorated with the Brazilian and American flags.

Aluizio never stopped trying to educate "his boys," the draftees. They were being taught reading and writing in the evenings. Tonight they were to learn something about waiting on tables. Adolf and I were instructed to direct the young men how to pass a plate on the left. This we were delighted to do, and the atmosphere became very jolly and informal. I could not take my eyes off one boy whose outer ears looked normal except for missing lobes. Upon inquiry I was informed that though he had been separated from his tribe at an early age, he had already been exposed to a tribal custom, the amputation of the earlobes.

(Recently the treatment of the Brazilian Indian population has come under much criticism. In 1945, we were told that there was little contact between the settlers and Indians living in the jungle.)

Mamoré was the far point of our journey. We were to return to Rio, stopping at the airport of Corumbá. Unfortunately, we were not flying in a Beechcraft with one of our regular pilots. Our craft was a Grumman amphibian manned by a bush pilot untutored in the use of instruments. He kept flying west into the sun, coming, to his great surprise, upon the Andes. It was too late to go on to Corumbá, so we landed in Santa Cruz, Bolivia. An ambassador is not supposed to land without permission in a country to which he is not accredited, so we hid in the bushes from the Brazilian air-force plane carrying General Moraes, the head of the Brazilian Expeditionary Force. It was landing, returning from an official visit to Peru.

We found a United States junior consul who put us up for the night, and we started off for Corumbá the following morning. It was a cloudless day. The air field was large, and there were no mountains; the bush pilot hit the ground with a thump, rose again, came down, could not control his landing, and went crashing into a barbed-wire fence. The barbed wire wound itself around the wheels of the plane, fortunately bringing it to a stop before it reached a steep bank where, had we gone over, the plane would have burst into flames.

The official Brazilian plane with General Moraes had already landed here, and the brass band tactfully refrained from playing as we walked, shaken and shamefaced, across the field. The Grumman, the pilot, and RDC personnel were abandoned to their fate while we bummed a ride on General Moraes's plane. We had a perfect flight into São Paulo, thanking God that we were alive.

≈ *31*

After V.J. Day, when Japan surrendered, ending World War II, we were anxious to bring Albert Spalding, the distinguished American violinist, to Brazil. "American cultural relations" were not part of State Department vocabulary at this time. Having granted priorities to a French cultural mission (far from pro-American) during wartime, the department declared that the Spalding visit would not help the war (now over) and delayed a visa for several weeks. Finally Albert and Mary Spalding arrived.

Albert had just returned from the war, where he had worked for the Office of War Information, and he had not given a concert for two years; indeed, he had hardly played the violin at all. As he practiced on the top balcony of the residence, Mary, Adolf, and I listened anxiously. At the Cultura, a small musical society, he was ill at ease, but he relaxed after the first number.

As we had hoped, he communicated with several strata of Brazilian society: with schoolchildren, for whom he gave a free concert; with the national orchestra, with whom he played the Beethoven violin concerto to enthusiastic audiences in both Rio and São Paulo; and with the *gran finos*. The *gran finos* were the Brazilian high society—the name derived from the French expression *grande fine*, which designates the best Cognac! The *gran finos* lived luxuriously, were collectors and patrons of the arts, and spoke perfect French—before the war they visited France at frequent intervals. Albert's patrons on this occasion were the Guinles, in whose drawing room hung a beautiful Fragonard.

The Guinle family was composed of a great variety of individuals: Gilda, wife of the banker Carlos, was an exquisite French-educated lady who thoroughly appreciated Albert's music; Octavio owned the Copacabana Hotel; another brother, now deceased, ran the best racing stable in Brazil, while his wife, dedicated, believing sincerely in the influence of moral forces in the world, had been most helpful in sponsoring a nursing school; Guillerme, the entrepreneur, had founded a center for the treatment of venereal disease, grew superb orchids, and declared, "I want to die poor."

Before Albert and Mary left we took them overnight to Teresópolis, then up into the glorious mountains on the other side of the bay, the Dedo de Deus (the finger of God), and on their last night we gave a dinner for them at the residence—sixty-six people sitting at small tables. We were happy to receive Heitor Villa-Lobos, the composer, who had been very critical of Americans but with whom we became great friends. The friendship lasted until his death. Portinari was there also, enthusiastic about Alice (sincerely so; he was known to dislike the genus *ambassador*), saying that he considered her very talented—as indeed she is.

Although an ambassador may be concerned with a great many aspects of life in the country to which he is accredited, his primary responsibility is political. Getúlio Vargas, dictator of Brazil for nearly twenty years, was a loyal ally of the United States throughout the war, and Brazilian soldiers had fought in Italy side by side with American GIs. Peter and I had been on the reviewing stand with President Vargas as the Brazilian Expeditionary Force returned at the end of the war. General Mark Clark and General Crittenberger were received as heroes, and they bestowed decorations on Brazilian soldiers in the embassy garden. But Vargas was a dictator, and more than one journalist we knew had been summarily arrested and imprisoned. Quietly we had tried to establish a counterforce; we invited to dinner an individual who we heard had been threatened with imprisonment, and the prestige of the United States embassy was sufficient to protect the dissident—temporarily at least. But there was growing ferment among all classes, and people were demanding elections.

It was a delicate situation. Vargas had declared that elections would be held in the near future, but few people believed him. Adolf decided to take Vargas at his word and made a speech at a meeting of journalists to which he had been invited, concluding,

> The pledge of free Brazilian elections, set for a definite date, by a government whose word the United States has found inviolable, has been hailed with as much satisfaction in the United States as in Brazil itself. Americans have not agreed with some who tried to misrepresent straightforward pledges and declarations as insincere or as verbal trickery....
>
> The happiness with which this steady march towards constitutional democracy has been welcomed is based on American experience. We have learned that the only way to be a democracy is to practice democracy.

The Queremistas, the pro-Vargas factions, were furious at Adolf's speech and threatened a coup, although Vargas himself had approved the text (which Adolf had shown him) with the comment *"Muito bem, muito bem"* (Very good). In accordance with State Department regulations, Adolf had submitted the text to the State Department, but no answer came until two months later, so that the day following, Adolf was alone out on a limb—although it was really a small rowboat on the Bay of Santos.

We had planned a fishing expedition for that weekend with the children. I do not recall that any fish were caught. Adolf, intensely worried and seasick, could not stop looking at the fort above Santos, fearing there would be a coup, with guns supplied by Americans used by Brazilians against Brazilians.

But fortunately there was no coup, no revolution. Vargas resigned three weeks later. In accordance with the terms of the 1937 constitution, the president of the supreme courts, José Linhares, became president.

Adolf persuaded his diplomatic colleagues and the State Department that the new government was constitutional and therefore could be recognized without additional formalities. A fresh breeze swept over Brazil, whose people had been apathetic and depressed. Many new projects were initiated during the two months the interim government was in power. We had good friends among the ministers; Adolf was consulted on matters of law, and I was asked to give my opinion on matters of health.

The election was held on December 7. Adolf visited more than twenty polling places and felt satisfied that the election was honest, with no evidence of coercion. Women, proud of voting for the first time, replied to the question "How did you vote?" with the triumphant answer: "This is a secret ballot!"

The presidency went to Gaspar Dutra.

Our assignment to Brazil was coming to an end. Adolf had stipulated to President Roosevelt that we would return when the war was over, and he stuck to his resolution in spite of President Truman's request that we remain.

We went home for Christmas. Flying in and out of clouds on our eighteenth wedding anniversary, we landed once more at Atkinson field in teeming rain, the base almost deserted, with only a few hundred men. Natal was the same way. After all, the war was over, and it would not be long before the jungle reconquered its own.

The inauguration of President Dutra was scheduled for January. We returned to Brazil for the occasion and for formal leavetaking. Adolf had arranged to have Fiorello La Guardia named as special representative for the occasion; Major General Walsh, Admiral Greer, and Phil Chalmers, a State Department official, were also included in the official party. All these gentlemen stayed at the embassy residence.

January in Rio is like August in Washington. Nevertheless, protocol decreed that delegates wear morning coats and striped trousers for daytime events; tails, decorations, and dress uniforms in the evening.

Fiorello hated protocol and dressing up. It was my job to impress upon him that although, after FDR, he was the best-known American in Brazil, he still had to conform.

Everything went off well, but for me it was a tough week — I could not get to the Santa Casa. Dona Maria, the housekeeper, and the laundress and I were endlessly busy with men's shirts, underwear, white uniforms to be washed, trousers to be pressed, and decorations to be sewn on or strung on a little bar.

During the last month of our stay we received a number of moving personal and official tributes. The Brazilian government decorated me with the Cruzeiro do Sul for the work I had done in Brazilian hospitals. Adolf, as American ambassador, was not permitted by our government to accept a foreign decoration, but the Cruzeiro do Sul was presented to him in 1949 after he had returned to private life. At the law-school graduation honoring the memory of President Roosevelt, Adolf was greeted as the Ambassador of Democracy — "so," we both decided, quoting Adolf's phrase, "it was worth risking one's political capital."

The most moving tribute was paid to me at an open hospital meeting at which I was speaking on American medical education. An unknown middle-aged woman in the audience got up: "I am a teacher. The United States gave me a fellowship to Columbia University. No conditions were laid down. It was hoped I would be a better teacher when I returned to my country. The representative of the United States has been helping my people. To her I present this ring—a doctor's ring. It was my brother's. He died a few years ago."

We left for home at the end of February. We were to return frequently over the next twenty years. As chairman of President Kennedy's Task Force for Latin America in 1961, Adolf made one official visit. All the other times we were private citizens, both cementing the deep personal friendships and continuing in our roles: Adolf the professor, Beatrice the physician.

After the War ≈

≈*32*_____

We returned to New York in late February 1946. We had spent five years in Washington and fourteen months in Brazil. Although Adolf expressed the feelings of the entire family when he wrote President Truman, "To Brazil and to Brazilians I am indebted for one of the happiest and most interesting years of my life," we came home, for we did not want to become expatriates.

Our home base was solid. The house on Nineteenth Street, rented during the war, was ours free and clear of mortgages. Konkapot, the "farm" in Great Barrington, was intact, not a teaspoon missing. This is what both Adolf and I had wished. "Political jobs and wars come to an end," he used to say. "I want to be able to come home and take up where we left off". He was fifty-one, I was forty-three — we were in middle life, mature adults with more than twenty years of future ahead of us. Our children would be shaping their own adult lives.

This period of our lives together turned out to be very satisfactory. As always, Adolf's activities were legion: his ideas enhanced through the publication of eight books and innumerable articles; his teaching at the Columbia Law School and Army War College; his participating in the Rockefeller brothers' project. He supported the Democratic and Liberal parties at home and democratic movements in Latin America, with a brief assignment in the Kennedy administration. Using the organization of Radio Free Europe, he was instrumental in creating Le Collège de l'Europe Libre. He was actively involved in inspiring new projects for research through the Board of Trustees of the Twentieth Century Fund. And withal he maintained a loving and sympathetic relationship with his children — not to mention his wife, who never ceased to adore him and marvel at his infinite capacity for generating new ideas! As in other periods of our lives, I took no active part in Adolf's political activities except insofar as Latin America

[181]

was concerned; here, the development of personal friendships and the use of Nineteenth Street to bring people together from both our individual worlds was a joint venture.

On my own, I endeavored, prematurely and therefore unsuccessfully, to develop the concept of primary medical care and genetic counseling, spending also a considerable time in the methadone treatment of heroin addicts.

But the first few days after our return, life looked dark and grim! We missed the sunlight of Rio. The front hall in Nineteenth Street was piled high with furniture and packing cases from storage. There must be no looking back, I said firmly. Adolf immediately resumed his teaching at Columbia University Law School and rejoined his brother at their private law practice on Pine Street. Alice had started her senior year at the Madeira School in Washington and would be ready for college in the fall. Beatrice enrolled in the Brearley School in New York, where I had been a student, and Peter entered the fifth grade at the school of Grace Church, the church where I had been christened, confirmed, and married.

I was a physician with no practice and no hospital connections. In Rio I had worked in the Santa Casa, a charity hospital, and learned a great deal about tuberculosis, intestinal parasites, and the life of the underprivileged—a fascinating experience but difficult to translate into American academic requirements that would make an appointment to a New York university hospital possible.

After reading a book entitled *Psychosomatic Medicine*, by Flanders Dunbar, a Brearley classmate of mine, and some articles by Harold Wolff and Stewart Wolf, I decided that I wanted to learn more about the relationship between mind and body.

At the New York Hospital and Cornell University School of Medicine, Drs. Harold Wolff and Stewart Wolf were studying the changes in color of the exposed gastric mucosa of their laboratory assistant Tom. A part of this man's stomach was visible to the naked eye through a stoma (opening) in the abdominal wall. Tom had been feeding himself through this opening directly into his stomach ever since his esophagus had been shut off when he swallowed boiling clam chowder in early childhood. This did not prevent him from leading a normal life—raising a family and working. For the physicians this stoma provided an extraordinary opportunity to observe and record changes in the gastric mucosa with differing emotional states—reddening during anger and paling during fright or depression. In other words, here was a perfect example of a visible bodily reaction to a feeling state. I longed to become a part of this medical group and boldly called for an appointment with Dr. Harold Wolff, Professor of Medicine and Neurology at the Cornell University School of Medicine.

Dr. Wolff's office was on the sixth floor of the New York Hospital. Miss

Helen Goodell, his research associate and co-author of many articles, received me cordially. Her manner was in contrast to the austerity of the office—a small room with one desk, two straight chairs, and many books, adjacent to a laboratory with few instruments.

Dr. Wolff—erect, spare, severe—was a man of few words who spread terror in the hearts of young interns who were not as precise in their thinking as he thought they should be. The interview lasted only a few minutes. I do not remember the content, but I left feeling that I had failed the examination. A few days later, to my great surprise and delight, Miss Goodell's cheerful voice over the telephone informed me that Dr. Wolff was prepared to take me on as a fellow in medicine. A medical clinic was being organized for the study and treatment of patients with various medical disorders such as diabetes, peptic ulcers, asthma, and headaches, which were thought to be associated with stressful life situations. This turned out to be the beginning of a most exciting intellectual experience, which developed later into a deep friendship among Harold Wolff; his wife, the distinguished painter Isabel Bishop; Adolf; me; and of course, Helen Goodell, the intercessor and promoter of the project.

The next question concerned Alice. We had not wanted her to miss a school year, so we had sent her back from Brazil to become a boarder at the Madeira School, where she had been a day student when we lived in Washington. She would be ready for college in the fall. A gifted artist, she had been painting since she was ten years old and been privileged to study with Portinari in Brazil. At this point, she wanted nothing to do with the eastern establishment and what she considered our overcomplicated, overluxurious ways of life. She wanted to be free.

Gently and lovingly, Adolf led her back to his own roots—together they went out to visit Oberlin College in Ohio, where Adolf's grandfather G. Frederick Wright had been a distinguished professor of geology and theology, and his mother, one of the early women graduates, had worked as a missionary among the Sioux Indians before she married. On the occasion of this visit, Adolf wrote, "President Wilkins, whose grandfather was a deacon in my father's church, had us to lunch during which we talked over all known problems. It was fascinating and emotionally luxurious to tackle international problems through the eyes of a college president whose great love is Romance languages, and especially through the eyes of Dante." Alice was convinced and entered Oberlin College in the fall.

Beatrice, a brilliant student, enjoyed the flesh pots as well. The subscription dances of prewar days still existed but were becoming increasingly commercial-

ized, so we decided to have our own parties in Nineteenth Street: black-tie dinner dances for about thirty people, music with records. I remember a very special
party attended by two Dutch girls, daughters of Max Steenberghe, Adolf's colleague at the Chicago air conference. They had spent the war in German-occu-
pied Holland; yet now Tienecke, age eighteen, pink cheeked, was laughing and
dancing as if she had never been threatened by the Gestapo.

Peter had his special activities — a Lionel train installed on a specially built
table with a hole in the center through which stationmaster Peter emerged and
controlled a complicated network of rails, tunnels, passenger cars, cattle cars,
and a whistling engine spouting smoke, this last provided by a loving friend,
Ernest Cuneo.

The kitchen on the ground floor was staffed by two White Russians. From
time to time volleys of sound resounded through the house; the house staff was
having an argument — or possibly only a friendly exchange? On our return we
had hired these two women because Adolf, who in the State Department had
spent a great deal of time working on refugee problems, wished to do something
directly for individual refugees, or displaced persons, as they were called at the
time. The experiment worked out well, and the food was good in spite of their
exaggerated fondness for dill and carp. The wedding reception for Nadia's
daughter, who was marrying a young architect, was held at Nineteenth Street.

The second experiment a few years later was not quite so successful. The
man, a Russian soldier wounded and abandoned by his army in Germany, had
been nursed back to health by a German *Schwester* (nurse), whom he married.
One day during the summer, he was about to hit our gardener in the country
with a hoe, when young Beatrice standing barefoot in shorts on the edge of the
garden, said calmly and firmly that this was not the way we settled disputes in
the United States. He stopped in his tracks.

While we were settling back in New York, many Brazilians beat a path to
our door, some just friends, with or without problems, bringing orchids and
the latest *trocadillos* (political jokes), others referred by the Brazilian consulate for
advice and help with medical and other problems. In fact, Nineteenth Street became known as the American Consulate for Brazilians in New York.

There were many different situations. As an example, one of my colleagues
arrived unannounced with his son, who had suffered a gunshot wound in the
eye. Through my New York Hospital connections I was able to arrange for a
consultation with an ophthalmologist. An enucleation was performed, and later
an artificial eye was provided.

Others needed help in choosing an appropriate school. Still others needed free room and board for a few days, since the state of the Brazilian economy and government regulations made the purchase of dollars prohibitive. We knew that Brazilian friendship was all-embracing and reciprocal, that when we or any member of our family came to Brazil they would be received and all their needs attended to. Such has proved to be the case, and now, almost forty years later, friendships on both continents continue into the third generation.

At the end of two years of college, Alice became engaged to a fellow student, Clan Crawford, Jr., son of a prominent Cleveland lawyer. College life at Oberlin thirty years ago was still quite simple. Students had no cars. When Adolf and I visited the young people on a Saturday night at college we found them gathered in a poolroom drinking 3.2 percent beer with their fellow students and singing gaily and loudly, "God bless free enterprise."

Alice wished to marry at the end of her junior year. We agreed, with the proviso that she obtain her degree by attending Ohio University the following year. This she did. Clan had been in the navy during the war and, like Alice, was determined to be independent and not to take advantage of his father's position. On graduation, he got a job in a company in Cleveland and was prepared to support his wife.

The marriage was celebrated in the garden at Konkapot on June 19, 1949. The garden had expanded since the first summer twenty years before, when Adolf and I had planted the delphiniums that his mother had given us. The sky-blue delphinium, mixed with the darker blue-violet King Arthur, were in full bloom on the lower terrace where Grandfather (Dr. A. A. Berle, Sr.), a stocky figure in black academic gown, the red Harvard hood over his shoulders, stood with the groom and the best man, waiting for the bride. She came striding resolutely across the lawn on her father's arm, her white satin gown and lace veil undulating gently in the breeze. Beatrice followed, dressed in white muslin and a blue sash.

It was an intimate and very personal wedding, with only close friends. Clan's mother, two sisters, and brother had come from Cleveland. Albert Spalding played the violin, accompanied by my cousin Alice Riggs on the piano and Peter on the recorder. The only formal note was introduced by Mauricio Nabuco, Brazilian ambassador to the United States, in top hat and striped trousers, presenting the bride with a superb aquamarine, a gift from Dutra, the president of Brazil. The wedding breakfast was served at small tables on the lawn. Fresh green peas from the garden, Perrier-Jouet champagne, purchased some years ago by the bride's European-minded parents in anticipation of their daughters' weddings, and a strolling accordion minstrel playing "Smoke Gets in Your Eyes" (a favorite of Alice's) contributed to the festive atmosphere.

Through the day I felt as if I were a spectator observing a distant scene. More vivid than the present were flashes of the past—the kids splashing and stomping in the mud of the newly leveled terrace, Alice standing on the back of Tiny the pony and directing a circus for my birthday....

When the time came for the bridal couple to leave, Alice threw her bouquet from the balcony right into the arms of Beatrice, standing on the lawn below. Laddy, Alice's beloved mutt, which she had picked up in the Washington pound, had been locked in a bedroom and was released in time to give his mistress a farewell lick on the nose. Adolf and I turned to each other with tears in our eyes.

Alice and Clan spent their first year of married life in a small apartment in Cleveland. Wiser than her parents, anticipating the nitty-gritty aspects of modern life without domestic service, Alice declined an oriental rug and a set of fine china that we were planning to give her, preferring solid but well-designed custom-made modern furniture.

As usual our lives proceeded on many different levels at once. Adolf had a remarkable faculty for reflecting, verbalizing, conversing with friends, and writing. In the flower garden, planting delphinium, foxglove, or Canterbury bells, his favorites, planning for the next season, or just digging up dandelions in the lawn waiting for the family to go out to dinner, he appeared to be meditating deeply, his lips moving in a whisper. The children, when small, had been cautioned not to interrupt Daddy when he was "burbling," to which Alice once responded, "Will he do a burble for me?" The burbling, or ruminating, was soon translated into conversation with me and with friends, usually over the dinner table or with house guests in the country.

These weekends were great fun—a combination of formality and informality. I remember one particularly lovely June afternoon when I was transplanting pink lady slippers with Pierre Bedard, an old friend, at the time director of the Parsons School of Design and now, alas, deceased. He and his wife, Gerry, and I were busy digging in under the pine trees, when Adolf and Peter crossed our path on the way to the pond, fishing rods in hand. I reminded them we were having a formal dinner party that evening. "It's only six o'clock," they replied airily.

The first guests arrived at seven-fifteen. No fishermen in sight. Mr. Bedard came down the stairs, impeccably attired in a white dinner jacket. I was still in shorts, basting the lamb. While Mrs. Bedard greeted the guests and I ran upstairs to put on an evening dress, Mr. Bedard went in search of the fishermen. No luck. Siiri, a fine Finnish woman who was working for us at the time, herself a fisherman (she caught trout with a worm, not a fly), started on the search. Still no fishermen. Her husband took the truck and finally returned with two disgruntled sportsmen and no fish. It was the magic hour when rises were appearing on the pond. Why interrupt it?

As Adolf walked through the door the telephone rang. It was President Pepe Figueres Ferrer calling from Costa Rica to announce that the negotiations with the United Fruit Company that he and Adolf had initiated had been concluded successfully. Five minutes later, Adolf reappeared in a dinner jacket, and we sat down to enjoy the first garden peas, fine wine, and great conversation.

≈ 33

Nineteenth Street and the farm continued as a base and a center of operations over the following years.

Old friends came to dine, spend weekends, and meet new friends. Peter was attending the Friends School on Stuyvesant Square. When the time came to enter college, we naturally hoped that he would choose Harvard, but he was not to be pressured and looked into several other colleges. The decision to enter Harvard was truly his own.

On September 20, 1954, he left for Cambridge in the Chevrolet coupe his father had given him. This was the end of a phase of life, and we all knew it. *"J'avais le coeur bien gros"* and tried not to show it. He was very sweet and affectionate the last two days. As he was stepping into the car he called, "I left a present for you, Mom, in the new room."

Curtly I replied, "Oh, you did, did you?" After the car was on the road, I ran in to open the package and melted into tears. The gift was a beautiful Swedish glass vase etched with the figure of a woman tossing a child into the air.

There really never has been, never will be, such a boy as Peter — the best I believe that America can produce — strong of body, honest of mind, and stout of heart, with a sense of responsibility, independence of spirit, and withal a sensitivity to the way the other fellow feels.

Adolf and I went up to rest in bed a while longer, watching the mist over the pond. It is a rich life we have had together these many years, I thought, and we thank God we have each other.

I had been thinking a lot about the new phase of life we were entering — with middle-older age should come more thought and repose. In my particular case, it is always a question of how life may be spent most profitably. My essential problem remains — too great an appetite, an unwillingness to limit the problem, trying to put five quarts into a four-quart bottle. The result—fragmentation, scattering of effort, and no accomplishment.

There was always a lot going on in our house—birthday celebrations among other things.

Dr. Berle, Sr., Grandfather, celebrated his ninetieth birthday in January 1955. His birthday was always a festive occasion. I made a point of giving him red roses—one for each year—plus a white one to grow on. About twenty of his cronies gathered around the dining-room table—champagne, of course, and a birthday cake with ninety candles. His friends, all in their sixties or seventies, were members of the "breakfast club," a group of men who gathered around Dr. Berle at the Harvard Club through the winter exchanging ideas on all subjects from Greek philosophy to current events. Adolf's sixtieth birthday, celebrated a few days later, was a quieter affair!

The Harvard Club was a happy winter home for Dr. Berle until he reached the age of ninety-two. Then he retired to his home in New Hampshire, where he was cared for by a dedicated practical nurse, Helen Lyons, and his physician, Dr. Rainie, until his death in 1960. In the fifties, the Harvard Club was a men's club. Lady guests were admitted through a side door and entertained in a special dining room.

Although Dr. Berle did not like physicians, there came a time when he thought medical attention might relieve a troublesome cough. He wished me to pay a house call at the club. Carrying my doctor's bag, I came in through the ladies' door and was escorted by a doorman across the hall to the elevator and admitted directly to his room. Fortunately, Dr. Berle appeared to be suffering only from bronchitis, which I was able to relieve with simple medication. He categorically refused laboratory tests, chest X rays, and so on. At the end of my examination, Dr. Berle telephoned for the doorman, who escorted me to the ladies' entrance along the same route by which I had come. Times have changed!

Dr. Berle was a remarkable man. Energy and independence of mind combined with great learning, a sense of social justice, and a willingness to fight for it, were, I suppose, his chief characteristics. Combined with these was a Teutonic temperament that seemed to make it necessary for him to dominate those he loved and to reject them when they showed signs of wishing to free themselves. This made life especially difficult for his wife and his two daughters. Mrs. Berle, who thought her own thoughts in her own quiet way, died of a cerebral hemorrhage at the age of seventy. Lina achieved her independence first as a teacher, later as the manager of her brothers' law office. Today, approaching ninety, she is beloved by us all and a wise counselor to the younger generation who confide in her. Miriam married Cassius Clay, a fine gentleman from Paris, Kentucky, who died a few years ago. Dr. Berle's two sons, Adolf and Rudolf, though recognizing their father's failings, maintained a warm relationship with him (between thunderstorms) and contributed to his support in his old age.

During the fifties, Adolf was busy with national politics and international affairs and also planning Le Collège de l'Europe Libre.

As an active member of the Committee for a Free Europe, Adolf felt that anticommunism was insufficient. A more positive approach was necessary, and young people who had been denied an education in eastern Europe, and had escaped from behind the iron curtain, should receive an education that would fit them to become democratic leaders on their return to their native countries when these were liberated. The committee organized Le Collège de l'Europe Libre at Strasbourg on this basis through Adolf's inspiration. We attended the summer sessions in Strasbourg.

I am not in a position to evaluate the political results, if any, of this enterprise, but for me, Le Collège was another example of Adolf's imaginative use of our friends, an activity in which I shared. Like a playwright and theater producer, he developed his characters and put them on stage. Plans worked out in his New York office and in Nineteenth Street were executed in Europe.

After several unsuccessful attempts to find a suitable American college president, Adolf invited our dear friend Jan Pelenyi to the position in Strasbourg. Pelenyi was a Hungarian nobleman trained in the Austro-Hungarian diplomatic service. He married an American when he was a consul in Cleveland in the early twenties. At the start of World War II he was Hungarian minister in Washington, but he resigned when Hungary was taken over by the Soviets. At that time, Adolf arranged for him to be named professor of political science at Dartmouth, and now, in 1952, as this distinguished European-American was reaching retirement age, Adolf persuaded him to take on the presidency of Le Collège de l'Europe Libre.

Adolf and I felt that Europeans should learn something about the unique political experiment of the Commonwealth of Puerto Rico, where a people elected their governor and managed their internal affairs, but their foreign relations remained under the jurisdiction of the United States and American companies were encouraged through tax exemptions to develop factories on the island. So Governor Muñoz Marín came to lecture at Strasbourg—a great success and also a romantic adventure. Muñoz turned poet again as he wandered singing by moonlight along the Strasbourg canals, accompanied by his wife, Adolf and me, and a group of students.

Thinking of Le Collège in American terms, Adolf and I felt that there should be a dean of women. Our dear friend Mildred Thompson was retiring from Vassar, and she agreed to come to Strasbourg to guide and supervise the women students. This proved to be an educational experience for both.

My beloved Mademoiselle Mulot was also brought into the picture. Together we translated some of Adolf's lectures from English into French. She was going through a very trying period. Hers was a cloistered order. When the Germans were approaching Paris in 1940, she led the evacuation of the school — nuns and students — on foot along the crowded highways to a convent in the center of France. After the war, it turned out that the small order to which she belonged had gone bankrupt, and she was authorized by the ecclesiastical authorities "to return to the lay state."

In due course she settled in a retirement home near Paris, where we visited her when we came to France. Later she joined us in Great Barrington on two occasions. But in 1953, here was this woman who had been cloistered for more than thirty years, suddenly thrust into the world. "I do not want to disgrace you," she said with a smile, "but you remember that the nuns took their meals in silence, so I have forgotten how to carry on a conversation." Such was not the case! Her knowledge of French history and literature was far more extensive than ours, and her gentle manners charmed us all.

Unfortunately the Strasbourg experiment came to an end in 1956 when, following the Hungarian revolution, Pelenyi suffered a massive gastrointestinal hemorrhage and no adequate leadership could be found to carry out Adolf's dream.

There were many other activities stemming out of Nineteenth Street. Adolf was working on Adlai Stevenson's campaign for president and starting on a project for the Rockefeller brothers.

The last session of the seminar in corporation law that he taught at Columbia always ended with a dinner at Nineteenth Street at which the students — at most fifteen in number — gathered around the wood fire in the library and exchanged views with the master on the future of the corporation. Their papers and these discussions formed a base for Adolf's forthcoming books.

For my part, in addition to operating a clinic in East Harlem, the publication of my book *Eighty Puerto Rican Families: A Study of Health and Disease in Context*, and taking care of a few private patients, mostly patients suffering from migraine who were referred by Dr. Wolff, I was engaged in orienting young physicians from Latin America in the ways of American medicine and of living in America.

The Kellogg Foundation offered six to eight fellowships every year to young medical graduates from South American countries on the understanding that the medical schools that had sponsored them would give them a teaching position when they returned home. They spent the first three months as graduate students at the Cornell University Medical College, doing their clinical work at Bellevue Hospital under the supervision of Dr. Thomas Almy and other members of the Cornell faculty, including myself.

Coming from hot climates, neither they nor their wives had warm clothing, although one young man came from Bahía, Brazil, with his uncle's overcoat, which had already spent several winters in New York with other members of the family! We kept a rotating supply of coats and galoshes for them and invited them to the house for dinner from time to time, to introduce them to young Americans.

In the winter our most satisfying pastime was reading flower catalogues, the only books of fairy tales remaining in the world. Adolf would say, "Listen to this — 'Outstanding masterpiece mums. Devote a bed solely for a sight you're not likely to forget. The best ever — sparkling clear color, weather resistance, early flower, myriad blooms. Cut all you want. You'll leave a throng of garden gems behind.'" Although these promises were never completely realized, we had a beautiful garden, and whenever possible, we spent stretches of time in the summer, as well as fall and winter weekends, in the Berkshires.

I rarely gave a thought to my unhappy early life. That was the past — a useful experience as a background for the practice of medicine. In July 1957, I received a telephone call from an electrician in Lenox informing me that my mother was "at death's door." I thanked him, saying I did not know that I could make use of that information. I called the local physician to inform him that I was available if my mother should wish to see me. Mrs. Hammond happened to be in the Berkshires at the moment and said that she had seen Mrs. Falk (Edith Nixon), but the trained nurse in attendance had not permitted her to see my mother. It seems that Mother had become semicomatose about a week before — a cerebral accident, I presumed.

I saw Dr. Whitman, the minister in Lenox. Mother had told him she knew she was dying and asked the Lord's forgiveness. She felt that she was with her neighbors in love and charity.

Mr. Falk, Edith Nixon's husband, was said to be in a state of advanced arteriosclerosis and had been a chronic invalid for the past year. I believe he died the following year.

The mills of the gods grind slowly. The Irish adventuress Edith Nixon Falk was to live another fifteen years alone with her fortune, which, according to the terms of my Father's will, went to Columbia University on her death. She died of senile dementia in a nursing home, attended only by a faithful Episcopal minister, Dr. Whitman.

Her career had been amazing. In her middle twenties she emigrated from Ireland and obtained a job as chambermaid in the Bishop home. Within two years, she had displaced the daughter of the house and presumably became the mistress of the master. On his death she inherited a part of his fortune, with the proviso that she continue to live with and care for his widow. I am not clear when she married Mr. Falk, but they continued to live with my mother and from all accounts took very good care of her and made her comfortable.

My mother, the beautiful Amy Bend, was born March 5, 1871. She belonged to an era that has passed, although narcissism and beauty culture are universal and highly prevalent today. Egocentricity in women today is primarily an expression of aggression, a defiance, not an appeal to men. In Mother's case, it was a declaration of dependence, with the expectation of being admired and cared for. From the time she was a child, she was told that she was beautiful, and she expected to keep men at her feet and to be worshiped by them. But she never grew up. Perhaps she did not have the capacity; certainly, no one encouraged her to do so or to take responsibility. Her paranoid turn of mind (which some authorities now believe may be innate) was fostered rather than checked, and it had dire results. But Mother's death was only the last chapter of a dramatic story that for me was no longer of any consequence.

Beatrice graduated from Vassar College in 1951—one up on her mother, since she had won her Phi Beta Kappa key in her junior year, whereas I did not get mine until I was a senior.

Beatrice also managed a gay social life that included going to football games at Yale, Harvard, Princeton, and finally West Point, where she met her future husband, Lieutenant Dean Meyerson, on a blind date. As they were about to become engaged, Adolf made it very clear to Beatrice that she must consider the implications of being an army wife. The army followed a rigorous tradition, different from ours, and we both felt strongly that marriage meant sharing and understanding each other's ideals and way of life. In the case of a man whose career was established, a woman should not expect him to change direction.

The marriage took place in November 1953, in Iceland, where Dean was stationed. Adolf, Beatrice, Peter, and I arrived in Reykjavik on Thanksgiving Day with a suitcase full of finery.

Today, thirty years later, I can only say that Beatrice and Dean and their three sons are people of quality and fine intelligence.

Latin America ≈

≈ *34*

Through the fifties and sixties we made frequent trips to Puerto Rico, Central America, and South America, forming deep friendships with Muñoz Marín in Puerto Rico, José Figueres Ferrer in Costa Rica, Rómulo Betancourt in Venezuela, and Alberto Lleras Camargo in Colombia and, of course, keeping up with our Brazilian friends. While Trujillo was in power, we did not go to Santo Domingo, Adolf's first port of call in the Caribbean.

In February 1952, we visited Haiti, where Adolf had been called to advise the government on some of their financial problems. Peter came with us.

There was a stopover between planes in Puerto Rico. I dropped off to sleep in the hotel garden. As I awoke, the day was breaking, and I saw two masculine figures silhouetted against the red sky—Adolf and Peter. Peter was the taller—at fifteen, already a man. I was filled with pride—and sadness.

In Haiti, though Adolf was busy, we managed to see something of the country. We rented a jeep and drove into the mountains, toward Lurie. After going as far as we could, we got out and, following the contour of the hill, walked along a stony trail created by the feet of men and beasts. Women carrying baskets of yams on their heads emerged from little huts surrounded by small garden patches. We exchanged greetings and continued in and out of light puffs of mist until, on a promontory about a hundred feet below, we saw a house. A small boy suddenly appeared before us.

"Is this the house of Pastor MacDonald?" we asked. He beamed and nodded in affirmation, disappearing as quickly as he had come.

Pastor MacDonald was a beloved Protestant missionary our Haitian friends had told us about. Just as we were realizing that our trail had reached a dead end and that the house could be reached only from the other side of the precipice where we stood, the child came running with a small bunch of nasturtiums and Chinese forget-me-nots. An offering in the name of Pastor MacDonald—freely given, freely accepted. In return we handed him a small gourd we had been using as a drinkng cup.

Unfortunately, we had to return by the same path and later transfer to a taxi. It was driven by a high-school-dropout, money-grubbing young Haitian who scorned the peasants. Pétionville, the town above Port-au-Prince, was crowded with the latest models of shiny American cars driven by Haitian politicians, racing past the barefoot women laden with their baskets of produce. The Haitians we knew were first-class, but there were very few of them: Two such were Dantès Bellegarde, Haitian representative first at the League of Nations and now at the United Nations, a brilliant scholar who upheld the notion of social responsibility against all adversaries; and Camille L'Hérisson, a fine physician with a degree in public health from Harvard, working to secure pure water and soon to be exiled by Papa Doc. He ended tragically and destitute on the ward at Bellevue Hospital in New York, where I cared for him in his terminal illness.

The following year, 1953, we visited Nicaragua as the guests of Dr. Luis Manuel Debayle, with whom we had become friends at the Buenos Aires conference in 1936. Luis Manuel was the brother-in-law of President Anastasio Somoza, with a considerable popular following of his own. He hoped that there would be an election and that he would succeed Somoza. This did not happen. An expansive and romantic liberal, Debayle took me out on horseback to look at the great volcano Momotombo. As we rode he vowed that he would support democracy and serve his country. Although I could not see any tangible results, he always claimed that he had a moderating influence on his brother-in-law and later on his nephew, Tachito, son of Anastasio Somoza.

While we were in Nicaragua, there was much talk of José Figueres, in Costa Rica, who was considered a communist by both Nicaraguans and American embassy personnel. Adolf decided he wished to find out for himself. A brief stopover in San José on our way home and a visit with José Figueres convinced him that this was not so.

We returned to Costa Rica many times over the next fifteen years, and Figueres—Don Pepe, as he is called—became a cherished friend. Short of stature, with a large head, a prominent nose, dark hair, and deep-set blue-gray eyes, swift of speech and movement, Don Pepe, today, alas, in frail health, represents an extraordinary combination of Iberian and American culture.

The son of Catalonian immigrants (Catalonians, like the Basques, are considered to be the most independent inhabitants of the Iberian peninsula), Don

Pepe had obtained an engineering degree from M.I.T. and returned to Costa Rica with an American wife, whom he later divorced. A progressive farmer and an able politician, he was elected president three times. His second wife, Karen, an American of Scandinavian descent, bore him four children and became an active promoter of his social programs, initiating many of her own.

Accompanied by Peter, we visited the Figuereses over New Year's, 1955. We were guests at the presidential house. It was a simple clapboard building converted into an official residence, a symbol of Costa Rican democracy, contrasting with the marble palaces built by Nicaraguan, Honduran, and Guatemalan dictators. On New Year's Eve, Peter was invited to a dance at the club whose members—bankers and coffee planters—were Don Pepe's political opponents.

When Don Pepe, Doña Karen, Adolf, and I walked down the street toward the main square, the president was soon recognized and people pressed in upon us. The crowd was friendly, but the pressure from behind could easily have knocked us down. Also, in view of threats of assassination coming from both the right (Trujillo, the dictator of Santo Domingo) and the communists, I was quite apprehensive. The other three appeared unconcerned, although Don Pepe carried a pistol in his pocket. We were practically carried up to a little rotunda where a band was playing. There we encountered two policemen, who directed the crowd to make a little circle, in the middle of which we stood. Everyone was shouting for Don Pepe.

He stood up on a chair and spoke a few words into the microphone. Hundreds of people milled around, wanting to talk to him, to touch him. One man came up to Doña Karen, threw his hat on the ground in homage, and presented his son, about ten years old, saying that the boy wished to be a doctor.

After about half an hour, an exit was worked out, and we managed to walk to the car. We went down the streets, Don Pepe driving and then later letting his bodyguard drive. The car went along very slowly; people talked to him and shook hands with him as we went through.

On New Year's Day we had a quiet lunch at the presidential house and then went to the bullfights—Adolf, Peter and I, Don Pepe and Doña Karen, and their baby. José, Jr., one year old, was the living image of his father. His mother carried him through the milling, shouting crowd and sat with him in the front row at the bullfight. People talked to him and patted him. He responded, putting his hand to his little ear, apparently unconcerned and quite comfortable.

A Costa Rican bullfight is no ordinary bullfight—the bull is not killed. Any man who wishes to chase him or be chased by him can jump into the ring. A few would-be *toreros* dash about waving pink comforters or other pieces of cloth. The majority chase the bull helter-skelter, and the bull chases them. When the bull is exhausted and falls down, people jump on him, pulling his tail. Then, at the blowing of a horn, four men on horses go out to lasso the bull, take him out of the ring, and let out the next bull.

Seven bulls were let out in the course of the afternoon. To taunt the bull to see how close you can get to him is showing off your courage. Some men grab the bull by the horn and ride him. In the case of two daredevil riders one was bounced off almost immediately and carried in triumph to the presidential box; the second one fell off, ran to the railing, and was hailed by the crowd. Then he walked along the edge of the grandstand, passing the hat.

There was a great deal of shouting in front of Don Pepe's box, and many climbed up to shake hands with him. There was also much buffoonery. One drunk asked for a coin to drink the health of the president. The president gave him a coin, and the drunk later returned, boasting that he had had a drink by order and at the invitation of the president.

When a man rolled over by the bull does not get to his feet, he is picked up by his comrades, rushed to the Red Cross station at the end of the ring, and pushed through a chute, at the end of which is, presumably, an ambulance. This first-aid treatment, I felt, must be more injurious than the original trampling by the bull. The papers reported that 192 men were injured during the season that year. I do not know whether the bullfight still takes place in 1983.

At the time of our visit, there was considerable criticism of this kind of sport, but I heard a number of men saying to Don Pepe, "Don't take this away from us." It is the best way for men to let off steam, to express their aggressive feelings — better than mugging or breaking shop windows.

After the bullfight came the real joy of this and every visit to Costa Rica, the trip to Don Pepe's farm, La Lucha. After about an hour and a half's drive out of San José, the last stretch along a winding road in the fog, we came to the iron gate across the road to the farm — a gate forged by Don Pepe himself. The headlights were turned on full so that we might pick out his motto in iron letters on the gate: *Lucha sin fin* (Struggle without end). The farm road zigzags down about half a mile to a plateau where the new house stands, a simple square structure of native bricks with a large terrace. It was built after the Communists destroyed the original farmhouse. Don Pepe showed us the spot where he, Padre Nuñez, a priest, and a few other men fought the Communists in 1948.

The new house has a view of the surrounding hills planted with pita, or sisal, a form of cactus, which is stripped and brought to a small factory in a gully below, where it is made into rope and baling twine.

A few minutes' walk from the house brings one to a glorious view of high mountains, which seem to stretch into infinity as the sun sets behind them. There were just five of us: Don Pepe, Adolf, Peter, El Capitán (Don Pepe's bodyguard), and myself. Karen had remained in San José with the baby and provided us with a casserole of hearts of palm for dinner.

Adolf and Peter brought in wood from the terrace as Don Pepe lit the fire. Then conversation began: What is the value system of democratic societies?

Developing a sense of personal responsibility through education is where you begin, Adolf was saying.

"That is what I have tried to do through the primer for voters that I have just finished writing," Pepe went on. Voters should understand where and how tax money is spent and select honest men to represent them.

"In a small country like Costa Rica," I said, "popular democracy is possible. Last night your people wanted to touch you, to speak to you personally, to know you and your family and have you know them. This give and take is impossible in a large country like the United States, except through the mass media, in which facts and personalities are manipulated and distorted."

The talk went on late into the evening, as Adolf discussed his ideas about the capitalist system and its potential for providing and distributing a greater measure of well-being to a greater number of people than any other economic system — provided the capitalists developed a sense of social responsibility. These ideas he had elaborated in a recently published book, *The Twentieth Century Capital Revolution* (1954).

Don Pepe and Peter talked about farming. Through high school, Peter had cut hay on our farm and developed a great love for the land, which continues to this day. Don Pepe was a coffee grower and proud that his trees, heavily pruned and fertilized, were covered with a second flowering of fine blossoms compared to the puny saplings on his neighbors' property across the road. "Those people," he explained, "belong to an old family who think they have nothing new to learn, since they have grown coffee for generations."

"Those old families," Adolf said, "have their traditions both good and bad, but the future does not lie with them. The future lies with people like you who are trying to improve agricultural and manufacturing techniques that will provide a better life for more people."

"Yes," Don Pepe went on, "my little sisal factory, which you see at the bottom of the hill, is exporting rope, and if we can make a profit, the workmen will have a better life. It is important for the privileged to have an understanding of the problems of the underprivileged."

Indicating Peter, Adolf said, "I agree. I would like you to take my son to work on your place, as a peon, so that he may penetrate beyond the surface of upper-class life."

This sounded to me like a tough assignment. Don Pepe thought so too; he suggested that Peter could live in his house at La Lucha for a couple of months. But Adolf and Peter were against any halfway measure.

As a result of this conversation, Peter worked and lived with the workmen cutting sisal for the little factory in the valley below. On his return he was pale, thin, tired—amoebic dysentery, was my impression. A stool examination confirmed the diagnosis. A heavy price to pay for a course in practical sociology, was my silent comment. Fortunately, with the help of Dr. B. Kean, the authority on tropical medicine at the New York Hospital, I was able to treat Peter immediately and effectively so that he never suffered from any sequelae.

Don Pepe, like Adolf, was interested in developing people's capabilities. This was particularly true in the case of Padre Benjamin Nuñez, the priest who had fought the Communists and who was sponsored by a liberal and educated monsignor. When Nuñez was named Costa Rican ambassador to the United Nations, Adolf and I came to know him well and to love him dearly. For the son of a poor blacksmith living under the famous volcano to be suddenly catapulted onto the world scene was, to use the modern term, something of a cultural shock. He suffered from severe migraine, for which I treated him. Adolf helped him to develop a postgraduate program in sociology and economics when his ambassadorial assignment came to an end.

But the conflict between the priest and the politician was not resolved. Was he in danger of losing his faith? That he could play both roles was demonstrated to us on the visit we made to Costa Rica in 1958. Don Pepe's party had lost the election. A proof of democracy was the opinion of people whom I spoke to casually: Let the other fellow have a chance! Don Pepe felt that his reforms, like the nationalization of the banks, were sufficiently institutionalized that they could not be destroyed.

We arrived in Costa Rica before the winning party had taken over and drove out to San Isidro, less than an hour from San José, where Padre Nuñez was running a church fair. He informed us that, being the organizer, he had tried to stay in the background and had encouraged many groups to take an active part. The Lion's Club, the diplomatic corps, the ladies of the government, the American women's club, the 4H club, and the Mexican club each had a booth. "Never before in the history of Costa Rica have we had a fair like this" he told us, beaming. "We expect to raise thirty thousand dollars for the benefit of a children's hospital." (They did.)

The fair was to be opened by a mass. At ten o'clock a band appeared on the steps of the church. The crowd was silenced. We were sitting close to the altar. Benjamin Nuñez, who had been a man walking about concerned with many details, became the priest who performed the sacrament of the mass, an outward and visible sign of an inward and spiritual grace.

There are many ways of attending mass. The padre was saying his mass as it should be said, with sincerity and devotion. Three old women sat on the bench saying their rosary mechanically, like a Tibetan prayer wheel. A dog, a boxer, who strayed across the steps was promptly chased under a bench, where he lay quietly, his front paws folded one over the other. There were the acolytes intent upon their job. There were the "queens" of the fair, concerned lest their skirts should blow over their heads. There were humble men, women, and children, their heads bowed, as the Host was lifted against the background of the cross of orchids. And there we were, deeply moved that this man, whose tribulations we had witnessed through many phases, was now a priest among his people!

The mass concluded, a few words were said by the chief pediatrician of the hospital-to-be. The queen was crowned by *la primera dama de Costa Rica*, Doña Karen de Figueres. Then we went in to lunch in the quiet of the padre's house. The padre seemed in fine spirits and discussed his university courses, which he gave beginning at seven o'clock in the morning, after saying his six-o'clock mass. In his house there was also a social-service office attended by a social worker who helped people with their material problems. He organized catechism classes. He expected to start an evening seminar in political science in which various members of the outgoing government would take part.

It was a busy life, but he felt better and in real possession of himself, as he had not for many years. "They say I am a good speaker," he told us, "but I speak because people listen, and I get more from them than I give to them. Most of all I get my faith from the simple people who have faith in me as a priest."

This visit to Costa Rica was followed by a visit to the newly elected president of Honduras, Ramón Villeda Morales. Adolf, as a private citizen, had managed to obtain the support of various branches of the United States government for the election by popular vote of a president in Honduras following the deposition of the longtime dictator Tiburcio Carías Andino. President Villeda

Morales had been at our home on Nineteenth Street, and we believed him to be a man of goodwill. He and his very capable wife, Doña Alejandrina, were anxious to show us their many projects. They drove us out to Sunyapa, about two hours from the capital, Tegucigalpa. A new road was to be inaugurated.

When we arrived at the village, the schoolchildren were standing in line singing the national anthem, and little black pigs were rooting under the stoops of neighboring houses. We walked a few yards in a procession to the entrance of the road. Engineer García, whom we had seen at work wearing dusty jeans, was almost unrecognizable in a sack suit. He explained that the road was five kilometers long, so many meters wide, and had taken so many pounds of this and that to be paved. It was not a final pavement; the macadam was to be covered over the small rocks and a final coating given later.

The president did not make a speech. The archbishop shook incense and holy water over the gauze strip that was tied across the road, and the president cut the strip. Then we got into the car with the president and his wife; we were to be the first to drive over the road.

One mile out, we met a man, a woman, and a child walking. The man was holding a chicken head down, tied by its legs. They, not we, were the first to inaugurate the road. It was hot, very hot. The president promised that trees would be planted along the road to shade pedestrians on the way to market.

Villeda Morales died of a heart attack a few years later. Were the trees ever planted? Who knows?

Later I visited three women doctors whom I had met on a previous trip to Honduras. Their practices seemed to be flourishing, but they were having servant trouble — the reason given was that prostitution was much more profitable than cooking or taking care of children. One of the doctors, who had four children, was obliged to close her office for two weeks when her only helper, an older woman, went on vacation.

A cheerful glimpse of the Honduran version of the American way of life was provided by a visit to a workers' new housing project, tucked away in a little valley between two hills. This oasis consisted of little block houses — about a hundred of them, with backyards and luxurious vegetation. A little boy, hose in hand, was watering a patch of green lawn — this in a desperately poor country, much of it a dust bowl. Was this real or just a mirage!

≈ *35*

From Honduras we flew to Puerto Rico, where Adolf was to attend a meeting of the Consejo Nacional de Educación Superior—the board of trustees of the University of Puerto Rico. Usually we stayed with Governor Muñoz Marín at La Fortaleza, a monumental structure, the oldest dwelling and fortress in the Western Hemisphere. But Adolf had not announced his arrival, and we found that the guest room was occupied by India's ambassador to the United States, G. Mehta, a fine gentleman whom we met the following day and whom I found particularly simpatico, since he had read all Adolf's books. So we spent the night in a hotel and since the meeting was scheduled for the following afternoon, we rented a car in the morning and went for a bumble. A bumble was an Adolfian specialty—a walk or drive with no particular end in view, following your fancy, going around the corner, the next corner, and the next, just to see what was there.

This time, I said, we should go around the corner and perhaps we'd see a *bumbulon. Bumbulon* is the word for tadpole in Honduras, an old Indian word incorporated into Spanish, perhaps. Anyhow, we had just learned it. I loved this word like a new toy. There did not appear to be any *bumbulones* around the corner in Puerto Rico. What of it? We found a small deserted inlet near Las Cobas and lay on rocks covered with soft seaweed, munching bread and cheese and watching the man-of-war birds and the changing lights over sea and sky, the dark blue El Yunque mountain behind us.

On the following day we moved to La Fortaleza and were installed in a bedroom on the top floor with a mammoth old Spanish four-poster, big enough to bed down a family of mother, father, and three children at least! The afternoon breeze was blowing in from the inland side, and the rays of the sun setting on the bay filtered through the white shutters. I came down the three flights of stairs to find Inez, the governor's wife, waiting for me in what I always think of as the enchanted garden.

We sat on the parapet, where the fortress wall drops some fifty feet to a small road at the edge of the bay. This was the fortress the Spaniards built to defend against Sir Francis Drake—but Drake never came!

Adolf and I loved Inez dearly. For us she represented the wise and loving Spanish matriarch, the woman on whom men and children depend. Men have the power, but women have the influence that guides the power.

On this occasion Inez expounded her views on the role of women. A woman is a person whose main energy and thought are concentrated on a man superior to herself.

What if the man is not superior? said I.

If she is good enough she can make him superior or at any rate make him feel that he is superior, and that is what really matters. Then the stage is set, she went on, for this man to fulfill himself and to be creative.

And as for the house and children? I asked.

That, said she, waving both her hands, is in the periphery. One must never be aware of that; it just has to work—the man is the center.

At that point I saw that she was looking through the laurel tree to see whether Muñoz had come. He was sitting with Adolf and two other men, who joined us presently, and we all went in to dinner.

A few days after our return to the States, Muñoz Marín came north to visit the dentist. He and Inez spent a brief weekend with us in the country. They were like children out of school, patting the snow, and we all had a very good time. The most amusing moment came when Muñoz went off Sunday morning by himself in one direction and Inez went in another. I came out to find the two policemen assigned to guard the guests standing around. When I asked where their charges were, they said they had not seen them and knew not where they had gone. It was wet underfoot and since one of the men had rubbers, I asked him to step over and ring the farm bell. He did so and at that point Muñoz and Inez appeared over the brow of the hill. Muñoz was in high spirits, considering that it had been ten years since he had been able to get a mile away from his keepers! It did not strike me until later that this was the supreme irony—a detective ringing the bell to find his charges.

We returned to Puerto Rico several times in the course of that year (1958), because Adolf was a very active member of the Consejo. Our next visit to the Fortaleza was particularly agreeable, since we were the only guests. A close feeling of understanding and affection bound the four of us together. Dining on the upper terrace in the light of the setting sun, Muñoz and Adolf dreamed long dreams. Operación Bootstrap, the plan through which American business had been encouraged to build factories on the island by means of tax exemptions, was being followed by Operación Serenidad—neon light advertisements were banned from the San Juan skyline, and undeveloped areas in the mountains and along the shore were to be preserved and turned into national parks. The *convento* that we visited the next day was one of these. A semicircular beach bounded by two headlands situated beyond Luquillo, the *convento* was free of buildings and dog wagons—a solitary spot except for a small air-conditioned house, which had been built as a retreat for Pablo Casals and other musicians. Isaac Stern and one of his friends were in residence when we arrived.

I walked alone along the edge of the water, following a fisherman who was holding a machete in one hand and his net in the other. Suddenly he flung his net into the sea and pulled it back—a glorious gesture. There were no fish this time. He flung the net again, undaunted. Unfortunately, I could not follow beyond the inlet, where he hopped into a small boat. Would he survive independent and solitary or would he be lured into the dirt and crowds of East Harlem? I wondered. Solitude is a rare bird—once lost, not easily recaptured.

As I turned toward the house, Isaac Stern was standing on the shore in his swimming trunks, small waves bathing his bare feet, his violin poised to play. We listened entranced as the sun was sinking into the sea and the great El Yunque darkened. The musician, his back to the sea, eyes closed, played Bach's Chaconne, transported in a world of his own beyond our reach. Adolf and I tried to recapture the lines from Keats's "Ode to a Nightingale":

> The voice I hear this passing night was
>   heard
> In ancient days by emperor and
>   clown;
> ....
>   The same that ofttimes hath
> Charmed magic casements, opening on
>   the foam
> Of perilous seas, in fairy lands for-
>   lorn.

Practicing Medicine ≈

Puerto Rico, Costa Rica, Honduras left me as a physician much food for thought. The people in Honduras appeared to be the most poorly nourished, although the patients in the Hospital San Juan de Dios in Costa Rica were a close second. According to my friend Dr. Miranda, a former Kellogg Fellow whom Dr. Almy and I had taught at Bellevue, individuals with a hemoglobin count of 5 cm (extremely low) were not rare in San José. Hookworm was disappearing rapidly in Puerto Rico, and gross malnutrition was rarely visible in East Harlem and on the wards of Bellevue. By the middle seventies, Puerto Ricans boasted of one car per three inhabitants, but the rates of drug addiction and juvenile delinquency were approaching those of the mainland.

The fundamental question remains unanswered — how is it possible to deal effectively with malnutrition and disease in the Third World without destroying the existing social and family structure? To adapt existing customs and traditions, which differ from culture to culture, so that populations may be guided to a realization of human interdependence and the need for moral values — integrity, responsibility, and love — is a task for priests, statesmen, and sociologists; a task not even begun!

I had been working at the New York Hospital for about a year, when I became ill myself — an unusual happening and an important educational experience. Every doctor should know what it is like to be a patient in bed. On my admission to the New York Hospital a diagnosis of tubo-ovarian abscess was made and chemotherapy was instituted. Proofs of friendship were not wanting on the part of my colleagues — besides the physicians who were taking care of me, Dr. Wolff paid a brief daily visit and brought me four red roses and a single yellow one.

More important, he took pains to reassure Adolf, who had an irrational fear of hospitals. Dr. Stewart Wolf, with whom we had established very close ties, gave me a pint of his blood when a transfusion was deemed necessary. Indeed, the doctors could not have been kinder or more efficient.

Not so the nurses. The following notes, written at the time, are still relevant today in many hospitals, although the nursing-school curriculum has been greatly improved.

> Fragmentation of Care
> From the point of view of the patient in bed, it appeared that procedure is the most important part of nursing.
> All technical procedures were most efficiently carried out, i.e., catheterization, assisting the doctor in taking a blood culture, or setting up a transfusion, etc.
> However, the various procedures were carried out as isolated items by different people on different days. Temperature, pulse, recording of stools might be Miss X's procedure today; tomorrow she might be "on medications". Miss Y was detailed to inquire about my symptoms today, but Miss X would inquire about them tomorrow.

I could not understand how the various fragments of information collected by so many different people could give the physician a complete and relevant picture of a patient's day-to-day course. I am able to recall no fewer than twelve individual nurses passing through my room during my hospital stay of nine days and nine nights. There probably were three or four more whose passage was so fleeting that I am unable to recall them. There did not seem to be any one individual nurse primarily responsible for my care. At no time did any nurse introduce herself to me by name. Their great number and rapid flitting in and out was very confusing during the first forty-eight hours.

I wondered how a patient established a rapport with her nurse or nurses. I was determined to accomplish this, so I asked every one her name, tried to remember it, and began to study her as a person. At the end of a few days, I had learned something about them and established quite a relationship with the student nurse who appeared to be more particularly assigned to my care. She got me extra coffee, gave me the lab reports, told me some of her own troubles, and consulted me on the management of a patient with a difficult emotional problem in the adjoining room. This was a distraction for me but hardly came under the heading of nursing care.

I wrote an indignant letter to Dr. David Barr, describing my dissatisfaction with the quality of the nursing care, but received no reply.

At the present time, there is a great shortage of nurses, since administration in business offices commands higher salaries. But a revolutionary idea confirming the obvious has suddenly dawned upon certain medical groups — the "primary nurse" is being re-created. This is a nurse who is expected to care for the patient's nursing needs throughout his or her illness, coordinating technical procedures that might be beyond her own skills but devoting herself primarily to her patient. Those hospitals which are instituting this program find that their enrollments have increased dramatically.

My troubles were not over. A year later I reentered the hospital for a hysterectomy. My reactions were interesting. Of course, I was scared, which brought me closer to an understanding of the feelings of Adolf, who was creating for himself ghastly pictures of septicemia and death. But I said to myself that, reinforced by sound medical knowledge, I must live up to my old code of behavior — self-control and trusting in the Lord. In preparation I obtained permission from my friend and surgeon, Dr. Gause, to watch him operate on another patient. The person on the table was draped so that only that portion of his body to be treated would be exposed to view at the appropriate moment.

Then came the time of my operation — a time for technique and the exercise of judgment and decision should the findings in the abdomen turn out otherwise than expected. In my case the decision to perform a hysterectomy was correct, and had surgery not been done, I would have languished for the rest of my life with intermittent abdominal pain and bouts of hemorrhage. Dear Dr. Wolff, who was in the operating room, later comforted Adolf over the telephone. All's well that ends well: Another ten years of life followed without illness.

Much as I enjoyed working in the clinic at New York Hospital, attending grand rounds and our own staff conferences, and taking care of a few private patients, I was not satisfied. Gradually, to use Dr. Wolff's expression, I came to "formulate" my real interest in medicine. At heart I was a country doctor. I would have liked to study and to care for families from birth to the grave, in a small community, keeping careful records of the course of their lives at work, at home, in sickness and in health, and of their relationships to each other. This, of course, was an impossible dream for a middle-aged woman with a family, living in a metropolis. How could one be a neighborhood physician in New York City? How could one study what Dr. Wolff was beginning to call human ecology — the whole man in his environment, both physical and cultural?

Through what source, I do not recall, I heard of the East Harlem Protestant Parish, with two or three churches and an office situated in the blocks between First and Second Avenues, and 100th and 106th Streets. On 100th Street everyone knew the Reverend Don Benedict and the Reverend Norman Eddy, and they knew everyone, calling them by name and asking about their families. It was a slum block inhabited by Puerto Ricans, blacks, and a few whites. No high-rise buildings: five- or six-story tenements with four apartments on a floor; bathtub in the kitchen, toilet in the hall, uncertain lighting and heating; women gossiping on the stoops in the summer; kids playing ball or lighting fires on the street with debris in the winter; a few dilapidated cars over which men gathered, peering hopefully under the hoods; a couple of small stores. Everyone knew everyone else, by sight, anyway. The clergy and families of the East Harlem Protestant Parish lived in apartments on this and neighboring blocks, as did a group of Catholic sisters. This was a neighborhood.

Encouraged by Dr. Wolff and the East Harlem Protestant Parish, I obtained a small grant from the Foresight Foundation. We rented a three-room apartment on the ground floor of 311 East 100th Street for eleven dollars a month and, with the assistance of a fellow in pediatrics, established a small medical office where we treated minor conditions in exchange for the opportunity to examine and study all members of a family. Presently we were joined by a team of social anthropologists. In due course I published a book entitled *80 Puerto Rican Families — Health and Disease Studied in Context.* The anthropologists, however, declined joint authorship and published their own separate and independent study. Such was the fate of interdisciplinary endeavors twenty years ago.

Gradually, the study developed into a family practice, with a new group formed by Margaret Grossi (then a young pediatrician, now deputy health commissioner of the City of New York in charge of maternal and health care), a Puerto Rican public-health nurse, and myself. All three of us were interested in continuing comprehensive medical care and vowed to practice together for five years. Several other physicians and nurses joined us on a part-time basis, but continuity was maintained, and every patient of the several hundred was known to at least one of the original team.

Two contiguous apartments were added to the original one, making the total rent forty dollars a month. Blood counts and urinalyses were done on the spot. We used the Health Department facilities for chest X rays and numerous stool analyses — hookworm was prevalent among Puerto Ricans at the time; now it has practically disappeared. Medical problems that were beyond our resources or capabilities were referred to specialty clinics at Mount Sinai Hospital, at 100th Street and Fifth Avenue. Obstetrical and pediatric patients were also referred for admission to that hospital. Other adult patients were hospitalized at

Bellevue, where I was an attending physician. Our contacts with Metropolitan Hospital, another city hospital, were unsatisfactory, owing to the crowded conditions and a lack of interest on the part of both administration and staff, but a step forward in neighborhood cooperation was taken when the new Metropolitan Hospital opened at Ninety-ninth Street and Second Avenue. Though Dr. Grossi and I were on the staff of New York Hospital, our patients were not "interesting cases" — they were just sick people, and so not eligible for admission.

In fact, apart from Dr. Wolff, my staunch supporter, New York Hospital physicians were rather scornful. "Since you are privileged to be on the staff of the New York Hospital and have a faculty appointment at the Cornell University Medical School, why do you want to go to the slums to practice 'poor medicine'?" We considered ourselves pioneers and longed to establish a vital relationship between our field station and the neighboring hospitals, believing that walking five blocks in the snow with a sick child for a daily penicillin injection was "poor medicine." We believed that families with small children should be treated near home by a family physician. We were able to pay house calls even after dark, since everyone on the block knew us and would open their doors for *"la doctora"* without hesitation.

This would not be true today. The construction of high-rise buildings and the demolition of Number 311 and other tenements, have provided central heating and sanitary housing, but the neighborhood in the terms that we knew no longer exists. At the time we were battling the rats, the lack of central heating and hot water, and uncertain electric lighting. In fact, my colleagues, the pediatrician Margaret Grossi and the psychiatrist Marie Nyswander, were prepared to quit if they saw any more little beady eyes peering up through the holes in the floor. After appealing in vain to the rat-control unit of the city Health Department, we were rescued by Angel, age fifteen. He was a member of the *"muchos"* family, known by that name because there were so many of them — nine children in and out of state institutions for behavior disorders or mental retardation. Angel was illiterate but most efficient in plugging up the holes.

This experience naturally led us to welcome the building of the high-rise housing developments with central heating and adequate plumbing and lighting. Alas, we learned that the improvement of physical environment can also involve unforeseen risks. Soon after the completion of one of the new buildings, the wife of a clergyman of the East Harlem Protestant Parish brought her nine-year-old girl to the clinic because she had been attacked in the elevator by an unknown man. (I examined her and was able to reassure both mother and child that fortunately, no physical harm had been done.)

[209]

At times, coming home either from East Harlem or from the New York Hospital or from an afternoon in my own office, I felt as if I had been a naked swimmer in the Amazon, being devoured by piranhas. It seemed as if people with all their troubles, no matter how insignificant they may have been, just clung and tried to tear their doctor apart in a vain effort to obtain relief. "They take pieces of you and throw them around," I said to a friend. "You know that they talk about you to their friends, that they both love you and curse you, and that you must remain always constant, perceptive, and unhurt, holding to the faith that life is worth living, that human beings are to be treated with compassion and love. There is universal order and design within which dedicated human beings can work and eventually achieve results." This was Adolf's and my faith, and we fortified each other.

Adolf was much interested in the East Harlem adventure and wanted me to publicize the work of the clinic for what it was: an experiment in what we now call community medicine and primary medical care. But none of us was a public-relations expert, and we preferred working in the field to promotional activity. As family physicians, we were able to sort out many minor complaints and convince men of their employability and children of the importance of school—as well as carry out appropriate immunization and contraceptive measures.

We soon found out that we could not ignore the drug problem. We were all neighbors. Heroin addicts stole from the clinic as they did from their own families—and if we were truly family physicians, how could we refuse to treat the son of one of our families when he had a boil at the site of an injection made with a dirty needle?

We were blessed by the arrival of Marie Nyswander, a psychiatrist with a long experience in private practice in the treatment of heroin addicts. She was discovering that psychoanalysis, with which she had been treating her patients, was not necessarily a cure for addiction. Together we tried out a buddy system. The addict declared himself willing to try to "kick" his habit and was put in charge of a "buddy," a nonaddict who promised to keep the patient locked up in his home for three days and to administer a prescribed dose of tranquilizers to mitigate the pains of withdrawal. After this the patient was to report for brief psychotherapy and medical treatment.

This method met with indifferent success—it depended largely on Dr. Nyswander's personal influence. She denied this, in spite of my observation that a confirmed addict of many years' standing, who had been visiting her for ten minutes once a week and had been abstinent, clean, and well dressed over a period of several months, reappeared in rags and in a stuporous state the week after she left on her vacation.

Bent upon research, Dr. Nyswander left us and joined the staff of Rockefeller University, where she and Dr. Vincent Dole discovered methadone to be an effective treatment for heroin addiction.

≈ *37*

Dr. Harold Wolff died in 1962. It was a dark cold February afternoon. At the clinic on 100th Street, the ceiling light was flickering. Were we about to be plunged into darkness? Where were the candles I had purchased last week? The telephone rang. Helen Goodell's voice said, "Dr. Wolff has suffered a stroke— he is unconscious in a Washington hospital. Isabel [his wife] has gone down already. Will you join me?"

We caught the next plane. It so happened that Adolf was in Washington on business. We four met at Harold's bedside. The following day he was transferred to the National Institutes of Health. His only response, an affirmative nod, came when one of his former residents, now on the staff of the National Institutes of Health, asked if Harold would like to be treated with hypothermia. At the time, lowering of body temperature was a new treatment used in neurosurgery to help to control hemorrhage in the brain. Alas, Harold never recovered consciousness. He died a week later. The original injury, an occlusion of the middle cerebral artery, proved intractable in spite of the use of the most modern machines.

It was both ironic and fitting that Harold should die in this way. He, who had observed and proved that man becomes ill when the strain of life as he perceives it becomes intolerable; he, who had witnessed so many cerebral accidents and demonstrated their effects at staff conferences in an incisive manner; he, who was deeply moved by the essential, unresolved problems of life and death— did not return "to tell us what it was like in 'limbo.'"

But as he always said, there is a lesson to be learned from every experiment that nature performs. Someone, someday, will return and be able to describe the state of hibernation; it will become possible to devise conditions that permit recovery after the original injury to the brain. Harold's disciples are working in many medical establishments, and it may be that his ideas will have a greater impact after his death than they did during his lifetime....

Dr. Wolff's death was a severe blow both from the professional and personal aspect. In middle life, Adolf, Harold, Harold's wife Isabel Bishop—a distinguished painter, and I had developed an unusual and special friendship. (As far as we know, Isabel and I are not related.) There were many points of contact between us, leading to continuing exploration of each other's views and tastes. We sometimes dined at the Wolffs' in Riverdale. The Wolffs sometimes came for the weekend to Great Barrington where we enjoyed discovering wildflowers together—lady slippers, hepatica, gentians—and skating in winter. Then around the open fire after a good dinner and a bottle of wine, conversation soared. Each developed his or her own ideas. Adolf was trying out his ideas on power, which would not appear in printed form for several years. Harold was working out his views on the importance of goals for human survival. In a study undertaken for the United States government, he was finding that the men who were able to pursue a goal in their thoughts were the ones who managed to survive privation in Japanese prison camps. The best example was the chief resident in medicine at the New York Hospital, who during incarceration maintained his goal of becoming a physician, then achieved his goal after his release. Isabel and I were good listeners, inserting challenging questions to encourage the discussants.

Shortly before Dr. Wolff died, we had spoken of the fact that the grant for the neighborhood clinic was running out. I said that a family neighborhood clinic had no business to exist in a metropolis unless it became formally attached to a teaching hospital to which clinic patients could be admitted when necessary, returning to their neighborhood physician on discharge. The clinic must be a place where medical students, interns, and residents could treat sick people in their homes, learning about the effects of illness within the context of daily life. Not every graduate of Cornell University Medical College was going to become a Nobel laureate—there must be some doctors to take care of people with common diseases.

The esoteric quality of medical education was borne in upon me when a student who had elected to spend a few weeks on 100th Street (with Dr. Wolff's help I had finally succeeded in planning and getting approval for an elective course on family medicine) became ecstatic on discovering a case of tonsillitis in one of our patients! He had been instructing me on the latest findings in the study of leukemia, but tonsillitis was new for him.

Dr. Wolff agreed with my goal, but he was no politician. His reserved manner did little to mitigate professional jealousies, although his international reputation and his scientific contributions were sufficiently important that his views could not be entirely disregarded by the Cornell—New York Hospital establishment. Unfortunately, the situation deteriorated as soon as he died. At my invitation, Dr. Dietrich, the dean of Cornell University Medical College, visited our clinic. His only comment on leaving was, "The streets are dirty." I knew I must look elsewhere for a sponsor.

I spent the next six years on this quest. Although Dr. Alan Guttmacher, professor of obstetrics at Mount Sinai, was my staunch supporter and had assigned several residents to see patients in consultation in my clinic, the department of medicine was not interested, so that door was closed also. I hoped that either New York University Medical College or Columbia University College of Physicians and Surgeons might be persuaded to establish a neighborhood clinic near Bellevue Hospital, where both these schools had important medical services at that time. Dr. Lewis Thomas, dean of New York University Medical College, and Dr. Dickinson Richards, professor of medicine at Columbia University College of Physicians and Surgeons and attending physician at Bellevue Hospital, visited the 100th Street clinic and were enthusiastic — particularly Dr. Thomas, who spoke eloquently of his father's experience as a general practitioner.

I resigned from the faculty of Cornell University Medical College, and in 1963 I accepted an appointment as associate professor of clinical medicine on the faculty of New York University Medical College, transferring my appointment as associate visiting physician at Bellevue Hospital from the Cornell to the New York University division. I hoped to be able to establish a family clinic in the Lower East Side. New York University was already sponsoring a clinic in the Gouverneur Hospital.

The development of a program for closer association both with the neighborhood and with Bellevue Hospital, as well as an elective course for both medical students and residents, sounded feasible. Unfortunately, Dr. Thomas left for a year's sabbatical in England, and his successor was not interested. Therefore, my elective course had no students, and no improvement took place in the outpatient division of Bellevue Hospital, where all efforts to ensure continuity of care — that patients should see the same physician on a return visit whom they had seen on their first visit — proved fruitless. I became greatly discouraged and decided to look elsewhere.

St. Luke's Hospital, I heard, had recently appointed a professor of community medicine. The problem in this case turned out to be the community itself. Representatives of various community groups could not come to an agreement with the hospital authorities on the organization and financing of the projected clinic. While the unsuccessful negotiations were going on, I became interested in the possibilities of genetic counseling as a branch of family medicine. Sickle-cell anemia was the most prevalent hereditary disease in the neighborhood.

It is found in persons of African and Mediterranean origin, but at this time (1967) the black population was so sensitive on the subject that genetic counseling was interpreted as a white conspiracy to bring about genocide of the blacks. Several years later, I treated a black patient whose child, he informed me, was suffering from sickle-cell disease—a very painful affliction. When I suggested that further pregnancies should be avoided, he burst into tears, exclaiming, "Why didn't anyone tell me this before?" Why indeed?

Finally, I decided to return to my old East Harlem neighborhood. The Mount Sinai School of Medicine had just appointed a professor of community medicine. After I had related my previous experience, he told me to secure a petition from residents of the neighborhood requesting the reestablishment of the clinic. Members and the clergy of the East Harlem Protestant Parish and a number of my former patients came forward gladly—but nothing happened.

As I was feeling more and more ineffectual, a friend and colleague, Dr. Joyce Lowinson, suggested that I join her in organizing a methadone maintenance program for the treatment of heroin addicts. I accepted and spent the last six years of my professional life as a medical consultant on the faculty of Albert Einstein College of Medicine, working out of the Bronx State Hospital.

The experience was an interesting one. I am convinced of the efficacy of methadone maintenance as a treatment for heroin addiction; however, the problem of addiction is worldwide, and so far little progress has been made toward its solution.

There are many reasons for my lack of success in promoting the concept of the family neighborhood clinic and in putting an end to fragmented medical care. For one thing, twenty years ago, even ten years ago, the time was not ripe. Today family medicine is slowly coming into its own. For another, at no time did I become what the French call *"de la maison"*—that is, I did not belong to the inner circle of the faculties. Naturally, I have wondered whether, had I remained in one place rather than tried to insert myself into different hospitals, the problem would have been resolved. I do not think so. Each time I made a move, it was on the basis of an assurance from an individual who shared my views and believed he was in a position to carry out a plan for the establishment of a neighborhood clinic designed to care for patients and to train family physicians—called primary-care physicians today.

The extraordinary scientific advances over the past twenty-five years that necessitate the use of increasingly expensive and complicated apparatus; the growing expectations and demands of the public in terms of health care; rising costs; and the problem of allocating health resources—all have resulted in the institutionalization of medicine and made the need for the primary physician greater than ever. And they have increased the difficulties attendant upon the education of such a person.

I believe that the primary physician should be a physician responsible for the comprehensive, long-term care of a patient and his family. As Stewart Wolf and I say in our book, *Limits of Medicine* (Plenum Press, 1978), this physician must be "a person highly educated and experienced, able to serve as a diagnostician, decision maker and advisor."

According to this definition, the responsible physician is *not* a superspecialist but is sufficiently knowledgeable to treat the majority of illnesses and to refer the patient to the superspecialist when necessary. The responsible physician evaluates the services offered by the superspecialist in terms of his patient's overall condition and continues to care for the patient after the technical procedures provided by the superspecialist have been completed.

I am hopeful that in time the medical schools will realize the need for the training of responsible physicians and the public will be educated to consult a responsible physician first rather than making their initial contact with a superspecialist. The establishment of residencies in family practice is a step in the right direction. However, the situation is not encouraging, as the results of a recent study indicate.

Not only is solo practice out of date, but American medicine has been taken over by profit-making corporations that own the hospital and the apparatus, hire the doctor, and fire him if he does not show a profit. In addition, forty-two percent of the nation's medical costs is paid by the government. Medicine is no longer a service, but a commodity.

Since I am too old to organize a campaign, I have tried to make myself useful to bewildered friends by interpreting the decrees and contradictory recommendations of superspecialists who do not communicate with each other or with their patients.

Once again, I am impressed with the importance of trust, in the doctor-patient relationship. Today the lack of trust on the part of the patient is one of the causes of costly malpractice suits while misplaced trust favors the charlatan. I remember my distress when I was externing at Bellevue and an old man on whom a spinal tap had been ordered refused to let anyone but me perform this procedure. I kept insisting to him that my colleagues were more competent than I — as indeed they were — but to no avail. "I trust you," he kept saying, "not the others." Not feeling brash, I nevertheless went ahead and, fortunately, hit the right interval between the vertebrae.

The Cuban Episode ≈

≈ *38*

In June 1960, Adolf was asked to join an appeal by intellectuals in favor of John F. Kennedy's nomination as the Democratic candidate for president. Ken Galbraith and Arthur Schlesinger had already signed. A few days later Adolf met Senator Kennedy with members of the Liberal party, whose support the Senator was seeking.

After his nomination in July, Senator Kennedy invited Adolf to organize a task force on Latin America to advise him. Adolf and I were in complete accord about the importance of Latin America in relation to the security of the United States. Adolf had many sources of information, and there was no doubt that Soviet technicians, arms, and equipment were being flown into Cuba with a view to establishing a military base on the island. On the other side, the plot to assassinate Rómulo Betancourt, the democratic president of Venezuela, was traced directly to the Dominican dictator, Rafael Trujillo.

In the task-force report presented to President-elect Kennedy at the end of the year, Adolf recommended, among other measures, financial support of Colombia and Venezuela and prevention of arms shipments to Cuba, Santo Domingo, and other Latin American countries. A long-term economic plan, which later became known as the Alliance for Progress, was outlined.

In order to end the stepchild status of Latin America in United States policy, Adolf urged the creation of an undersecretaryship of state for the Western Hemisphere, this official to report to the secretary of state and have access to the president.

Arturo Morales Carrión, secretary of state for the governor of Puerto Rico, Muñoz Marín, and a professor of history at the University of Puerto Rico, was one of Adolf's most active collaborators in drawing up the report. I was particularly happy that a Puerto Rican should have a leading part in this task, and since much of the work was done at home in Nineteenth Street and in Great Barrington, I followed with interest and approval. On New Year's Eve, we three went to Puerto Rico to be present at the inauguration of Muñoz Marín for his third term as governor.

On January 8, 1961, Dean Rusk, secretary of state–designate, came to lunch alone with us at Nineteenth Street. He was inviting Adolf to take a position in the new administration.

From my point of view this was 1938 all over again — with an important difference: Adolf would be sixty-six in a few days, and I was fifty-eight.

Power without Property, an elaboration and an updating of the now classic, *The Modern Corporation and Private Property*, published in 1932, had just appeared and was going well. The previous summer Adolf had had a brilliant encounter defending enlightened capitalism against the distinguished French Socialist Jules Moch, in Geneva. We had gone to Brazil for additional lectures. In fact, Adolf appeared to be more and more creative as he worked in the garden ruminating on the concept of power — ten years later he published a book under that title.

I was running my neighborhood clinic on 100th Street. It was a satisfying and exciting little venture and had a future if only I could succeed in interesting a medical school in training the needed physicians. Peter, our son, had married the previous spring — the young couple were in the Philippines, where Peter was serving as a second lieutenant in the air force. We were living a productive, interesting life. But Adolf, unalterably both scholar and man of action, wished once more to play a part in the international scene.

"This will shorten your life," I said. "It may even kill you."

"I am willing to take the risk," he replied. "Are you?"

"Yes," was the only answer I could give.

The position turned out to be anomalous. The undersecretaryship of state for the Western Hemisphere was not created, nor has it been created. Dean Rusk was suggesting that Adolf accept the title of ambassador at large or presidential assistant, working directly with the president. Mindful of past struggles between the White House and the State Department, Adolf refused an off-center position. Believing that foreign policy must be handled through the secretary of state, he became instead chairman of an intradepartmental task force for Latin America with headquarters in the State Department.

Our move to Washington was preceded by a trip around South America. When we settled in Washington this time I was the commuter, returning to run my clinic as often as possible.

The Alliance for Progress speech written by Adolf and Dick Goodwin, special adviser to the White House, was delivered on March 13 by the president. It recommended measures for long-term economic development in the hemisphere. I commented at the time that judging from the reactions of Brazil and other countries we had visited, the Cuban danger remained unchanged, and when the chips came down no one would provide a gun—the United States would stand alone and be expected to accept the challenge and stand the criticism. Also, it did not follow that Congress would vote the necessary appropriations to make possible the program as outlined. Actually, funds were appropriated, and both Brazil and Venezuela were substantial beneficiaries.

There I was in Washington, in a fancy house, without much to do. It was unthinkable that I should not be there with Adolf. Up to a point it was easy to do nothing, to enjoy pleasant sociability, to expend much effort in arranging a dinner party and making sure that the white tablecloth was perfectly pressed, the menu and wines well chosen. Yet if the day seemed a bit empty, when Adolf came home I knew why I was there, and I had no regrets.

The Cuban situation was becoming more critical every day. Of course, I knew nothing about the plan for the Bay of Pigs. On April 19, the day of the unsuccessful invasion, we had had an exhausting reception for Thomas Mann, our newly appointed Ambassador to Mexico, and his wife, Nancy. The atmosphere was tense and gloomy.

At 1:30 A.M., we were both asleep, when a consistent banging of the front-door knocker finally came through to me. The State Department duty officer was there to take Adolf to the White House. I woke Adolf; he got the president on the telephone, then told me he would probably leave for Florida to see Miro Cardona and Tony Varona of the Cuban Revolutionary Council. He dressed. I made coffee. We packed a light suit, a shirt, shaving things.

The duty officer called the White House, announcing that they were on the way. "What is the news?" I asked him.

Hesitation, then: "Nothing new since what you heard on the radio before you went to bed."

Adolf and I kissed several times—casually. There was another trip upstairs to find the house keys. We checked on who was due to come for dinner the following night. Then he was gone into the night with the duty officer. I tried the Cuban radio, which was silent—and finished Hartog's *The Inspector*. It was 3:00 A.M. when I turned out the light. I thought of those who were praying for Adolf, and I prayed too.

I realized that this was a test of wills, of national strength and survival, such as we had never faced before and that most of the United States did not realize it. It affected Adolf and me individually as nothing else had. The immediate issue was drawn: We could not tolerate the Soviets in this hemisphere; but did the exiles miscalculate their strength, would this turn into a long-drawn-out bloody civil war in Cuba, with the rest of the world standing by and criticizing our involvement?

For me at the moment, it meant waiting for Adolf—being there when he returned and meanwhile doing lots of inconsequential things to pass the time. Ours had been a good life, but no life is without its periods of disaster, national or personal, and somehow one must continue to have faith.

The White House also was going on about business. There was a dance and reception for members of Congress, and the work continued upstairs in private afterward.

Adolf returned the following night. He had gone to Florida with Arthur Schlesinger to bring back Cardona and Varona. He had asked the president to see them, which Mr. Kennedy did.

The "invasion beachhead" failed. The president told the newspapers that we were in for a long pull. He appeared determined and clear-headed. "Nixon is *not* president, thank goodness," I commented in my diary.

The severity and reality of the Soviet threat became obvious in the confrontation with the Soviets the following October.

Soon after this, I went up to New York for a couple of days. It was an exquisitely lovely spring—so cool that the tender, tiny green leaves were still with us on the first of May.

In addition to working at the clinic on 100th Street, I held my appointment as assistant clinical professor of medicine at Cornell University Medical College in New York and was acting as adviser to the Kellogg Foundation fellows. On this occasion, Gilberto Freyre, the Brazilian sociologist, the first scholar to point out the contribution of blacks to American culture, joined me and a group of ten young South American medical students at Nineteenth Street. He had dined with us in Washington a few days before, hopefully discussing the future role of Brazil in Africa as the mediator between civilizations.

The evening before this gathering with the students, walking along the canal in Washington, Adolf had expounded to me the objectives and the working of socialized capitalism in the United States, and I duly relayed his ideas to the young physicians. Gilberto Freyre concurred, emphasizing the archaic nature of capitalism in São Paulo at this time. Together we tried to explain that American manners were different, inferior probably to Brazilian manners, and that when a busy intern or attending physician with whom one had had an exciting exchange of views on the previous day rushed by without even saying hello, this was not to be taken as a personal insult. It was a very satisfactory evening.

We had good evenings in Washington, too. Muñoz Marín, his wife, Inez, Arthur Schlesinger, and Kenneth Galbraith disagreed with Adolf's views on the Bay of Pigs, considering that using main force at this time would have created more problems than it solved. But that did not prevent us from enjoying the evening as we ate *poulet à la reine*. Friedl, our fine cook, declared that she had cut the recipe from the newspaper and that this was the president's favorite dish. We drank Tavel through the evening, a Uruguayan played the guitar, another read some of his own poetry. Then Muñoz Marín explained Operación Serenidad. People, he said, might build large houses if they wished, but access to the sea and to the beach must not be preempted by the real estate operator, for all men have a right to beauty.

As June wore on, Adolf became more and more disgusted with the rabbits in the State Department, who he felt were sabotaging not only his reports but also direct orders given by the president. "I have been in the State Department," he commented, "when the secretary did not speak to the undersecretary or the president did not speak to the secretary of state, but never before has the State Department not spoken to the president."

Before leaving Washington, we helped our daughter Alice to arrange a one-person show of her paintings in a new gallery. She is a professional artist whose dedication and continuing growth have not ceased since she was Portinari's pupil in Brazil at the age of fourteen. The show was well attended, and she sold several pictures.

It was time to get a new perspective. We decided to go around the world, visiting Peter and Lila in the Philippines, touching base in Great Barrington before leaving.

I galloped across the field on horseback, shouting, "Hello!" to Adolf in the canoe as he pulled in a trout. It was the magic hour, as he called it—we would have great adventures together again.

Post-Kennedy ≈

≈ 39

We had no experience and little knowledge of the East. Peter was a first lieutenant in the air force, and Lila had joined him after their marriage in May 1960. Peter had exercised the proverbial Berle initiative and succeeded in getting an assignment that permitted him to go to Singapore and learn something about jungle warfare and parachuting. This information he was making available to the American forces in the Philippines.

When we arrived, he was receiving a special award for his work. We were much impressed. It was a credit to Peter that he had been able to organize an independent project within the army and a credit to the army that they recognized individual initiative. Apparently the staff thought well of him and recommended that he make the army his career. "But," said Peter, "they were offering me security, emphasizing fringe benefits—not a challenge."

Since Peter had two weeks' leave, we decided to travel together to Japan and India. In New Delhi we stayed with the American ambassador to India, Adolf's old friend Kenneth Galbraith. Galbraith saluted Adolf as one of America's most durable politicians! We met Nehru and Adolf chatted with him for about fifteen minutes. (Unfortunately, there is no note of the conversation in either of our diaries.) We also wanted to see the mountains, but it was the wrong season; our only view of the Himalayas was obscured by clouds and fog.

I cannot say that the voyage was an unqualified success. We were both tired, Adolf especially, and our background knowledge of the countries we visited was insufficient for us to be more than casual tourists. How could we at our age undertake a study in depth of these ancient civilizations, so as to try to understand their current problems? Europe beckoned to us, to me especially. I wanted to learn more, to appreciate better the world with which I was familiar. As a result, instead of getting off the KLM plane in Lagos, we stayed on and arrived in Zurich. How happy I was to see the fir trees, to watch peasants making hay on slopes, to drive along the road to Geneva and find our friends the Georges Henri Martins, with whom we shared an association of twenty years.

When we got back to New York, we picked up where we had left off before going to Washington.

Even though Adolf did not have another "major rendezvous with destiny," as he had hoped, the next decade, the last ten years of our lives together, turned out to be productive and happy. Many of the personal friendships and Latin American activities in which I shared came to fruition. Adolf published two important books. The first, *The American Economic Republic* (1963), had a wonderful dedication to Beatrice Bishop Berle, "Baccalaureate of the University of Paris, Master of Arts in History, Ambassadress of the United States, whose skill and hearth and heart have been open alike to the high and the humble of many lands, this book is dedicated in admiration, friendship and love." The other, *Power* (1969), crossed many academic lines long before interdisciplinary studies had become popular. Adolf's death in 1971 prevented him from keeping lecture engagements when he would have been able to present the book to diverse audiences. In this book, Adolf was endeavoring to stake out the laws of power, believing that political science would not be a science until laws governing political activities could be formulated. According to Adolf, power is always personal.

1. Power will invariably enter and organize any situation threatening chaos or disorder.
2. Power is always personal, coming to rest in a man or men.
3. Power is invariably supported by, and usually invested in, institutions, organizing its exercise and its application.
4. The institutions for the exercise and application of power are invariably based upon a philosophy or idea system.
5. The institutions of power and the power holders and the idea structure are invariably confronted by a field of responsibility, be it acknowledged and recognized or unrecognized and inchoate.

One person who understood this concept was Fred Lawrence Whipple, the astronomer and discoverer of comets, who, on listening to Adolf's presentation at the American Philosophical Society, became very enthusiastic. "These are laws indeed; they fit the facts as we know them and produce a rational explanation."

As these books were being written and published, Adolf enjoyed discussing them with friends, walking around the garden in Great Barrington or sitting around the dinner table in Nineteenth Street. One of his favorite interlocutors was the Jesuit priest Paul Harbrecht, sent by his superiors to study under Adolf at the Columbia Law School, where he wrote a book on pension trusts. I thought of Paul as Adolf's spiritual son; he became friends with our children as well and godfather to one of our grandchildren. On the pond at Great Barrington, he guided the stern paddle of the canoe as Adolf cast a fly for the elusive trout. Unfortunately, Father Paul was caught in an agonizing personal dilemma. After spending seventeen years studying to become a Jesuit, he fell in love with a young woman and, following a painful struggle, returned to the lay state so that he could marry her. They had two children. Regrettably, since Adolf's death, the Harbrecht family has disappeared completely from our lives. I hope that Paul's scars are well healed.

Another family friend was Nelson Rockefeller. The social relations between our two families antedated the war, and when Nelson came to Washington as coordinator of inter-American affairs, Adolf tried to protect Rockefeller, the outsider, from the snipings of the regulars in the State Department. Adolf's political association with Nelson over the years is fully discussed in *Navigating the Rapids*. I will speak here only of the many friendly contacts between parents and children, which continue to this day. The high point was reached one spring day when Nelson took Adolf to a storage basement on the Rockefeller estate in Tarrytown, and together they lifted a Mexican stone monkey into the trunk of our Chevrolet. This object was the work of Mexican children working in an art school in Mexico, a school sponsored during the war by the coordinator of inter-American affairs. The monkey was set on a stone wall in our garden — a dry wall, which he succeeded in toppling because of his heavy weight! But he was not like Humpty Dumpty — we were able to lift him up again in one piece.

There were other personal political ties, since the Rockefeller and Berle houses were the only ones in which Rómulo Betancourt, later a democratically elected president of Venezuela, was received during his exile in the United States, at a time when the State Department gave him a cold shoulder.

Rómulo Betancourt dined with us the night before his return to Venezuela to run for election. He, like Count Sforza, fifteen years before, came to say farewell to Adolf, the exiles' sponsor. Betancourt was duly elected, and he governed wisely and effectively, building up a strong party, so that Venezuelan democracy is now well established.

We visited Rómulo several times in his house at Altamira on the outskirts of Caracas and in Switzerland after his retirement. On one occasion in 1964, the government party was holding a convention for the selection of the next presidential candidate, and the Communists warned the public that they would sabotage the meeting. With Rómulo, we watched on television as thousands of people walked to the hall, notwithstanding a driving rainstorm.

One bomb went off, and three Communists were shot by the security police. The following morning it was business as usual. While the armed guard walked up and down the garden wall, Adolf, Rómulo, and I swam in the little pool at the residence discussing the development of the new city, Goyania, on the banks of the Orinoco river.

Only the previous year, Rómulo had barely escaped assassination at the hands of an agent of the Dominican dictator Trujillo. Liberals and democrats like Rómulo Betancourt, Muñoz Marín, José Figueres, and those who have come after them are targets for both the extreme left and the extreme right.

≈ *40*

Adolf never ceased trying to bring the hemisphere together. One evening Luis Manuel Debayle of Nicaragua and Pepe Figueres sat together in our living room under Catherine's portrait. Would she have been surprised? I wonder. Unfortunately, the conversation did not lead to any practical solutions, but after Somoza's assassination, when his oldest son, Luis, had succeeded him, Adolf and I went to Nicaragua to meet him, at the invitation of Luis Manuel.

The Somozas arrived at Debayle's house in the country above Managua at eight o'clock. The señora, American-born, was the mother of seven children. Luis, a big man in his forties with a double chin, had a persuasive manner and told his stories well. I felt he would have no difficulty in imposing his will on his subordinates. That evening, he wanted to impress us, and he talked at length about his school program, agricultural reforms, labor relations, and so on, promising elections in 1963.

It was a long evening. The gentlemen retired after dinner and remained closeted until 2:00 A.M. while the ladies were left to entertain each other with fitful conversation between yawns. A few months later, Luis Somoza died of a heart attack. He was succeeded by his brother Tachito, and the subsequent bloody revolution in Nicaragua is not over yet. Had Luis lived and been able to put through the reforms he discussed with Adolf that evening, things might have been different. But dwelling on historical might-have-beens is a futile pastime.

On this same visit to Central America we went to Guatemala, where Adolf had been invited by President Miguel Ydígoras Fuentes to advise his government in reorganizing their finances.

I believe President Ydígoras and his able and ambitious aide, Roberto Alejos, were sincere in their efforts. I do not have any information about the circumstances surrounding the overthrow of the Arbenz government, so I will make no comment. However, we could not help shivering a little as we looked at the bullet holes made by the shots that had been aimed at Carlos Castillo Armas.

We were guests in the Casa Crema, the presidential palace. Not a breath of fresh air in the bedroom; the windows were boarded up with sheet metal to protect us from bullets.

The following evening a *banquete* was given by the president in honor of the United States ambassador and ourselves. There were thirty-four people in all: ministers of state and members of the United States embassy. Alejos was the protocol headache—not a minister and yet more than a minister, an able and energetic man in his forties who was being lured by the siren "power" against his wife's wishes. In fact, she had a severe migraine the following day when Ydígoras named Alejos his general coordinator.

As we went in to dinner, Ydígoras pointed to the bullet holes in the dining room, calling them "the two eyes."

"The Sword of Damocles," replied Adolf.

For most of the guests it was a stiff and dull occasion—indifferent food and wine, fine glass and china, beautiful tablecloth. The chief butler, the president pointed out, had served five presidents and seven imposters (the junta). The president, on whose left I sat, was fascinating as he spoke at length about schools, the interest of Indians in industrial development, cotton growing, and so forth.

He talked to Adolf at length across the table, so we sat from nine-fifteen to eleven-thirty—he might have lifted the siege and gone outside to talk to Adolf, but he didn't. I tried to pass the conversational ball to the ambassador's wife, but she dropped it—hopeless.

The president found out I was an M.D., so he ordered me and the minister of public health to sally forth at eight the next morning. Dr. Manuel López Herrarte turned out to have been a surgical resident at New York Hospital from 1940 to 1944. We understood each other at once. He was trying to maintain his organization, but the United States government bureaucracy had a master plan into which his scheme did not fit. Also, the new hospital, the "Roosevelt," did not have funds to open all its wards. It practiced academic medicine at $8.00 a day while the "Bellevue" of the city cared for patients at $3.50 a day. As far as I know, there has been no study comparing the mortality rate or the quality of care in the two institutions!

On Sunday morning I wandered around Guatemala City watching people going to church. An older woman, a woman in her thirties, a girl of ten, a babe in arms, all starched and booted, were getting out of a taxi in front of one of the churches. The babe was carried by a barefoot Indian girl—no shoes for the servant.

Inside the cathedral were all kinds and manner of men, women, and children. A hard-faced older Spanish woman—aquiline nose, over-red lips, a mantilla; another in black with puffy eyes and a blank expression sitting next to an old Indian man in patched clean clothes. Before the elevation, the bells rang out, a child wailed, and we all knelt respectfully. At the end, we pushed out through the doors to the blue sky and the vendor of balloons. The bunco steerers, as Adolf called street vendors, had charming wares: little jumping monkeys, whirling plumed little noisemakers. A well-dressed, starched family was delightedly playing with a little girl taking her first steps, the father commenting as she lurched, *"Como si tuviera su jaibolito."* (Just as if she had drunk a little highball).

I chatted with a man sitting under a tree with his wife and three children. He had the classic spongy gums of scurvy. He had been out of work for three weeks, and the three weeks previously he had held a carpenter's job. He considered that he could not afford to pay for Social Security. Apparently it is not obligatory for small concerns and their employees. Arevalo was his hero, but from Arbenz on he considered that all governments, including the present one, were grinding the faces of the poor.

Before leaving, Adolf spent some time with the United States embassy staff, as he always did on similar occasions. He ran the meeting like a Columbia seminar, developing the views of the staff and interjecting his own at appropriate moments.

In Miami, on our way home, we dined at the Chesapeake East—good crabs and seafood. As I saw Adolf settling at the table, I counted myself indeed blessed; the idea of spending the next two hours exchanging impressions with him and listening to him filled me with joy and anticipation. I was not disappointed!

"Nada es verdad ni mentira en este mundo traidor. Todo es según el color del cristal con que se mira." ("In this treacherous world there is neither truth nor falsehood. All depends on the color of the glass through which you look.") Calderon de la Barca, as quoted by Luis Manuel Debayle.

≈ *41*

Although Santo Domingo (now the Dominican Republic) had been Adolf's first love in the Caribbean, we did not go there until 1964, three years after Trujillo's assassination. We went on our own—just to see! The government was composed of a triumvirate, pending elections.

When we arrived in July of that year, Donald Reid Cabral was the man in charge. Although his brother had been killed by the dictator, Donald had managed to survive. His father, a Scotsman, had come to Santo Domingo many years earlier as manager of the Royal Bank of Canada and had married a Dominican lady. Donald characterized his father as a Scotch Presbyterian and a most rigid and moral man. "He was hard, and I am glad he was. I learned to work very early. I have always worked long hours, and I believe in work—hard work."

The following day we rented a car, driving on a four-lane highway most of the way. Dictators build roads for military purposes, but the roads have other uses too! Coming over the crest of the hill into Santiago de los Caballeros, the road became a six-lane highway. A little brown pig crossed the road nonchalantly while we gazed, appalled, at a hideous column. This, it seems, was put up by Trujillo. It was topped by an enormous statue, which was broken up when Trujillo's fall came. We were told that the head is preserved in a private museum just to show how ugly and awful the statue was.

Santiago was the town from which Adolf had written his first letter to me in 1925, after our meeting under the Washington Square arch. Although Café Eden had disappeared, Adolf thought the town had changed very little. We took a back road, driving slowly through clouds of brown dust, waving to the brown children, who waved back smiling. Adolf wanted to show me the hills where his Dominican adventures had begun in 1918, at the time of the occupation of the island by the American marines.

"At that time," he told me, "I was working on the verification of land titles for the Central Romano, a sugar company. This was during World War I, when the United States needed sugar very badly. By the time the titles were established, the war was over. We did not need the sugar, but the Central is still functioning today!

"My work took me into the back country. One day I got lost in the hills you can see from here. A great storm blew up. Torrential rain, in the tropics, pours down as if every hydrant in the world had opened up. It can be quite frightening. Night falls quickly here—there is no prolonged twilight, as there is in temperate zones. Then I saw a small, isolated house by the side of the trail. Fighting the driving wind and rain, I went up to the door and knocked. A man came to the door, and I asked for shelter. Leaving the door ajar, the man turned to people inside whom I could not see, and there was a brief whispered conversation.

"*Entre, señor.*' The door was opened, and I went in. Three men and a woman were sitting around a table. The house had a dirt floor and adobe walls, one window in the rear, an oil lamp.

"We spoke of the weather and the crops. I was invited to share rice and beans with them. The storm abated. I rose to leave, expressing my appreciation. They looked from one to another. The father stood in front of the door. *'Un momento, señor; hay peligro. Mi hijo va con usted.'* His son would pilot me down the mountain's circuitous trail.

"We went past a number of small houses; a little light flickered through the one window of each. Only later did I learn that in the recent shooting of hostages by the American occupation forces, a relative of the boy who guided me had been killed. The population was prepared to shoot any American who ventured into the neighborhood. But the boy's presence had shown them that I had broken bread with the uncle of the victim. I was safe. Such is the meaning of friendship."

When we returned to the center of the town, we were informed that we were to be received by the governor of the province of Santiago, an energetic and competent woman. She was accompanied by the bishop, who showed us Madre y Maestra, the new Catholic university, under construction. It was completed and is now functioning well. In view of the Communist infiltration of the national university, the church was endeavoring to establish a counterforce.

The governor took us to her home, where we met her mother, her husband, her pretty daughter, and her fifteen-year-old son. When we arrived, the youth was in the yard, washing his jeep. He offered to drive us "wherever you want to go." This sounded like our son Peter! The minister of health, also a guest, told us that the boy was working on malaria control with a crew of youngsters.

After returning to Santo Domingo city, we drove out to Central Romana. The firm's old accountant still remembered Adolf. The others working there were young Americans who lived in a world of their own.

Before we left the island, Adolf had a number of serious conversations with Cabral. Politically, his problems were similar to those of Betancourt in Venezuela: How to lead a people long oppressed by a brutal dictatorship into the ways of democracy, to avoid an army takeover on the one hand and Communist domination on the other. But the Dominican Republic does not have oil, and a one-crop sugar economy is not sufficient for survival.

From the Dominican Republic we flew over to Puerto Rico, where Adolf tried unsuccessfully to persuade Governor Roberto Sánchez, Muñoz's successor, to recognize the legitimacy of the current Dominican government and to work out a plan for economic assistance. Nevertheless, although the economic problems of the Dominican Republic are far from resolved today, the continuing political stability of the country is a cause for rejoicing.

≈≈≈ *42*

Our only trip behind the iron curtain took place in 1966, when we attended the meeting of the International Political Science Association at the invitation of Jacques Freymond, our friend from Geneva. We wanted to see for ourselves how a Communist regime provides for its people.

We stayed at the Europejski Hotel in Warsaw, where visiting Americans of Polish origin entertained their Polish relatives with fine meals, paying in dollars and thus helping the Polish economy. On our arrival, I asked the chambermaid to have two shirts washed for Adolf. She replied that she would do them herself. Since we did not have the exact change in Polish currency, we gave her two one-dollar bills. The poor woman burst into tears and threw her arms around my neck. I was in tears too. As we were communicating in broken German, she explained that she would be able to buy meat for her children on the black market; none had been available in the government stores.

She was a tall, well-built blond woman who bore a striking resemblance to Josephine, our beloved housekeeper in Great Barrington. Josephine's mother and father were poor Polish peasants who emigrated from Poland to the Berkshires before World War I. Josephine, her sisters, and their husbands owned their own homes and their cars, and their children are in college — her youngest son was graduating this year with a master's degree in electrical engineering. This is a familiar story, but the American liberal too often tends to forget it and to point only to the failures of the American system — which, alas, are many and must be corrected.

We were enthusiastically received by the friends and colleagues of Dr. Pyka, our neighbor on Nineteenth Street who had come to the United States as a displaced person after World War II. Not being party members, his friends lived in straitened circumstances and were denied promotions but at that time were not being molested. Those who were sufficiently distinguished and were known abroad were permitted to attend medical conferences in the West. The travel allowance was so small that it was necessary for their American friends to supplement it when they were in the United States.

The meetings of the international conference were held in the nineteenth-century palace of Jablona, which had been built for one of the Polish kings and was now a conference center.

At the conference, Adolf set forth his views on American capitalism. The Soviets were somewhat vituperative, but they calmed down at breakfast the following morning, as they were spreading scrambled eggs over their beards, and explained that they were making a discovery: They improved productivity by giving a bonus to good workers and discharging poor managers!

We wanted to see something of the countryside and managed to rent a Fiat for two days. We found the fields on the way to Kraków well cared for. Each was plowed by one man driving a horse. Women were digging potatoes and weeding, all by hand—no tractors in sight. We were told in Kraków that the state had recently returned these fields to their peasant owners.

The hotel was modern and comfortable enough. In the restaurant on the square, we saw two women guests, made up fit to kill. They and their escorts were treated with great respect. "Party members," whispered the professor whom we had invited to join us. I see them coming in here frequently. *I* can afford to come here only at Christmastime. Beauty parlors," he went on, "are private enterprises, and everyone somehow manages to afford a hair do." Indeed, not only the party members but the waitress and other women walking in the square had heads surrounded by fluffed-up beehives.

The waitress took our order—fish and Yugoslavian wine—while the customer at the next table tried to kiss her hand to attract her attention. As we were eating, an old woman with broken shoes and very swollen legs was sweeping up the dust with a broom made of twigs.

The unhappy events of the last two years have magnified these small incidents in my mind. My heart is full of sympathy for the brave, warm-hearted Polish people.

When the time came to leave Poland, we were glad to fly once more to join our friends in Geneva.

A few days later, we flew home. Leaving for a trip and coming home were equally happy experiences. We enjoyed both our homes, and so did our friends.

We had many friends—some we had known and loved over many years, some more recent ones. We liked to think of a friend as one who came into our home, who shared a bit of our lives, and for whom the memory of time spent in Great Barrington or in Nineteenth Street became a part of our joint heritage—theirs and ours.

Frequently it turned out this way. People whom we knew when they were children now bring their own children. "This is the place," a father may say to his son, "where I fell through the ice when I was your age." Another will remember the raspberries or the vegetables we picked together to put in the freezer in July and enjoy together in January. Indeed, the garden at Konkapot was a constant source of wonder and delight.

Since Adolf had been working in his garden for more than forty years, it was beginning to catch up to "the year before last," which his mother had always declared was the time to start a garden. The arbor vitae, though not equal to Italian cypresses, which Adolf always longed for and which do not grow in the Berkshires, were now six feet tall; clematis climbed over the wall, and delphinium, sky blue, dark blue, and violet, prospered. The lawn was almost dandelion free, since Adolf dug these intruders out while patiently waiting for me and the house guests to finish dressing for dinner.

Nineteenth Street had acquired a patina all its own. The library on the ground floor was Adolf's room. The facsimile of the Declaration by the United Nations, the document that preceded the U.N. Charter and that Adolf had helped to draft in January 1942, hung over the mantelpiece. On the walls hung Adolf's many commissions: assistant secretary of state, ambassador to Brazil, and others. The signed photographs of Presidents Roosevelt, Truman, and Lyndon Johnson were there. The bookcases contained copies of Adolf's own books, many books by his favorite authors, Isaac Walton's *The Compleat Angler*, the biographies of Sir Philip Sydney and Sir Walter Raleigh, and others. Although the drawing room was a formal room over which the portrait of Catherine Lorillard Wolfe, by Cabanel, and my portrait, by Albert Sternes, presided, the orange-gold curtains, the fire burning in the fireplace, the bookcases filled with all manner of books, and the Adam and Hepplewhite chairs, light enough to be moved about to form small groups for conversation, created a welcoming atmosphere.

The drawing room opened into the dining room at the rear of the house. It seems that we were always celebrating someone's birthday. We both enjoyed good food and good wine, and I spent considerable time planning menus with the kitchen staff. The results were usually excellent.

On the occasion of our fortieth wedding anniversary, Adolf in his morning suit, with striped trousers, and I in my wedding dress, came down the stairs as a brass quintet played a fanfare. The salute had been organized by our friend Carleton Smith, flute player and musicologist. Then came champagne, dinner, and a performance by a group of young singers, who extolled the glories of marriage in several languages, to various melodies.

We had come a long way from the glacial atmosphere of Sixty-seventh Street! On each side of the door at Konkapot were two Portuguese tiles, on which are inscribed the following maxims:

> If you come to my house with God in your heart, you may share my bread.

> The pride of my home is to receive without prejudice both rich and poor.

≈ *43*

We were gradually letting up on our activities, spending most of the summer in Great Barrington, with a few trips to New York for both of us, and flights to Ohio or Michigan for Adolf in connection with the Nationwide Insurance Company.

My beloved Mademoiselle Mulot — my adopted mother, I called her — joined us in Great Barrington in the summer of 1970. She had made several trips to the United States already. She and I were hopeful that the Meyerson boys, Dean's and Beatrice's sons, would take to learning French. Down in the garden where I was picking beans, I could hear Mademoiselle's beautiful enunciation and clear tones: *"Comment allez vous aujord'hui?"*

Not a peep out of Win, age fourteen. I decided it was not worth the trouble, so I persuaded Mademoiselle to join in our bucolic activities instead. Armed with a pair of scissors and a basket, she delighted in cutting the dead roses while chatting with Adolf about de Gaulle. Neither of them were admirers of *le général.*

There was always a lot going on. Though we had both a gardener and a house staff, Adolf and I both worked hard. He felt that there must be flowers in bloom all summer, lots of them. So coxcombs and chrysanthemums were transplanted from the lower garden as delphinium and madonna lilies faded. And of course, there were always dreams of how to do better next year.

Adolf was the real innovator. He decided that the old barn blocking the southern view from the house should be moved down the hill.

I was the conservative. "It won't work," I said, but it did, and Adolf had a wooden balustrade made to circle the lower terrace where the barn had been.

We had a large vegetable garden, a raspberry and a blueberry patch, expecting to feed our numerous house and dinner guests on perfectly frozen raspberries and small and tender peas and beans, picked and frozen before they became gigantic and hard. In the picking, preparing, and all the rest, Mademoiselle, I, and the others all took part as Josephine, our invaluable helper and friend, and Crétan-born Christine and her family ran the proceedings.

Still, it was an uneasy summer. Adolf was very unhappy about the state of the world. For once, he could not see a solution, while resisting strongly the desire of the New Left to destroy existing institutions and discard the benefits that had accrued in spite of injustices. "The younger generation," he would say, "has an unparalleled range of choice in making their daily lives. They have not had to work to achieve these choices, and they have not had passed on to them a system of values giving them a guide to the choices they do make."

On August 11, I put Mademoiselle on a plane for France. All summer, time had slid along like water over sunlit stones in the brook. In a way, it had been a blessed summer. Somehow I realized that we were living in an enchanted enclave of time and space.

Adolf's diabetes, which had been diagnosed ten years before, was becoming difficult to control. Also, he was coughing more than he should and had neglected to get his spring chest X ray. On August 12, he went to see Dr. Timpanelli. The X ray showed an infiltration in the right hilar region. We put him on antibiotics, and he stopped smoking. The cough stopped, but the infiltration had not changed on the X ray taken six days later. Two sputum examinations did not reveal any tumor cells. Both Dr. Timpanelli and I knew that statistically this was a tumor. Against that possibility were the patient's age and the fact that he was a diabetic. This could also be an indolent fungus or other infectious process.

When the possibility of a tumor presented itself, I felt deep physical pain through my own chest and abdomen. The night of the 13th, we went up to Picasso, a cottage we had bought as an investment. I called it a sophisticated Swiss chalet with a view. It was beautiful and remote—and we were together.

Before going to sleep, Adolf looked at the moon through the dormer window. "I will be with you," he said, "but in a different way."

I remained wakeful. The same pain went through my chest, and I had problems with my bowels.

Of course, the returns were not all in yet. Adolf felt well and considered that at the age of seventy-five and a half, he was bound to have a time bomb somewhere in his body.

Should it not be a tumor, or should we have several years more together, it behooved us to decide how to make life rich and beautiful in individual terms, since we could do nothing about the problems of the world. "We are what we are and can stand up with strength, love, and dignity as long as we live," was our conclusion. "Though I walk through the valley of the shadow of death I will fear no evil, for thou art with me."

Further investigations were carried out through the Pittsfield General Hospital and a very competent Berkshire medical group. No tumor cells were found. We declined to submit to further exploration, feeling that the possible therapeutic procedures for this type of tumor (assuming it was a tumor) would be so destructive to the quality of our lives that we preferred to take the risk of letting nature take its course. This we discussed together in total frankness and came to a complete agreement.

We did not go to Spain in September, as we had planned to do, but flew out to Jackson Hole, Wyoming. The altitude affected both of us, so we did not walk as much as we had on previous mountain trips.

Adolf fished and fished, but ne'er a trout was seen.

At night we dined well, at a table next to the hotel's plate-glass window, which gave onto the great Teton range.

Perhaps it was the underlying anxiety that affected me, but the Tetons seemed cold and distant. I longed for the Alps—mountains where men had lived, not just passed through.

We continued our trip to Santa Barbara where a discussion on the reform of the presidency was taking place at the Center for the Study of Democratic Institutions. Adolf's paper had the usual combination of idealistic and practical common sense. He and Arthur Schlesinger had good talks together, since we shared a cottage.

Back home in New York and Great Barrington, life went on as usual. This meant Twentieth Century Fund business, a lecture trip to Loyola University in New Orleans, and so on. Repeated X-rays showed no change. Dr. Timpanelli did not change his verdict of probable tumor but accepted our decision regarding treatment.

We went up to Great Barrington for Christmas. Adolf was very short of breath. The night of New Year's Eve was very dark. Adolf, flashlight in hand, directed the grandsons, who were to toboggan down the hill. This was a custom started a couple of years before. At the top of the hill, he shouted, "On your mark, get set, go!" Then, covered with snow and laughing, we came in and sang "Auld Lang Syne" while Adolf stirred the hot poker into the mulled wine.

I knew—*we* knew, though we did not talk about it—that this was the beginning of the end. It was to be our last night together as man and wife. During the next six weeks, Adolf went to Washington, taking part in a so-called leadership group organized to support the foreign policy of the United States—notably the White House and Henry Kissinger. He attended the regular insurance meeting of Nationwide Insurance Company in Columbus, Ohio, and signed a contract with Bill Jovanovich for the publication of his journals.

We thought he might be more comfortable in a warm climate, though of course, that was not a solution. We flew to Puerto Rico. There Adolf gave a last lecture to the law students at the University of Puerto Rico and looked upon his mistress, the Caribbean. Muñoz Marín and Inez were away, but we had many loving friends, including the Becerras and the Agraits. Best of all, Roger Baldwin, Adolf's oldest friend and his companion in many a battle for liberal causes, spent many hours with us as we took little drives or picnicked under the coconut trees. It was a fitting and quiet farewell.

On our return home, Adolf's condition deteriorated very rapidly. One day he awoke quite disoriented. "Do you know where you are?" I asked.

"In Brazil, of course," he replied.

A neurological examination did not reveal any localizing signs, and his mind cleared. Our beloved Carlos Chagas, with his wife and his daughter, were with us in Nineteenth Street. This seemed very fitting and was a great comfort to me. On the last morning, Adolf seemed quite himself, *A bençaõ da saude*, (the blessing of health), Carlos called it. Adolf and I sat together hand in hand, enjoying the pink hyacinth brought down from the country. He dressed and came down for lunch. Lila joined us. We spoke of the grandchildren and of Peter, who was a member of the state assembly at Albany.

After lunch, walking across the drawing room, Adolf collapsed into unconsciousness. I picked up his right arm, then all four limbs—they were paralyzed. I ran upstairs to get adrenaline and a needle and shot the hormone into his heart, but in ten minutes, he was gone.

The funeral in Stockbridge was attended by the family and a number of friends. The weather was New England at its worst, as Adolf would have said; wet snow fell as a slow procession walked up to the old cemetery where the ashes of Adolf's father and mother were buried. Alfred Starrett, the former rector of Saint Paul's Church in Stockbridge and a close friend, read a prayer he had composed:

> Almighty God, we are grateful for the life of your servant Adolf, in

whose presence we have had a special vision of your creative action. In him we knew the brilliant light of intelligence, combined with child-like simplicity; the responsible use of great power, together with a capacity for gentle tenderness; the ability to call forth growth in a man or in a flower; love of the competitive excitement of urban living, added to love of woods and hills and all of nature; the tireless service of a citizen devoted to his country and yet one who was able to continue to demand higher levels of public responsibilities toward the powerless and the poor.

We thank you for a good and generous man who brought to marriage the capacity for lasting friendship, tender affection, and fascinating companionship; who shared himself deeply with his children; and who gave both happiness and inspiration to his friends.

In ways beyond our knowing, may he receive the honor due for work well done, and may we demonstrate our thankfulness by living our remaining years in as much of his tall spirit as is possible for us. In Christ's name, Amen.

(February 20, 1971)

After the service, friends came into the house as they had when we had skating parties. Joined as we were in fellowship and love, we knew that Adolf's spirit was with us and always would be.

The following spring, as I looked down the field, my heart leaped as I heard the familiar click of the gate closing. Little Adolf, our grandchild, was coming through, pole in hand, triumphantly carrying a trout on a cleft stick.

I grieved but was determined to carry on. The rich legacy of love and fulfillment that came from our long and happy life together was to be shared with our friends. Adolf's papers and ideas were to become available to a larger public. For the first two years after Adolf's death, I worked with Travis Jacobis, the young professor of history at Middlebury College whom Adolf had selected shortly before his death to work with him. He and I edited a selection of Adolf's papers, which was published in 1973 under the title *Navigating the Rapids*. Adolf was a brilliant writer and the papers selected from a diary he kept intermittently over the years make a fascinating historical record of events and people as Adolf saw them over his long and varied career from 1918 to 1971. The book sold only fifteen hundred copies.

The bulk of his papers, letters, and speeches I gave to the Franklin Delano Roosevelt Library at Hyde Park, where they have been admirably classified and are available to scholars.

Continuing to live in Nineteenth Street and in Great Barrington, I felt and still feel that his spirit is very much with us. Our mutual friends continued to visit me, among them André Cournand and his wife, Ruth. It was Ruth who introduced André to me after reading my book *Eighty Puerto Rican Families*, which she had come across while working at Bellevue Hospital.

At a meeting of the Twentieth Century Fund in 1963, André and his colleagues had presented the work of Gaston Berger, a French philosopher. Called *Prospective*, it is a systematic approach to shaping the future. From that time on, André, Adolf, Ruth, and I had become great friends.

Ruth died very suddenly in 1973. It was a terrible shock. André and I shared our grief.

In the spring of 1975, André invited me to accompany him to Lindau to the triennial reunion of the Nobel laureates in medicine and physiology. He had been awarded the Nobel Prize in 1956. The moonlight over the Lake of Constance, coupled with the learned scientific discussions, added a new dimension to our friendship. We were married in August 1975.

Ours has been and continues to be an extraordinarily rich and happy life. André's affection and admiration for Adolf are important factors. We accept each other's pasts. My early French education and André's American career make for additional points of interest and mutual understanding. We share each other's families and friends, and we have made new friends together. We respect each other's liberty within the cultural framework of our shared French and American experience.

When this book appears in print, André will be eighty-eight and I will be eighty-one. We will not last forever—but as André wrote when we were getting married, "Ours will be a wonderful life, whatever the duration."

So it is.

Index